THE WHEEL OF CREATIVITY

THE Wheel OF Creativity®

Taking Your Place in the Adventure of Life

Katherine Robertson-Pilling

Art & Soul Productions LLC

Art & Soul Productions LLC

P.O. Box 2248, Boulder, Colorado 88036-2248

Copyright © 2012 by Katherine Robertson-Pilling

Library of Congress Control Number: 2012919909

ISBN: 978-0-9885111-0-1

Cover and interior design by Sue Niewiarowski
n-design.com

Cover illustration by Greg L. Golden

Cover photo by Aaron Bennett

Author services by Pedernales Publishing
www.pedernalespublishing.com

In memory of Shaka Taylor (1976–2008),
whose creative spirit lit up every room he entered.
May his short life remind us all not to wait for life's
creative adventure to begin, but to take our places
in it today.

Acknowledgments

My life is a creative adventure. Everyone who has crossed my path has been my collaborator. You have made me who I am and contributed to this work. To each of you who has participated in this journey, I thank you:

— My gorgeous, generous and loving husband, Ian, for his unrelenting support in every way through this process

— My beautiful stepchildren, Kristian and Regi, and their partners, for their open hearts and unique ways of seeing the world

— My mother, Juanita, for showing me that I could achieve whatever I set out to do. And my father, Cecil, for demonstrating that *being* trumps *doing* in every game

— Mary Carol, Dale, Anne and all my precious family, for reminding me that, at the end of the day, this book is a thing, and we are all human beings doing the best we can

— Dear friends on three continents, for being cheerleaders, critics, organizers, advisers, comforters and devil's advocates: Anita, Anne, Carol, Connie, Diane, Jennifer, Kathy, Penny, Peter, Samantha, Shelley, Suzy and Terry, and too many more to mention

I am particularly grateful to everyone who has helped me evolve this material from a small seed of an idea into a finished product in the world:

— The students who participated in workshops, courses and retreats, for showing up with curiosity and continuing with generosity and love, especially Petra, Diane, Anna Maria, Delphine and Lane

— My private mentoring clients, for trusting me with their creative process, business development and personal growth

— The generous souls who agreed to share their stories in these pages

—The FocusBarflies, Barbara, Deborah, Diane, nikO and Suzanne, for their informed, intuitive and pointed feedback

—Suzanne and Meri, for their faithful trust and faith through years of creative evolution

And I would especially like to acknowledge the people who have contributed directly to the creation and production of this book. I am deeply grateful to each one, without whom I could not have done this:

— My salt-of-the-earth editor Ron Silverman, for his professionalism and competence, and for giving me confidence in the manuscript by calling things as he saw them

— The gifted artists and technicians who made this book beautiful to look at: Sue Niewiarowski, Aaron Bennett, David Fennell, John Balodis and Jose Ramirez

— Greg Golden, for his visionary, alchemical illustration of the Wheel

— Louella Santobello, for reading the early versions and not holding back

— Tessa Allen, for proofing to ensure the baby was ready to leave the house

Contents

Part One Discovering the Wheel of Creativity

INTRODUCTION Creativity, Source and Me   3

The Wheels of Life   13

The Wheel at a Glance   29

Part Two 12 Stations on the Creative Journey

STATION 1 Hunger: "Something's Missing"   43

STATION 2 Appetite: "You're All I Want"   55

STATION 3 Anorexia: "Don't You Dare"   65

STATION 4 Launch: "Into the Wild"   77

STATION 5 Isolation: "There's Nothing Out There"   87

STATION 6 Crisis: "Catch Me If You Can"   99

STATION 7 Conception: "Wade in the Water"   109

STATION 8 Gestation: "Sittin' on the Dock of the Bay"   119

STATION 9 Breakthrough: "Free at Last"   129

STATION 10 Nurturing: "Someone to Watch Over You"   141

STATION 11 Pruning: "Time to Say Goodbye"   153

STATION 12 Harvest: "Homeward Bound"   165

Part Three Coming Home to the Adventure of Life

Taking Your Place in the Adventure of Life   181

CONCLUSION The Wheel Will Bring You Home   193

Part One

Discovering the Wheel of Creativity

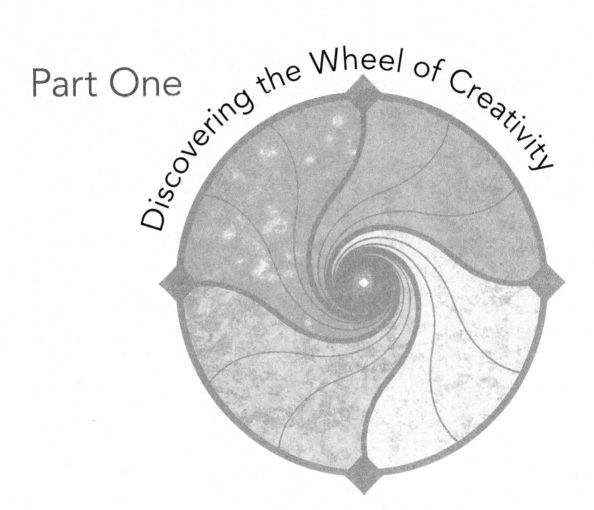

For the hero, fear is a challenge and a task,
because only boldness can deliver from fear.
And if the risk is not taken, the meaning of life
is somehow violated, and the whole future is
condemned to hopeless staleness. . . . C.G. JUNG

INTRODUCTION Creativity, Source and Me

Living is a form of not being sure, not knowing what next or how. The moment you know how, you begin to die a little. The artist never entirely knows. We guess. We may be wrong, but we take leap after leap in the dark. AGNES DE MILLE

My most important lessons in creativity have not come in the classroom, but on the street. I have always been curious. How does this thing work, and why? Why do you do the things you do? Why do I? There have always been gaps throughout my life between a relentless string of questions and the answers to those questions, between having ideas and implementing them. It is into these gaps that I love to go.

Half a lifetime ago, I decided that questions never have final answers, that life is meant to be explored, and there is always new territory to discover. Answers come in bite-sized pieces, revealed in the context of the language I understand at the time. Whatever knowledge I gain today will be replaced by something new tomorrow. My life rolls out before me in never-ending, unceasing cycles, one giving way to the next in a great wheel of evolution.

This book explores the territory between the questions and their answers—the mysteries of life and its manifestations, the unseen and the seen— the landscape where spirituality and creativity converge. This book is about how you can use the creative process to explore that territory yourself. I tell you my story not because I believe I am unique, but because I believe, at the deepest level of our humanity, we are the same. Through seeing the process unfold in my life, you can learn to recognize it in yours. And that is the beginning of the adventure!

Splitting Life in a Second

So many of the great adventures of my life have arrived as the unannounced afterthought at the end of a road. At the time, most of these experiences felt like the end of the world. For all my talk of questions, living through them is not an easy path. It is not comfortable. But perhaps comfort is not all it's cracked up to be.

In one split second, on May 7, 2009, all my plans changed. I was in the prime of my life. I was newly married to an amazing man, living in three countries, working on a meaningful project with the ideal client, and beginning to go public with my heart's desire to sing. I had lots of plans.

On that sunny afternoon in Nice, France, having just returned from England, I left my apartment to walk to the store to buy food. I crossed the street and stepped up onto the sidewalk. The curb in that spot was about four inches higher than normal. My foot did not clear it, and I fell. Arms full and unable to break my fall, I landed on my right hip. I tried to move, tried to stand; but my leg lay there beneath me like a tree trunk in the forest.

In that instant, though I pushed my mind to stay open to a better possibility, I knew what had happened. Two hours later, the young emergency room doctor at Saint-Roch Hospital confirmed it: I had broken my hip. It was a clean break, severing the head of the femur from the rest of the bone. My heart sank. Young Dr. Roux performed emergency surgery at 10 that night. And I began the long process of recovery. It would be four months before I would walk again, and a year before I would feel close to normal.

Resting there on the sidewalk, even as my body slipped into shock (paramedics measured my blood pressure at 80 over 50), my heart responded, "Okay, if this is what is next, let's go." That spirit of acceptance and willingness made the long months of recovery—which could have brought misery and angst with the pain and complications—rich with treasures, discoveries, blessings, friendship and love.

There on that sidewalk, Life took the lead, and I embarked on a new journey. Like countless others throughout my life, this process showed me my place in the adventure of life, required me to respond, and invited me to collaborate in creating the outcome. The cycle I went through, like all the others, had specific stages, which I identify now as The Wheel of Creativity.

The Wheel of Creativity is a map of the creative process, each point of which I have verified by going there myself many times. In addition to showing you that map, this book retraces my steps along the way so that in your own life journey, you can learn to recognize the stations I have visited. This book also presents others' stories to show the diverse applications of the process. And it offers you the tips I have learned at street level for how to get the most out of your trip.

This book is not just for artists, though artists certainly will find the material useful; it is also for the rest of us. It is for the everyday people in all walks of life who are unceremoniously doing their best to make something of value with their time on the planet. This is a guidebook for the adventure of being alive.

The Place I Had to Leave

I can't say exactly when I first had the idea for this book, but its roots are there in my earliest memories of childhood. Not so much from what I was given, but from what I was given to work with. So many experiences, as I look back now, showed me whom I was by showing me what I was not. So I begin with my own personal story—the soil into which my roots reached out, where I was nourished, inspired, humbled and compelled.

I was born in Houston, Texas, in 1956, the daughter of a child psychiatrist and a self-made entrepreneur who left school at 15. I would have been an only child, but six months before I was born, my father's niece and nephew, who had spent 10 years in an orphanage, arrived to make their home with us.

Ours was a religious home. Sundays and Wednesdays found us at South Main Baptist Church. And I was proudly presented at Sunday School practically before I could form a thought. I learned to think and act in the context of Jesus's teachings and someone else's interpretations of them.

Ours was a fearful home, with right-wing political leanings and well-researched fears about the dangerous changes happening in the world. My mother—a pediatrician turned child psychiatrist in 1960—protected me as only a trained shrink can. My father, less educated in his anxiety, also believed the world a dangerous place for his daughter and tried his loving best to keep me safe. They protected me by instilling their fears in me. I say this with the deepest appreciation for their loving intentions and complete forgiveness for their human limitations. As I have taken responsibility for my own limitations along the way, I have come to understand the origins of theirs.

I was a sensitive child. According to my mother, by the time I was able to sit up in my high chair, if

I spilled my milk I would burst into tears. I was extremely fearful about doing anything wrong. At the same time, I was a big and colorful character, and was probably overindulged as the only child born to parents late in life.

I vividly recall one night, when I was three or four, being in the family room with my parents and cousins (19 and 14 by then), whom I idolized as sister and brother. I was doing my usual bouncing-singing-dancing thing around the room, when suddenly a dark cloud of worry came over me with a message: "These people are really uncomfortable with me. This is really bad, that they feel uncomfortable. It's obviously my fault. Therefore I am too big." It led to one of those decisions you never really make but changes your life all the same. I began to reel in my energy like a school of fish caught in a net, tighter and tighter, until I felt it was safe to be there, safe to be. I was born into a world of other people's agendas for me. So are we all.

Conformity Comes Home

At age six, because of my mother's desperate campaign to keep me safe from the sex, drugs and rock 'n' roll in public schools, I was sent to a strict parochial school. My childhood fears took root in the school's narrow judgments about what was right and what was wrong. Seeing the harsh punishments inflicted there on those who ventured out of bounds—forced to stand outside the classroom facing the wall, sent to the principal's office, hit with a paddle—terrorized me. Order in the classroom was maintained. And I was conditioned for a life of conformity.

The education at St. Thomas was excellent in classical academics—math, science, English, Latin—and the arts had their tiny extracurricular place. In addition to chapel singing, competitive Scottish dancing and needlepoint, there were occasional Christmas concerts and plays. Once, when we performed Shakespeare's The Merchant of Venice, I played Portia. There was no structure to develop skill in or understanding of the arts; they were the seasoning on our

---

GEORGE WASHINGTON
By Kathy Robertson

When George Washington was a boy his father had pigs, cows and horses. George had a pony of his own, Whitefoot. He rode Whitefoot around in the fields every day. When George was eleven years old his father died. One day when George was at his mother's house he found some old tools. "Those tools were your fathers tools," said George's mother. "Can I have them"? said George. "Yes", said his mother. "He meshered land with those tools", said his mother. "I want to learn how to mesher land," said George Washington. "You will have to go to a man in town", said his mother. So George went to town. He said, "Sir I want to learn to be a sirvaer", said George Washington. "To be a sirvaer is hard work", said the man. "I know sir", said George Washington, "But I want to be a sirvaer sir", said George Washington. "Okey", said the man. One night when George was out with the sirvaing party he saw an Indian war dance.

---

intellectual buffet. We were being groomed—with math, science and language—to get into good universities and to excel and compete in the world. I am grateful for the benefits of this training, and I regret its costs.

In this creative outback, there was one woman who saw me. Mrs. Homer T. Bouldin, my first-grade teacher, was writing a book on teaching children to read and write phonetically, which she called An Acorn in My Hand. To demonstrate how her method could work, she selected my story and published it exactly as I had written it, exactly as you see it here.

I was six years old, still innocent of the judgment and shame in words like mistakes, and right and wrong. I was so proud. I am proud to this day—of the sweet little girl who set out to write a little story in the best little way she could. Lesson one: I can do it and it's fun. But that changed the next year.

In second grade, we learned to write cursive, and Darcy Dunn knew how to make her ovals right. I can remember looking at my page, looking at her page and feeling bad. No matter how hard I tried, I could not get my ovals to look like Darcy Dunn's; I could not get mine to come out right. Lesson two: You don't always get what you want.

One day, in third grade, I dared to play a little. It was Halloween time, and those little white-yellow-orange candy corn pieces were a favorite. Quite uncharacteristically on a dare, I broke off the white part, went to the teacher with "my tooth" in my hand, and asked to be excused to the bathroom. I shall never forget the terrible feeling of waiting in the principal's office, crying my eyes out. My inner shame was punishment enough. I never dared anything like that again. Lesson three: Don't you dare!

By fourth grade, I had learned it was not safe to not know. If I had a question in class, I would not ask it; I feared I would be reprimanded for not knowing the answer. So for me, learning came not from passionate curiosity but from the need to be right, to do it right, and above all to not be wrong. Lesson four: Take no chances!

I stayed at St. Thomas until my last year of high school. Though one year I tried another private school, I returned. I was fused to it. It was the cloth I was cut from. What drove me to excel, despite my innocent love for life, was fear. Year after year, the lessons taught without words took me farther away from myself.

Spirit Breaking Free

Outside school, my mother ensured that I was exposed to all the traditional art forms. There I dared to dream, to explore, to reach out for something more. My introduction to creativity was learning-how rather than listening-to.

There were lessons for everything, starting at age six. There was dance—ballet, tumbling and tap—which I adored but did not continue. There were piano lessons with Mrs. Clark—strict, academic and constricted—and the terrible stage fright at every recital, which I am finally mastering today. There were painting lessons, and private voice lessons as well, as it seemed I was gifted in this area.

Outside school as well, what began as a delightful

dream soon deteriorated into work and fear. I could only envy the pleasure of friends who played piano by ear at our parties. I stopped studying piano when I was 12, and I always regretted it. I avoided dance again until my 40s, when I discovered Gabrielle Roth's *5Rhythms*. I never painted again. I learned to plant the seeds of work and pleasure in separate gardens.

The one place in my life where pleasure and work flowed together was on the back of a horse. With all my other pursuits, I could go through the motions in my head; but I had to be in my body to stay in the saddle. Those strong Arabian spirits settled me down, and I was passionate for them. Horses gave me my first physical experience of an unseen force that flowed through all living things, connecting us to each other. Deep within I knew that this force was truer, stronger and more important than anything I was learning in school.

God Gets a Box

One Sunday morning, when I was 11, I felt this force in a new way, like a knock at a door deep inside me that I hadn't known was there. I responded in the way it was done there at South Main Baptist Church: I left my pew and walked the long aisle to the front, where, met by the preacher, I was guided to ask Jesus to be my Lord and Savior.

In that moment, I stepped into the box where others would define that unseen force for me. What the filmmaking Wachowski brothers called the Matrix, I call the box.

I was a good learner, and all my questions found answers there, for a while. From the innocent awakening of my young heart, I was taught to *have the answer* for the rest of the world. I was taught to be *right*. In the context of what felt to me like loving and caring, I learned fundamentalism. But along the way I misplaced my direct connection with the unseen force that had called to me in the first place, the force that was flowing through me all the time.

For the next 10 years, Southern Baptist Christianity would be the only box I knew. Eventually, that box became my launching pad. Life's journey has led me far from the shores of that safe haven and back, beyond the box to the unseen force beyond definitions, back to myself.

God Is in the Guitar

At 14, I picked up the guitar. Three easy chords to that first song, *House of the Rising Sun*, moved me. Perhaps it was the vibration of the instrument in my arms. Like my Arabian horses, the guitar was another relationship, between a very limited human girl and the mysterious, uncontrollable force I longed for.

I started to write songs. They were desperate songs, angry songs; but the voices inside me that could not find expression anywhere else found expression there. The words and music flowed together through me, from somewhere beyond me. I was plugged in. I was free—from the opinions of others, the instruction of experts, and the right and wrong way to live my life. The energy flowed to me directly from the source. I was alive.

The more I felt alive, the more I felt angry. It was there in my music. It was there in my attitude. After one particularly memorable blowup with my parents, I feebly tried to take my life. My mother's solution was a tranquilizer and a trip to see our church pastor. I rejected the first but consented to the second because I felt safe with this man. I walked the two blocks to his house that night in darkness, inside and out.

He listened to me compassionately and then told me a parable, which went something like this:

"Once upon a time, there was a young goat who lived in a beautiful green garden. He had everything he needed in this garden: plenty of grass to eat, a clear running creek to drink from, and full, mature trees to shade him from the hot sun.

"But the goat was obsessed with the fact that there was a wall around this garden. Every day, from dawn till dusk, he spent his hours trying to jump high enough to overcome the wall. Every day he would collapse in the green grass in exhaustion and frustration that he could not surmount this wall, see what lay outside and escape to his freedom.

"You are like this goat, Kathie. You can spend your life butting your head up against this wall and miss all that you have right here in the beautiful garden where you live. And it only makes you unhappy."

On the surface, in our days of present-moment spirituality, the moral of this story rings true. But it did not satisfy me very much. What if we were all contented like this? What worlds would lie undiscovered, what cures still dormant, what problems unsolved?

I went home that night feeling nothing. My heart was numb. I sat in a chair in my room, wrapped in a blanket, knees-to-chest, and didn't move for hours. I could not think. I could not feel. But in my heart, I knew I was not content to live within those walls and pretend that the world outside did not exist.

Something died in me then, and I spent the next 30 years trying to keep it buried, for the resurrection of it would surely destroy the world I called home.

What I didn't know then was that ash is the most fertile of all soils, and that the ashes of that neat little world would nourish the seeds of a vast new world beyond the walls of my imagination.

View From the Ivory Tower

Going away to college in Chicago opened the box for me, but only slightly. I was a smart young woman and had been well prepped for a good education. Following in the pastor's footsteps, I applied to only one school. *Time* magazine called Wheaton College "The Harvard of the Evangelicals"; we affectionately knew it as Billy Graham University, as he had gone there too.

Wheaton was a new piece of the same fabric: religious, strict, conservative, uniform. Even when transferred to a new garden, this little goat still jumped to the same height. But somehow from this ivory tower, I began to get a glimpse of life *out there*, beyond the unilateral vision of my childhood. More than 200 denominations were represented at Wheaton, from Quakers to Catholics. Not everyone thought like my parents.

I became a tourist in a new world of thought. I had my favorite stops on that tour: psychology, philosophy, astronomy, drama, art and music appreciation, and pottery making. I longed for new vistas I had not seen before. Each stop was a feast of new ideas and experiences—just enough to keep a "starving girl" alive.

My favorite professor, Robert Webber, incited us to think differently, to question our ideologies, to acknowledge the absurd and shadow side of our beliefs. He won me over when he provoked our Bible class with the words, "Kill a Commie for Christ!" I liked his shocking way of making a point. It blew the top off the box, if only for 45 minutes.

I approached Wheaton the only way I knew how to approach school, for strict academic pursuit. I might have majored in art, but because I did not draw, I believed I could not be an artist. Though I had studied voice and Wheaton had a renowned conservatory, I did not even consider music. Looking back, I believe these life-limiting choices demonstrated my prejudice at the time that creativity was exclusive and reserved for a select few. But they also drove me to keep searching.

View From the Floor

Secretly, privately, the creative voice in me longed for expression. With the same guitar in my arms, on Saturday afternoons when everyone else was outside, I sat on the floor in my dorm room and wrote songs of longing and discontent.

Of all my creative endeavors, it was while writing songs that I felt the unseen force flowing; something beyond me was coming through. I was connected with the creative spark of Life, the Source, the Life Force, what many call God. It was using me to express something. I was a channel. And I was Alive . . . with a capital *A!* But despite this bliss, there were long periods of silence when I abandoned my creative process.

View From the Floor

Always sitting on the floor. Guitar in hand, on the floor, in hand, on the floor. A single piece of paper and a pencil or pen. Sitting . . . lying . . . writing . . . trying. Something coming first. Could be the chords . . . a single line of melody . . . a few words . . . a feeling . . . an idea. A single drop . . . followed by others . . . the flow increasing . . . becoming steady . . . and strong . . . love growing in my heart. From the chords, a progression . . . and rhythm . . . from the words, a verse . . . then a refrain or chorus . . . a story emerging in song . . . building . . . building . . . then settling . . . coming back home. Swept up in this wave . . . of love . . . seeing the newborn growing in me . . . knowing I am not the source of this . . . loving . . . settling down . . . in admiration.

I had been trained to take the safe road. And so I studied what I knew from childhood—psychology—and proceeded down the path of science. What makes us tick, and why we do the things we do. It was another route to my feelings. It was the route my mother had chosen before me: not the expression of feelings but the study of them. But I never stopped stretching to see over that wall. Ultimately, answering our questions about life can never replace the direct experience of it.

Something Out There Calling

In my senior year at Wheaton I discovered Rainer Maria Rilke's advice in his *Letters to a Young Poet*. It was as if he was writing to me:

> "… be patient toward all that is unsolved in your heart and … try to love the *questions themselves*…. Do not now seek the answers, which cannot be given you because you would not be able to live them. And the point is, to live everything. *Live* the questions now. Perhaps you will then gradually, without noticing it, live along some distant day into the answer." (Rainer Maria Rilke, *Letters to a Young Poet,* New York: W.W. Norton & Company, 1934)

I exhaled completely. I wrote those words on a tiny brown piece of paper and carried it with me everywhere. For years. Those few words changed the course of my life. They move me still.

This was my first big clue from Life: "Love the questions," he said. And for the first time in my life, I began to do so. I loved them as an expression of all that was good in me. I loved them as an expression of God. What I found, when for the first time in my life I allowed myself to ask my questions, to live my questions, was that the answers I heard from the powers in the box were too small for me. Each time I heard an answer, I had a larger question. And then, I exhaled again.

In Peter Weir's 1998 film, *The Truman Show*, Jim Carrey plays Truman Burbank, the unwitting star of an elaborate TV show, whose entire life has been created and sustained for a television audience. The film comes to an end as Truman discovers the edge of the set and a tiny door in an expansive section of a painted blue sky. As director Christof tries to persuade him to stay, Truman responds, "In case I don't see you, good afternoon, good evening, and good night." He bows to his audience and steps through the door into the real world he knew not at all.

Like Truman in that closing shot, I had found the edge of my box. In his advice to his young poet, Rilke had returned to me my compass of curiosity. And that was the beginning of living for me. As bruised and scratched as I might have been along the way from living my life on that edge, it has been my liberation. It has led me to my purpose.

The Mystic Creative

Religious traditions of every culture seek to answer the same fundamental question, "What's it all about?" While I grew up in the Christian tradition, I have long been in awe of the unintentional parallels between different religions' elaborately distinctive answers. Since stepping out of the obligatory exclusivity of my childhood religion, I have found in this vast array a beautiful testament to the creative diversity of Life. I have sought to find the common ground—deeper than ideology and belief—among them all. For me, this ground is the creative process, and it is a mystical path through life.

According to the *Stanford Encyclopedia of Philosophy*, "The term 'mysticism' comes from the Greek μυω, meaning 'to conceal.' In the Hellenistic world, 'mystical' referred to 'secret' religious rituals. In early Christianity the term came to refer to 'hidden' allegorical interpretations of Scriptures and to hidden presences, such as that of Jesus at the Eucharist. Later the term began to denote *mystical theology*, including direct experience of the divine."

Typically, according to *Stanford*, mystics seek to know the deeper truths of life through their direct experience, and they interpret these mystical experiences not as the end goal but as participation in the larger process of human transformation.

Every major religion has a mystical tradition deep within it or on its fringes, depending on your point of view, where believers seek to know the deeper hidden aspects of God through personal and direct experience.

Judaism's mystical tradition is found in the Kabbalah, a set of scriptures outside the biblical set. These esoteric teachings explain the nature of an eternal God (the Creator), God's relationship with the finite world (the creation) and the way life creates a path to spiritual attainment.

In Islam, the mystical knowledge is held in the Sufi Way, defined in the 15th century by Shaykh Ahmad Zarruq as "a science whose objective is the reparation of the heart and turning it away from all else but God." Sufism teaches the seeker, or Dervish, how "to travel into the presence of the Divine, purify one's inner self from filth, and beautify it with a variety of praiseworthy traits."

Mysticism is also a core tenet of Hinduism. Most Hindus believe that the soul is eternal and that the goal of life is freedom through merging your soul with the Supreme Soul. Hindu texts and wise men teach followers to attain this by seeking awareness of God in everyday life. Practices including yoga, singing hymns, chanting mantras, reciting scriptures and worshiping through daily chores are the very heart of the religion.

The one tenet that all mystical religious traditions share is that knowledge of God, spiritual truth or ultimate reality is possible through direct personal experience. A common tenet is the ultimate oneness of the individual and all of reality. Mystical practices have as their goal to experience that oneness by shifting focus away from the physical experience of separation.

In general, Christian mysticism teaches that this direct awareness of God can be cultivated through interpretation of scriptures and the practices of prayer, meditation, purification and contemplation on Jesus Christ and the Holy Spirit. According to the *Encyclopaedia Britannica*, mysticism was an important part of life within the Christian community and led the human community to higher consciousness.

For as many years as I could frame the thought, I have experienced Life itself inviting me to know it through my own experience and to dance with it through my response to it. Life invites us all, whatever our culture, creed or belief system, to step outside the box of our conditioning, to come closer, to know it in this way.

The Way of the Nomad

When I graduated from Wheaton College with my BA in psychology, there were new questions to ask, each being some version of, "Where to now?" I stood at the intersection of two paths: (1) I could continue my education and get an advanced degree for the practice of psychotherapy, or (2) I could take the creative route I had always loved but avoided.

Once I had agonizingly ruled out the traditional commercial routes of both paths, someone came into my life just long enough to make the suggestion, "What about movies?" A creative impulse, inspired by someone I have long since forgotten, synthesized two seemingly opposing passions: my love of creative expression and my fascination with the human spirit. I had lived my way into the next step.

After a year in a master's program in broadcasting, with core skills and experience, I left school. I began weaving my way through the world with my creative process in my handbag, in search of a job. I was already a nomad.

Though it would be years before I would recognize it, knowing what I didn't want was guiding my life, moving me away from the boxes that didn't fit and creating questions that moved me down new paths. My future unfolded before me as one synthesis after another of seemingly disparate passions. And while I felt lost much of the time, I wasn't at all.

This book, through The Wheel of Creativity, can help you to define the nature of humanity and eternity through your own experience, and to give meaning to your place in the stream of life, bridging the shores between the two. It does not require that you believe a certain way, or adopt a creed, or abandon your tradition to benefit from it. By following the principles and practices you learn here, you can:

- Come to know yourself more intimately than ever before
- Find and strengthen your authentic connection with the unseen force that flows through us all
- Develop your capacity to live your life in the joy and power of the creative process
- Take your place in the adventure of Life's great unfolding
- Produce the outcomes in your life that flow from your innermost essence
- Live the life you dream of

The Wheels of Life

Some people will be very disappointed if there is not an ultimate theory,
that can be formulated as a finite number of principles.
I used to belong to that camp, but I have changed my mind.
STEPHEN HAWKING

The Value of "This Isn't It"

This is a chaotic time in the world. The attack on the Twin Towers on September 11, 2001, effectively collapsed a grand American myth—that our strongest structures are secure enough to protect us from harm. The shockwaves from that collapse have spread throughout the world, and today the shadow of once-sacred institutions grows darker everywhere we look. In 2012, the crisis still paralyzes economies around the entire world, replacing optimism with fear and blocking the flow of energy into new endeavors. And no matter how hard we try, we cannot get our leaders back up on their pedestals.

In times of crisis, in times of chaos, people become frightened:

"It's not supposed to be like this."
"We want to go back to the good old days."
"What was I thinking?"

These are instinctive responses for the human animal, who loves comfort, security and order. The brain stem, the oldest part of the evolving human brain and what scientists call the reptilian brain, is in charge of your survival. When it perceives a threat (real or not), the reptilian brain automatically kicks into a fight-or-flight response, often overriding the logic and reason of other parts of the brain.

Chaos enters our lives unannounced, but forward movement, growth and transformation do not come without it. A forest is more fruitful after it has burned; chaos initiates rebirth if you work with it. So, you must learn to work with chaos, and with the primitive reactions that rise up in you in response. For without the dissolution of old forms, there are no new forms; the future simply recycles the past.

Science recognizes the progressive nature of knowledge, with each theory constructing itself in response to what came before, even when the previous theory is disproved in the process. Albert Einstein himself expressed the belief that the evolution of physics has occurred through a series of successive approximations. Predictions become more accurate and more widely applicable over time, but no physical theory yet is believed to be precisely accurate. This is not required. Such is Life as well.

13

Without a doubt the evolution of my life, and of this material, has been a series of successive approximations. From the narrow confines of my childhood box, each step has led me closer to myself and my connection with the unfathomable mysteries of ultimate truth. I had been working with the idea of the creative process as a series of stages for years when one day, as I was sitting in meditation in the sunshine, it all came together for me. "It's a wheel!"

Through the serial synthesis of disparate passions, I conceived The Wheel of Creativity. That moment turned my search in a completely new direction, for evidence of my theories in human nature, culture, science, mythology and nature, in business, family, politics and religion. In the chapters that follow, I will trace what I discovered and how it changed my life, and I will show you how to use it to change yours as well.

The Wheel

Throughout history, the wheel has been generally recognized as humanity's first great invention. The word *wheel* is derived from a Proto-Indo-European word that means *to revolve* or *move around*. Always circular, often spoked and capable of rotating on an axis, the wheel made it possible for humanity to move across distances, to transport goods and to develop machines for achieving previously impossible tasks. Revolution empowered evolution.

The wheel is thought to have originated in ancient Sumer (modern Iraq) around 5000 BC, when it was created for throwing pots. Over the next several thousand years, it showed up in India and Pakistan on burial carts, in southern Poland on four-wheeled wagons, in China on chariots, and in Europe. The appearance of spoked wheels around 2000 BC made vehicles lighter and faster. As time went on, wheels were adapted to create new technologies, such as the water wheel for milling, the spinning wheel and ancient instruments of astronomy.

With its revolutionary impact on humanity through the millennia, it is not surprising that the

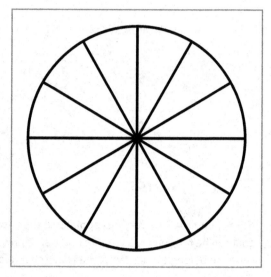

The Spoked Wheel

wheel also took on strong cultural and spiritual significance. Across cultures and epochs, it became a metaphor for the cycles of life and the processes of growth and change. It still has deep symbolic meaning in most religions today.

The Wheel of Fortune. For the Romans, the wheel was associated with the sun (as the wheel of a chariot that moved across the sky) and thus with life. The goddess Fortuna held the Wheel of Fortune in her hand, causing lives to change as she spun it, some for the better, some for the worse. Consequently the wheel endured for centuries as a symbol of the capricious nature of fate.

Ezekiel's Wheel. In Judaism, the wheel is associated with Ezekiel's vision (Ezekiel 1:15–22), in which he sees four creatures descend from heaven. Twice, he says of these creatures, "the spirit of the living creatures was in the wheels." "Wherever the spirit would go, they went, and the wheels rose along with them; for the spirit of the living creatures was in the wheels."

The Rose Window. In Christianity, the wheel motif appears in almost every major cathedral in the world, in the jewel-toned emblem of the rose window. From the Roman oculus, a round skylight, the rose window developed in the French Gothic period, when geometry played a symbolic role in cathedral design. Every angle carried meaning.

The Mandala. The wheel is also a central feature of dharmic religions, such as Hinduism and Buddhism, in the mandala—a representational sacred space of concentric circles from its outer edge to its ornately decorated central square. For thousands of years, Tibetan Buddhist monks have painstakingly created mandalas in intricate patterns of colored sand as metaphysical symbols of the cosmos, a microcosm of the Universe from the human perspective. Many Tibetans also pray using a prayer wheel, a cylinder on a stick with a strip of paper prayers wound inside, which they turn back and forth to release the prayers into the world.

The Medicine Wheel. One of the most sacred traditions of the indigenous people of North America is the medicine wheel, symbolized by a configuration of 36 stones on the earth—a circle with a cross inside. The circle itself, also known as the sacred hoop, represents different stages of physical life and the influence of the nonphysical world as well. According to Jamie Sams, author of *Sacred Path Cards*, "This symbol of all of life's cycles has given the People of Native America an evolutionary blueprint for centuries. Each cycle of life is honored in a sacred way, giving us a way to see the value of each step of our pathway and a new understanding of our growth patterns."

Turning on Opposites

Years ago, in a television interview with Bill Moyers, I heard the pioneering mythologist Joseph Campbell interpret the biblical story of creation in the context of archaeological evidence across cultures, throughout the ages. Throughout my 18 years of biblical training and Christian education, I had never heard such an interpretation—and a light went on for me then.

Genesis 3 tells the story of what Christians call the Fall of Man, but Campbell describes it in very different terms. The moment when man "ate of the tree of the knowledge of good and evil" Campbell describes as humanity's entry into the dualistic world of opposites. Innocence is lost in the physical world. Humans live life in the realm of opposites, where the infinite gives way to the finite, measured against opposing sides: good and evil, light and dark, male and female, here and there, etc. Campbell's interpretation opened my mind to the idea that an eternal spirit lives between these opposites and encompasses them both.

The tree of the knowledge of good and evil stands between heaven and earth, and by eating its fruit we fall from the eternal bliss of heaven into the finite and often painful experience of earth. But why? Why would eternal souls floating in unending bliss want to leave that perfect state? Why would anyone choose endings, limitation, restriction, suffering, and pain? There are probably as many answers to those questions as there are souls, each of whom expresses some aspect of the Divine in the world. The first answer that made sense to me was, "Because it's interesting. It's entertaining."

One of my favorite representations of this idea is found in Wim Wenders's cinematic masterpiece, *Wings of Desire.* The infinitely better basis for the Hollywood film *City of Angels,* Wenders's film contrasts the intimate sufferings of postwall Berliners with an army of angels who keep continual watch over them. The angels can neither touch nor be touched by anything. They are eternal, always standing by, giving comfort, observing.

This causes great sadness for lead angel Cassien, for he longs to become human. He longs to hold a pencil, to have fingers dirty with newsprint, to love, to bleed, to hurt. He sees a woman and falls in love. He longs to do more than watch her and comfort her from afar; he longs to touch her; he longs to feel. He longs to enter the physical world of opposites, where he can no longer be everywhere at once but must be either here or there. He longs for the exquisite experience of being human. Since the first moment I saw him, I have been moved by the way Cassien's hunger dignifies the human experience, all that we have and take for granted, whether we consider it good or bad.

This dualistic experience of life appears again and again in explanations of life with very little else in common. Having rejected the one-answer-fits-all exclusivity of evangelical Christianity, I find freedom and dignity in this inclusivity. For me, it is in this understanding where The Wheel of Creativity begins to turn.

Yin and Yang. Buddhists, and particularly Taoists, celebrate the world of opposites with the ancient symbol of Yin and Yang. They see life as an eternal and harmonious cycle, unifying two complementary opposites without merging them. Yang is the light, active, positive principle, associated with the Masculine, while Yin is the dark, passive, negative principle, associated with the Feminine. The two are in continual dynamic relationship, maintaining balance through constant change.

Over the years, I have come to recognize that the Feminine Yin force, referred to as negative, is as important in the creative process as the positive Masculine force of Yang. Without the destruction or dissolution of the old form, no new form can come in. Recycling the past can be imaginative and exciting if we are mindfully engaged with the process, or it can be counterproductive and draining if we are unconscious of our participation in it.

The Human Brain. The human brain itself is divided into two connected but separate cerebral hemispheres (right and left), each controlling complementary but separate functions. In his research in 1861, French physician Paul Broca was one of the first to identify brain functions as being two-sided. Most recently, neuroscientist Jill Bolte Taylor has beautifully illuminated the individual powers of each hemisphere from the inside out, through her vibrant description of her own stroke in her best-selling book, *My Stroke of Insight*.

The left brain processes information in a linear, sequential, logical and analytical way. The right brain processes information in a holistic, simultaneous, intuitive way. The left brain is verbal, while the right brain works in images. The left-brain is oriented to the past and future, while the right brain focuses

Yin and Yang

on the present moment. In mathematics, the left brain counts and measures, while the right brain perceives form and movement. In language, the left brain works in words and patterns, while the right brain works poetically in tone and context. Either, without the other, is an incomplete experience of life. But when the two are working together as they are designed to do, the whole brain emerges with the integrated experience of life we have come to recognize as *normal*.

Vive la Difference!

Dualism has had a bad reputation in recent years, but we live in this world of opposites for a reason. The Wheel of Creativity celebrates the fundamental opposites of life because the energy released by moving between opposites creates momentum. If we are willing to move, the process of Life itself moves us forward; if we are not, it drives us further into our polarized positions.

The two opposite forces at work in the process of creation exist in the two founding principles of Life: Masculine and Feminine. You have only to look at animal physiology to understand them. The Masculine stands still, erect, powerful, single-focused, moving out into the world. The Feminine is soft, flowing, relaxed, welcoming and receiving. (I am not referring to sexual preferences, but to procreative principles at the heart of Nature.)

These two forces, which Taoists call Yang and Yin, can also be described as active and receptive. Together they form the harmonious creative force of Life. Life progresses through a continual interaction of the two, one moving into the other again and again and again. One must have the other, or the process of Life is blocked.

The Cycle of Birth and Death

In every cycle of creation, these two forces are present. The constructive force is the one we usually associate with the creative process; but, before anything new can be created, another equal force is required. The force of destruction, or what the Hindus call dissolution, is as integral to creativity as the force of construction.

Form comes into being through energy, but energy is only released through the destruction of another form. Both of these processes are recognizable throughout Nature, from the cells of the human body to the stars in the heavens. The Wheel of Creativity integrates both forces, empowering you not only to deal with the times when the Muse is upon you, but also the times when your world is coming apart.

In the Cell

I know this cycle now in my bones. Two months after my accident I had a setback. I had done everything right, according to the doctors. I had just started to put a bit of weight on my leg in physical therapy when my foot became extremely painful, swollen and red. Through a series of tests and scans, I was diagnosed with a condition called algodystrophy, an inflammation of the nerves in a traumatized limb that causes the bones to decalcify. The bones in my right leg were so fragile that I broke my heel simply by stepping on it. It would be six more weeks minimum before I could walk, and I had to have daily calcium injections, which made me very sick.

The radiologist who read the scintigraphy confirmed the diagnosis and mentioned in passing that this was a problem of metabolism. The next day, when the nurse came to my home to give me my first injection, I asked her about the connection. She explained that there are two forces in human metabolism: catabolism and anabolism. She explained that catabolism breaks down tissue, and anabolism builds it up. With algodystrophy, these two forces are out of balance. My body was breaking down the tissue but not rebuilding it.

I was astounded by that conversation and amazed by the timing. I suddenly realized that this was just the material I needed for this book. I suddenly realized that the crisis on my doorstep eight weeks before had carried within it the missing elements I had been asking for, and that Life was asking me to step up to the plate and play ball.

Creation and destruction are at work even at the microcosmic level. *Encarta World English Dictionary* defines metabolism as "the ongoing interrelated series of chemical interactions taking place in living organisms that provide the energy and nutrients needed to sustain life." Through the processes of metabolism, any living organism, such as your body, converts one substance into energy and then uses that energy to build and rebuild all its structures.

In humans, catabolism breaks down molecules of food, through digestion, to make energy available to the body. Anabolism uses that energy to build new structures, cell by cell, through the process of synthesis. In metabolism, catabolism is the destructive force; anabolism is creative.

My prayers had been answered in a much deeper way than I could have imagined. I knew that my love of ideas had me stuck in my head. Ideas were coming fast and furious for this book, but I knew I needed to ground the ideas in my life before I could express them meaningfully to others. The cycle had to find its completion in me before I could articulate it. Then Life—through what might have been a catastrophe—met me and gave me an opportunity to learn the meaning of the concepts in my very bones. If the first big clue in my life had been, "Love the questions," the second was, "Trust the process."

In the Cosmos

Ever since my college astronomy class, I have felt a special connection with the stars. To step out of my warm bed into the cold night air to see a certain predictable celestial alignment reassures me. What astounds me is that the same two forces of creation and destruction are also at work at the macrocosmic level in the birth and death of stars. What astronomers observe, when they're lucky, is the cosmos's continual process of flowing energy into form and out again.

Stars are born in areas of the cosmos called giant molecular clouds (GMCs), which astronomers also call stellar nurseries. Typical GMCs average hundreds of light-years across, are millions of times more massive than our sun and millions of times more dense than all the empty space in a galaxy.

As a GMC orbits a galaxy, it might encounter any of several events that disturb its gravitational balance and trigger its collapse. It might collide with another GMC, or pass through dense regions of spiral arms. It could run into matter from the explosion of a nearby supernova. Sometimes even galaxies collide, triggering massive bursts of star formation.

Stars are formed from the fragments of these collapsing GMCs. As the fragments give way to the pressure of the collapsing gas, energy is released in the form of heat. As pressure increases, the fragments begin to form rotating spheres of superhot gas known as protostars.

According to Ron Cowen in *Bang: The Cataclysmic Death of Stars*, "Gravity is responsible for setting newborn stars aflame, by squeezing atoms of hydrogen in the star's core so tightly that they fuse to make helium. The fusion generates light and heat and also exerts pressure that allows the core to withstand the enormous weight of the star's outer layers."

Cowen continues: "But when the core consumes all of its hydrogen, gravity compresses it. The tem-perature of the shrinking core rises to about a hundred million degrees, hot enough for helium nuclei to fuse and make carbon. The new surge of energy keeps the core from collapsing much further."

The cycle that creates stars also destroys them. The forces of destruction and creation are always in delicate, violent balance. From there the process differs depending on the size of the star and its proximity to other stars. But the internal forces to expand and the outer gravitational forces to contract are in constant battle, accelerating at exponential rates until the internal fuel is exhausted and the star either collapses or explodes.

The forces of Nature show us the inescapable truth that you cannot move on indefinitely in one direction. Creation of form must follow release of energy, or the creative process leads to destruction. At a personal level, this implies a responsibility to work with whatever you have been given, and to choose how you work with it.

"Yet the legacy of supernovas is as close as our own bodies," Cowen writes. "The carbon in our cells, the oxygen in the air, the silicon in rocks and computer chips, the iron in our blood and our machines—just about every atom heavier than hydrogen and helium—was forged inside ancient stars and strewn across the universe when they exploded billions of years ago. . . . All the elements are there in the debris of fallen stars." (Ron Cowen, "Bang: The Cataclysmic Death of Stars," http://science.nationalgeographic.com/science/space/universe/cosmic-explosion/)

I have often heard the advice, "When you're feeling bad, go out into the night and look at the stars." Why it is so healing is a mystery, but it has something to do with remembering my actual position in it all. At a deeper level, knowing that we are made of the same elements grounds me; sensing that the same process forms us from those elements moves me to my core.

I could not have predicted in my college astronomy class that my fascination with the mechanics of the universe would have led me to take my place in it. It was only after years of life experience that I began to find myself on the same map with the stars. We are part of the same process. The continual exchange of energy and matter that creates the stars creates us as well. It is this force that moves the world forward; and we participate in it, consciously or not.

What would it mean if we fully accepted and applied this principle? Perhaps it is there to show us our place in this universe we share with the stars. We can use it to understand our lives. We can harness its power to change our world. This is the power of The Wheel of Creativity: to make us conscious of our relationship to this force and to put its power in our hands.

The Heavens on Earth

Humanity is fond of creating explanations for the workings of the universe from the knowledge it has at the time. Today we call our explanations scientific. But every generation has a science of its own.

Human beings have been observing the movements of celestial bodies for at least as long we have recorded our stories. As the earth keeps turning among them, our experience of time unfolds in regular cycles and rhythms. This force is no more broadly demonstrated than in the simple change every 12 hours or so of day into night into day. We are born and we die. Our stories, like our projects, each have a beginning, middle and end. Our lives unfold in seasons.

Human beings have marked the cycles in the earth's annual journey through the heavens for thousands of years by celebrating the summer and winter solstices (the days with the most and least sunlight respectively) and the spring and autumn equinoxes (the days when night and day are approximately equal in length). Why? At the most fundamental level, seeing the cycles of our own lives mirrored in Nature comforts us.

It is believed that humanity's oldest religious festival marks the winter solstice, when daylight hours on earth begin to grow longer. Ancient cultures—Celts, Romans, Saxons, Mayans, American Indians and others—marked equinoxes and solstices with sacred structures, such as Stonehenge, and sun-honoring ceremonies. To them, heaven and earth were mysteriously linked, and human beings lived their lives on the precarious edge between the two.

Though science has largely demystified the mechanics of solar movements, contemporary cultures—from Asia to the Americas, the British Isles to the Middle East—still celebrate their meaning. Darkness and light still belong to a single cycle, one giving way to the other. And human beings are still in awe of it, for it mirrors us our own experiences of the vicissitudes of life, and our hope that there is a force at work behind it all.

Through rituals like these, we celebrate Nature's creative process in four seasons. Each season gives a vital energy to the repetitive nature of Life. Spring is a time of rebirth and new beginnings. Summer is a season in full bloom. When summer has reached its peak, autumn brings the harvest. And when the harvest is done, winter offers rest and repose.

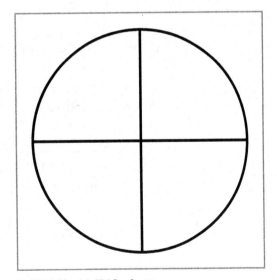

The Wheel of Creativity With Four Quarters

Drawing on the rhythm of Nature's cycles, The Wheel of Creativity uses four quarters to understand the cycles of the creative process. Just like the different energies of the seasons, the four quarters of the Wheel reflect distinct energetic states, which appear in human creativity as well as Nature.

- Quarter 1: Vision is where new things begin, in the form of ideas.

- Quarter 2: Exploration is where new things are sought and pursued.

- Quarter 3: Incubation is where new things are sown and protected.

- Quarter 4: Cultivation is where new things are developed and grown.

Each of these quarters corresponds to one of four elements, named by philosophers dating back to 5000 BC as the fundamental stuff of which life is made. The process through which we create is the same process through which we are created, the same stuff of which we and the stars are made.

- The Vision Quarter expresses the energy of the element Air and is the realm of the mind and thought.

- The Exploration Quarter expresses the energy of the element Fire and is the realm of the spirit and intuition.

- The Incubation Quarter expresses the energy of the element Water and is the realm of the heart and the emotions.

- The Cultivation Quarter expresses the energy of the element Earth and is the realm of the body and action.

The Four Elements

In the fifth century BC, the Greek philosopher Empedocles proposed that the universe is made up of four "roots" (Earth, Air, Fire and Water), which Plato later named elements. Similarly, Empedocles theorized that the human body was made of four humors, corresponding to these elements, which were later developed by Hippocrates.

Empedocles stated that the four elements were mixed and separated by two opposing forces—

Love and Strife—to produce the nature of the universe at any given time. The same dualistic forces that keep us separate and distinct also bind us together. This sounds a lot like construction and destruction to me.

The Buddha, who lived on the other side of the world from Empedocles, taught that the same four elements form the basis for our observations of physical sensations. But he also taught that they are false, and that form is actually made up of much smaller particles, which are constantly changing.

These are the elements of which we are made, and with which we work in the process of creation. Empedocles's names made them personal. The Buddha's warning revealed the doorway to our personal participation in the process. The Wheel of Creativity helps us find the building blocks of the future in our present circumstances, as we play our part in bringing Life's ideas into form.

As The Wheel Turns

The primary defining characteristic of a wheel is that it turns on an axis. It can be still from time to time, of course, but its function and its usefulness is in its turning. The Wheel of Creativity is a model that describes the process that turns and moves you through your life. The Wheel of Creativity is equally a system and a set of tools that assists you in moving through life deliberately.

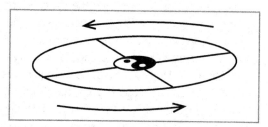

The Wheel of Creativity Turning

Two hundred years after the Buddha's death, Aristotle proposed a fifth element, based on his observations of heavenly bodies and his belief that they could not be understood according to earthly elements alone. Aristotle's fifth element was Aether, what we might call Space or Void. It is as integral a part of the beliefs of Hindus and Buddhists as of the ancient Greeks.

Taoism gives Aether the name Qi (Chi) and refers to it as a force or energy rather than an element. The Taoist universe consists of heaven (made of Qi) and earth (made of the five Chinese elements). These are the major themes of China's oldest written system of cosmology and philosophy, the *I Ching*, which describes the balance of Nature in the interactions of two cycles, a generating (creation) cycle and an overcoming (destruction) cycle. All that exists moves through these life cycles in this dance between heaven and earth.

On The Wheel of Creativity, Aether takes the name Essence, which is the Wheel's axis. From this still point at the center of the Wheel to its constantly spinning perimeter, the four elements interact together in a continually evolving dance of creation. Essence is made into Form at the perimeter, and Form is dissolved into Essence as it cycles back to the center.

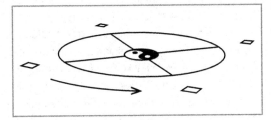

The Wheel of Creativity: Four Quarters Around Essence

Consciously or unconsciously, all human beings participate in this evolution. When we create anything—from a letter to a meal—we bring energy into form through the deconstruction and reconstruction of elements. The process begins even before we have the idea. With the realization that something is needed, we put ourselves in the gap between what is and what is not yet, between what is not yet and what is to be. We engage in the transformation of form into energy into form by expressing our own essence in the world.

The Chakra of Creation

Both Buddhist and Hindu philosophies describe human energy in terms of seven primary centers, ascending from the base of the spine to the crown of the head. Each of these chakras (Sanskrit for *wheel* or *disc*) spins at a different frequency in the energy system of the human organism, each governs a different aspect of the human experience, and each is associated with a different element.

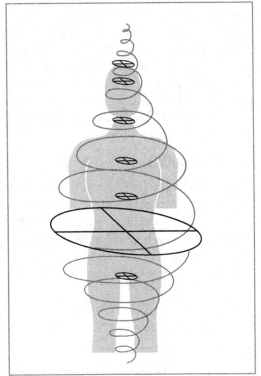

The Wheel of Creativity Within the Seven Chakras

Like the chakras, and perhaps unifying them, The Wheel of Creativity spins on the axis of our innermost essence. Like the chakras, when it spins freely, creative energy flows; when it doesn't, it doesn't. Learning to align ourselves with the natural turning of The Wheel of Creativity brings us power, balance, harmony, energy and a sense of connectedness with all of life. When we try to force the movement it becomes blocked, and we fail to experience these most nurturing aspects of Life.

Writer's block is a familiar term that expresses the moments when "it" is not flowing. Each writer has techniques to unblock the blocks. One of the most effective of these is house cleaning; simple, repetitive tasks get us up out of our chairs and out of our heads. They free us from our illusion of control. And then creative energy can once again begin to flow through us.

Every living thing engages with Life through its own Wheels of Creativity. As we respond to external events and our inner intuitions, hunches and inspirations, we weave webs of energetic patterns around us. When we open to Life's flow, we connect with the Source of all life and with each other. When we do not, we block Life's movement through us. Making this process conscious not only changes the quality of our lives, it changes the quality of our contribution to the lives of others. We do this through diligence, practice and presence in our daily lives.

The Wheel in 3-D

While it is helpful to view the details of The Wheel of Creativity in two dimensions, it does not move in two dimensions alone. When we look at the third dimension, the Wheel becomes visible as a whirlpool, a whirlwind or a vortex.

The Wheel of Creativity as a Vortex

The *Merriam-Webster Dictionary* defines a vortex as "a mass of fluid (as a liquid) with a whirling or circular motion that tends to form a cavity or vacuum in the center of the circle and to draw toward this cavity or vacuum bodies subject to its action." Yourdictionary.com defines a whirlpool as "water in rapid, violent, whirling motion caused by two meeting currents, by winds meeting tides, etc. and tending to form a circle into which floating objects are drawn." Following similar principles, a whirlwind is defined as a whirling mass of air in the form of a column or spiral, which rotates on an axis.

The Wheel of Creativity is a mass of whirling, spinning energy, your mass of energy, and you are responsible for its use. This spinning—caused by the continual cycling of destruction and creation—creates a vortex, and a vacuum in the center. The vacuum draws in everything close enough to be subject to its force. This vortex is your place in the stream of life, and you exert a force on the world around you, for better or worse. You can be consciously connected with Source, or you can be aligned with Form. In either case, Life seeks to flow energy through you all the time. Your experience of your daily life springs from your response to that flow.

Scientists recognize that a researcher cannot observe a subject without exerting an influence on it, so great effort goes into minimizing that influence. Journalists are trained to minimize the influence of natural filters—their background and experience, worldview, personal issues, etc.—on their stories. Learning how to responsibly use our energetic influence on that which we encounter in the world is our work as human beings. The Wheel of Creativity shows us how to channel the creative energy that moves us forward as we impact our world.

The perimeter of The Wheel of Creativity is the edge of the vortex. At this edge is where you encounter matter: your body, your possessions, the people you know, the people you don't know, your city, country, continent, the entire physical world. Here on this edge, in the material world, your perception is that things are specific and individual, that everything exists in separation. Movement is the rule. Change is the only constant. Time is linear, and what was yesterday is different today.

At the center of the Wheel lies Essence, the non-material aspect of matter, pure potential, that from which Form is expressed. The center is still, unaffected by time and space. Through the continual spinning of this vortex, the center of the Wheel descends. Below the level of the perimeter, the center of the Wheel sits deep down in a pool of collective consciousness. Here, in stark contrast to the edge of the Wheel, where matter separates into distinct forms, everything exists undifferentiated, commingling as fundamental particles of energy. Here at the center you perceive the oneness of things, people and the world. Everything exists in union.

For everything made of energy—in other words all things that exist—energy flows from the pool of collective consciousness up through the center of the Wheel (Essence) to the perimeter (Form). At the center of the Wheel, the experience is nonphysical, eternal, infinite and still. At the perimeter it is physical, temporal, finite and changing.

As a conscious human being, you can move through the Wheel at will. Your relationship with an experience will be different than mine, depending on where you are on the Wheel at that moment. Your experience will be different from moment to moment in relation to different aspects of your life, as each aspect has its own cycle.

You can be peaceful at home and in complete drama at work, depending on whether you are identifying with Form or Essence. If you focus on the perimeter of the circle, life will feel changeable, speedy and dramatic. If you remain at the center, you will experience it as still, peaceful, spacious. There is room for both of these experiences in life, and both are available at a moment's notice with a simple shift in focus. Movement between them is the creative process. It is a natural process that you influence by the choices you make in response to whatever is in front of you at the time.

When we know that our positions on the Wheel are a matter of choice, there is a sense of power, freedom, even play. Awareness enables you to trust the process. Practice empowers you to make the most of it. The descriptions, tools and practices you will find throughout this book will empower you to take your place, to play your part, in the process, to manage its inevitable discomforts and to maximize its power.

When we do not take responsibility for our experiences, we judge them, labeling one good and another bad, and spend untold amounts of time and energy justifying our lives accordingly. Throughout time and across cultures, human beings have developed myriad methods for managing this experience. Religious faith, metaphysical practice, physical training and psychological counseling can empower human beings to work with the personal impact of interactions with an environment we cannot control.

Whatever name it is given—meditation, prayer, mindfulness or presence—the practice of moving awareness from Form to Essence brings peace of mind. Shifting focus from the physical and sensational on the perimeter of the Wheel to the nonphysical, eternal and infinite at the center brings the timeless, spacious experience of stillness.

Artists experience this timeless, spacious relationship with life during acts of creation. The artist's work is to bring something from Essence into Form. In most of Western society, artists are revered for their ability to bring an original idea—through research, skill, practice and magic—into the physical world. But artists are not the only people on earth to do this work; the magic is available to us all.

In other cultures, especially the so-called primitive cultures, art is not an elitist role. It is neither professionalized as work nor trivialized as a hobby, but recognized as a fundamental aspect of being human. In these cultures, every member of society practices creativity, because it is held as essential to the health and life of the society where all the members play their parts.

There is an invaluable place in society for the work of the artist, and I do not intend to suggest that anyone can produce great art. At the same time, tribal cultures have recognized for millennia that the creative process is a human birthright and a responsibility, and they have built their societies around it. Only when we recognize this force in our modern-day world—in business, science and politics, as well as music, theater and dance—will we reap the full harvest of human creativity.

This harvest is far more than product, for when they engage in it consciously and deliberately, the creative process transforms accountants as well as artists. To make yourself a bridge between Essence and Form is to open yourself to the full force of Life flowing through you. It is to position yourself between stillness and change, spirit and matter, heaven and earth. Not only are you creating a New Thing, you are changing your environment, and you are transforming yourself. From Vision through Exploration, into Incubation, and through Cultivation, you can continually create that which nourishes you. The Harvest is your harvest of life itself.

A Field of Wheels

As the stars fill the heavens, we populate the earth. Everything—living and not living—is made of energy. This is a well-accepted scientific fact. Everything that exists is in a continual process of creation, using energy to create new forms, and destruction, destroying those forms to release more energy. Everything is grounded in Nature by this force.

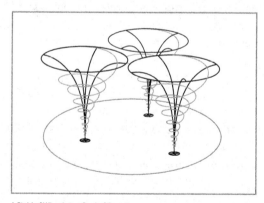

A Field of Wheels in a Pool of Consciousness

Today, it is commonly accepted that all objects have a magnetic energy field around them. This magnetism is classified into various types, from the spin around elementary particles to stellar magnetism around the stars.

All living organisms, including human beings, give off an energetic (electromagnetic) force. The

world's oldest philosophies give this force names like Prana and Chi, and we have modern names as well, like Life Force and Aura. As a human being, you are at the center of many energetic fields—from your circulatory and nervous systems, organs, muscles, glands, cells, molecules, right down to the electrons and protons of which they are all made.

At the nonphysical level of Essence, all these magnetic fields interact with each other. Buryl Payne, PhD, author of *The Body Magnetic,* notes that research findings "all point to connections between living organisms, spin and geomagnetic activity. All living organisms seem to be in resonance with earth's dynamic magnetic aura." And, he adds "Earth's magnetic field is in turn a function of solar activity and the positions of the Moon, and at least some of the planets." Life is moving in you all the time, and in relation with everything around you.

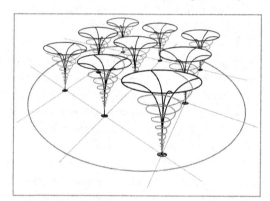

The Creativity Highway System

On earth today, there are more than seven billion Wheels of Creativity turning all the time. They are all bumping into each other, interacting, overlapping, cross-pollinating, for better or worse. Our connections with each other form a vast network—a highway system—through which one creative force expresses itself in seven billion different ways.

Different cultures have different myths about the earth's subtle energy currents, or electromagnetic fields. In England, they call them ley lines; in India, snake lines; in China, dragon lines; and in Australia, the song lines.

In his revelatory book *The Songlines*, Bruce Chatwin revisits the tracks of Aboriginal creation myths on which the original creator-beings created heaven and earth in the Dreamtime. The legend holds that these beings manifested the world as they wandered by naming in song everything on their path, from birds to rocks to waterholes. The term *songlines* identifies the intricate arrangements of lines between their stops along the way

As part of their rich and ancient cultural history, the indigenous people of Australia have told this story and shared these songs of creation from generation to generation. Native Australians still sing the songs today, following the footprints of their ancestors found in tracks laid down among the stones and sands of the Australian landscape. Through their journeys, they discover and reveal a deeper pattern, not readily visible but accessible through a mystical process of connection. This is what they call *walkabout*.

Each of us, through our own personal Wheel (and Wheels within that Wheel), receives and transmits energy along infinite energetic highways. Each of us stands at an intersection where the forces of Life pass through us, are processed and released—or blocked. The center of the vortex of each of our Wheels drops deep down into the collective pool of all that is, a single pool of unmanifest reality, where we are all connected, Source. Everyone is grounded in this same energetic Source by the creative force. Everyone has access to this energy all the time, and we are always creating with it.

We have given that Source many names, depending on the cultural influences of our birthplace: God, Allah, Great Spirit, the Universe, Mind, to name just a few. I call it Source, but at its most fundamental, and nonexclusive, I like to think of it as that which keeps my heart beating, the grass growing and the planets spinning.

We do not produce creative energy ourselves, but it flows through us. It not only gives us our ideas but the power to realize them, and we can either develop the skills to receive and use it or keep trying to do it on our own.

Weaving the Fabric of the Universe

The need to create is a large part of what makes us human. Our creative longing binds us together. Our ideas, whether thoughts alone or fully realized projects, change the world.

The physical separations that once made the world huge and impenetrable are now being dissolved, as the car, the telephone, the airplane, the television set and the Internet link us. You and I do not exist in a vacuum, untouched by each other or our environment.

As you are reading this book now, we are connected. We are here together, each with our lives, our circumstances, our dreams and our fears, all of which make up our personal creative process. Consciously or unconsciously, we are creating our worlds by our thoughts, words, emotions and actions, not only for ourselves, but also for those with whom we share the earth. We are alone here together, weaving the fabric of the universe. The idea of The Wheel of Creativity can help you make your creative process conscious. What do I mean by that?

In the textile art of weaving, two distinct sets of threads are interlaced at right angles to form a fabric or cloth. One set of threads, the warp, runs the length of the cloth, and the other set, the weft, runs from side to side. Cloth is usually woven on a loom, which holds the lengthwise warp threads in place while the weft is woven back and forth through them using a shuttle.

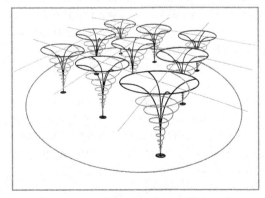

The Field With a Weaving Pattern Between Heaven and Earth

As weavers of the fabric of the universe, we use distinct threads as well. The vertical, or warp, threads are signals from Source to us: the continual transmission of Life expressing itself to us and through us. The horizontal, or weft, threads are the particles of matter that make up our world. Heaven and earth form the loom, and we (our thoughts, feelings, words and actions) are the shuttle.

Life expresses its desires to us, for us and through us, throughout our lifetimes; we respond to the best of our ability. Matter vibrates, waiting for our direction. Our shared experience of heaven and earth holds us all in place. And we move between the two, creating our lives as well as the world around us.

Whether meditating or singing, trying a new recipe or swimming in the sea, you move the weft back and forth through Essence and Form, between heaven and earth. Every time you reach out for Life, you dip your awareness down into Source, into the pool of consciousness to access the eternal, and come back up again into the material world.

If you imagine that we are all doing this with every thought we think, word we speak, feeling we have and action we take, the importance of these threads of our lives, which we take for granted, becomes very clear. Consciously or unconsciously, metaphorically and literally, we are continually creating our bodies, our relationships, our lives and our world throughout our lifetimes.

A cloth is not woven with one pass of the weft, but with pass after pass after pass. This is what makes the fabric beautiful or not, depending on the color and quality of the threads, the stability of the warp and the hand of the weaver. The point is not perfection, but rather the daily practice of resting in Source, moving between Essence and Form, collaborating with Life's desire to express itself through us. In this way, we welcome Life to move through us. We create what we think, and we transform ourselves, in joy or misery. And this is how we weave the fabric of the universe.

Transforming Your Patterns Is Your Adventure

Human beings are creating all the time. We are distilling ourselves in the world. We are synthesizing the raw experiences of our lives. The possibility of consciously cocreating this world together excites many people these days.

One of the contemporary pioneers in the concept and practice of cocreation is Findhorn in northern Scotland. According to its website, Findhorn was founded on the principles of "deep inner listening, and acting from that source of wisdom, co-creation with the intelligence of nature, and service to the world." Findhorn's founders, Eileen Caddy, Peter Caddy and Dorothy Maclean, applied deep inner listening to the task of growing Findhorn's first garden. "The inner source of wisdom they contacted daily included the intelligence of nature, and when they listened to and applied the wisdom they received, the garden flourished. As they progressed in their practice of attunement to the intelligence of nature, they came to understand that they were actually engaged in a process of co-creation with nature." Through their results they came to public attention, and today they inspire others to work in this way.

When I look at the world, I see this cycle of creativity everywhere. The cycling of the Wheel occurs on many different time scales at one time. Even on one plant, you can see all these processes at work at once. One branch is budding while another is dying. There are seasons, growth and dormant periods, in different areas of our lives all at the same time.

Everyone encounters blocks and gets stuck, in personal as well as professional life. The only way out is through. If you really engage yourself in the work of each stage, especially where you get stuck, you have the power to shift the energy. The Wheel of Creativity allows you to identify where you are in this natural cycle of creativity, to understand what you need at any point, and to take constructive, compassionate actions to accomplish what you need to in order to move forward. The process itself can become a pleasure no matter what your circumstances are.

We are all always on The Wheel of Creativity. If we're not conscious of it, we're creating by default. We're producing the results that we have in our lives. Whether it's a bitter fruit or a sweet fruit, that's what we're doing. The opportunity is always there to engage with the Wheel consciously, actively and proactively. Take that opportunity now

How Do You Live?

What distinguishes us as creative is neither innate nor environmental—whether you are particularly talented, rich or famous—it is experiential and inspired. How do you live? Whether solving a mathematical problem, composing a song, or building a business, human beings are most closely connected to the Source of all things, whatever they name it, when they are creating. When unexpressed, however, the same creative force deteriorates into the malaise, cynicism and anxiety so many people feel today.

The Wheel of Creativity is a concrete model of the process of creating anything new—a business, a work of art, a scientific explanation, an athletic performance, a new career or a new day. It enables you, whether you know you're creative or you're sure you're not, on any given day, in relation to any situation, to determine where you are in the cycles of Life's creative process. Awareness is the first step.

Knowing where you are in any creative process in your life (and there are many happening simultaneously all the time) gives you the information you need to respond. The actions required in the Vision Quarter are very different than in Exploration. One requires waiting with the process, the other requires gathering steam and moving out in search of the unknown. What is supportive of a project at one stage will shut it down at another. First you must know where you are; then you can determine where you want to go from there.

The Wheel at a Glance

Life is either a daring adventure, or nothing. HELEN KELLER

Helen Keller arrived at her assessment of life through her hands-on exploration of the world around her, and she expressed her experience in a language all her own. Keller might have spent her life institutionalized in sensory isolation, or medicated to control her emotional outbursts. Instead she made unprecedented contributions to the world as an educator and author, not despite her deafness and blindness but because of them. The limitations of Keller's physical body shaped her genius. She became a hero to our world because she accepted the role of hero in her own. For Keller, the ultimate creative adventure was being alive.

By our cultural standards, Keller was as creative a human being as ever lived. Not only did she take what she had been given and make a better life with it; she also grounded her personal achievements in tangible results that would change the world. A life is created stone by stone, particle by particle, and, as with Keller, the quality of our lives rests in our own hands.

Life itself is your greatest creative collaborator as you dance your way through the process. Some-times the dance is a waltz, sometimes a tango, sometimes it's nothing more than wild, ecstatic abandon. Sometimes Life leads the dance, and sometimes you do, but you are always participating in the process together. It is easier and more enjoyable when you know the steps.

I have observed the creative process at work throughout life, synthesized a wide range of descriptions of this process and created a model to help you find and take your place in it. No matter how wealthy, how beautiful, how intelligent, how popular or how far from these things you may feel, you are here on earth for a reason. You have a contribution to make, and making it will change your life, not only by the results you produce but also by the way you undertake the task.

Life does not come with a set of instructions; each of us must find our own way. But when someone comes along who has been on the same street, that person can guide us. If you can, with a little help, see your life from a higher viewpoint, you can relax and trust the process just that much more.

The Wheel of Creativity is a framework for a

The Wheel of Creativity®

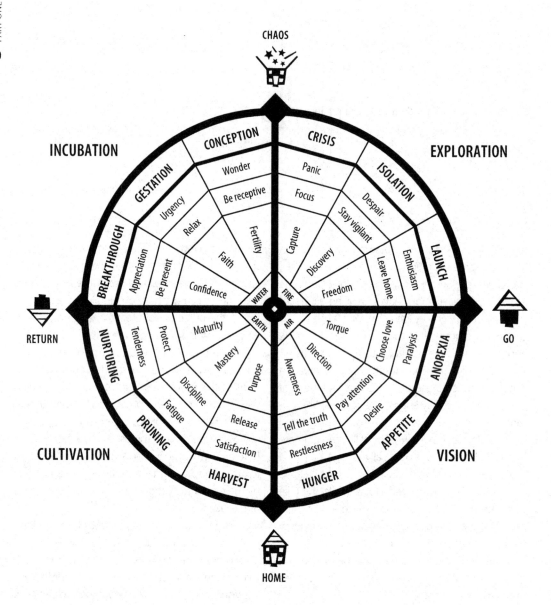

CHAOS

INCUBATION

CONCEPTION
CRISIS

EXPLORATION

GESTATION
Wonder
Panic
ISOLATION

Urgency
Be receptive
Focus
Despair

BREAKTHROUGH
Relax
Fertility
Capture
Stay vigilant
Enthusiasm
LAUNCH

Appreciation
Be present
Faith
Discovery
Leave home

Confidence
Freedom

WATER FIRE

RETURN

EARTH AIR

GO

NURTURING
Tenderness
Protect
Maturity
Torque
Choose love
ANOREXIA

Mastery
Direction
Paralysis

Discipline
Purpose
Awareness
Pay attention

Fatigue
Release
Tell the truth
Desire

PRUNING
Satisfaction
Restlessness
APPETITE

CULTIVATION
HARVEST
HUNGER
VISION

HOME

process as ancient and intimate as Life itself, and I have tested and refined that framework through the experiments of my own life. It is more a poem than an equation, waiting for you to enter the spaces in between and find yourself there. Enter the Wheel with me to discover what it has to say to you about your place in life, and how to jump in and participate in the greatest adventure of all.

The Landscape

In the previous chapter, I established the basic structure of The Wheel of Creativity: a circle with four quarters, each of which contributes a different vital energy to the process of creation. I also presented the context in which the Wheel organizes the energy of cocreation in the physical world. Here we will take a closer look at what happens inside the Wheel as you live your daily life in that world.

The Wheel of Creativity is a map of the creative journey. The journey has 12 stations, which take you through all four quarters of the creative process: Vision, Exploration, Incubation and Cultivation. Your ticket, which every human being receives at birth, gives you access to all 12 stations, and they must all be visited. You need not visit every one on every cycle, and they do not necessarily appear in order. You can get stuck in a station or a quarter when the work you need to do there is particularly difficult for you. But the Wheel is always turning and will move you forward through your life if you will trust and commit yourself to the process.

Each station has a unique and recognizable feeling. It calls you with a distinctive voice. Each has its own task for you to achieve, and its own reward to win. Knowing where you are on the Wheel with regard to a single project will enable you to gain the most from the experience and to transform yourself through it even as you create.

Station by Station

To help you understand what occurs through the Wheel as a framework for the creative process, I will outline the journey here station by station. This is the process in its most natural and organic state, as it turns unobstructed by personal agendas or issues.

Think about yourself as you read this. Think about a project you're dreaming of, or one you're already in the midst of. And follow along on the Wheel as we go through, to see what fits for you here. Where do you find yourself in The Wheel of Creativity?

HOME. The starting point on the Wheel is always Home. This is the status quo, the world as you know it, normal everyday life. While this is not necessarily your literal home, it is an experience where everything is familiar, stable, orderly and known. Most of the time, it is lovely to be at home. Grounded in the community you know, it is comfortable and safe and secure. And then one day, suddenly or gradually, you begin to feel restless. You start to feel that you want something more, there's something missing. It is this restlessness that casts you into the Wheel and starts you on the journey.

STATION 1. That feeling of restlessness is the first station, which I call Hunger. It is a vague feeling that something's missing. You don't really know what it is; you just know that something is not right. It could be that something is worn out in your life—a relationship, a job or a hometown—but it is always evidence of an inner hunger, a desire not quite yet formed. Station 1 can lead you to the start of any new project. You can find yourself here at midlife, or at any transitional time. It is a clear indication that the-way-things-are needs to die in order for the-way-things-could-be to be born. As you sit with that and begin to tell the truth about what you hunger for, what is missing starts to become clear; you become aware of what you're longing for.

Nalin Patel is an MIT-trained computer programmer who grew up in the Gujarat region of India. Encouraged by his family to become an electrical engineer, he was in college when he first felt his life didn't fit. "I liked Indian robotics, being a part-time gadgeter," Nalin told me one day as we sat on a park bench in France. "So I got into the best engineering

ol I could and took electrical engineering as
te to making robots." Leaving his sheltered
for the first time at 16, Nalin felt out of place
India's future electrical engineers at college.
"They would spend all their time reading and talking
about it; and I couldn't wait just to be done with my
assignments."

Nalin's restlessness with his choices pushed him
to look outside his childhood box, and that led him
to the point where he found something that did fit. "I
started exploring other things just to keep me sane.
I started taking philosophy classes and, eventually, a
short-story writing class run by a very old Polish lady
who had been a writer for years and had stories of
cafés in Poland and Paris and the writer lifestyle, and
I found that it just fit. Something clicked."

- Where in your life are you experiencing
  creative restlessness?

- What other doors do you feel drawn to
  knock on?

STATION 2. From the vague feeling of something
is missing, you begin to notice something on the
horizon. Soon you realize that it is calling to you. That
calling makes the vague hunger into something specific. This is the second station of the wheel, which
I call Appetite. It is the feeling of desire. It's the big
"Yes" that leaps up in you: "That's what I want!" For
some, it comes as a clear certainty of what to do next.
Joan of Arc called her guidance "voices." For others,
it could be simply the awareness that something
like that might be better than this. It can lead you
to a new town or job or out of a bad marriage, but
it is the first stop in a process, and you cannot know
now where you will actually end up. Whatever the
form, it is the point of clarity when something comes
into focus outside, and your heart spontaneously
responds. Yes! Yes! Yes!

Marti Cate, a performing artist and teacher, enjoys spotting the creative process at work in everyday life. In an interview, Marti told me:

"I watch kids on the beach playing with stones.

The stones may slip as they try to move them from
one place to another; but they never get discouraged. They just do it and do it and do it; and then
they get it, and then they get better at it, and then
they get great at it. There's a lack of self-conscious-
ness because they are just finding the depth of the
well of unlimited possibilities.

"I find that these days in partner dancing. For
example, I was in the countryside in Italy, and there
was this moment. The waiter, the music, the floor,
there we are. We were total strangers, listening with
all our senses to this moment and cocreating it. And
it's just brilliant and exciting and fulfilling. And that's
what I would like to share with people in my work."
Whether it's children on the beach or her own personal pleasure, Marti is always paying attention for
signs of what she wants on the horizon.

- How do ideas on the horizon get your
  attention?

- What do you do to be available to them?

STATION 3. After the expansive "Yes" of Station 2,
a natural contraction follows. It is the habitual "No"
in your life, and it comes down like a crashing wall.
I have named Station 3 Anorexia after the eating
disorder, because essentially it is the avoidance of
what nourishes you. In this station you must not
only release control, you must also choose what
you believe will nourish you. You may second-guess
yourself, or the voice of doubt may come from your
family, your friends or your culture. "You'll never have
that. Don't you dare try." As inner and outer voices
come up to test and build your resolve, the pressure of your longing builds. It is a time of resistance,
whether from outside or within. Your inertia may
look really cozy as you cling to the familiar past.
Even though you long for change, you are paralyzed.

As he moved further from his sheltered upbring-
ing into the world, Nalin Patel began to see the origins of his inner restraints. "Within my region of India,
creativity is thought of as a luxury of the idle rich,
not something that any sane person should focus

on. Children who enjoy writing are told, 'Fine, you do that on the side, but get your career in pharmacy so you have a stable living.'"

By aligning his choices with what clicked for him, Nalin gradually overcame the internal prejudices against creativity he had learned in childhood. It was in Los Angeles, when he joined a writing group at a club of Indians in the film industry, that he realized the extent of his internal resistance. "I was the only young person there. Everyone else was the age of my father. This class of people I had always thought of as disciplinarians, people who hated creative pursuits, were all sitting around drinking and smoking, talking about art and poetry. And suddenly I realized that Indians do have strong creative instincts."

- What prevents you from going for it in your life?
- What kinds of new choices do you need to make?

Hunger, Appetite and Anorexia are the three stations in the Vision Quarter, where the work is primarily internal and receptive. As you move among them, these stations work together to build a kind of torque, the energy to push you from your internal idea out into the external world. When your desire to pursue the vision exceeds your reluctance, there is an energetic shift that allows you to break through your inertia and take action. If, however, you sit in the process too long, the energy can become extremely destructive. You must harness the power of your thought to be able to move on.

GO. Once you've moved past the paralysis of Anorexia, you move through the Go Gate into Station 4.

STATION 4. Launch is exhilarating, energizing and exciting. Finally leaving the familiar shore can be an act of faith or an act of desperation, depending on how you handle the risk. If you've been resisting the commitment out of your fear, you might let go and leap from sheer exhaustion. But inherent in this station is the natural enthusiasm and excitement of beginning something new. Whether you are beginning a new project or a new relationship, Station 4 is the high dive, and once that leap is taken there is no turning back.

Through 30 years of research into changes in the sun's activity, solar physicist and computer scientist Peter Fox has learned to "look for the unexplainable" in his intuition. "As a scientist, you have to have some element of confidence in yourself," Peter told me on the phone, "because otherwise you don't open yourself up to the creative thought. There's the point where you have to trust that at some level your intuition is right.

"Early on, self-censorship doesn't exist, because we're just like children, experiencing everything. And then in the period of training—graduate work, postdoctoral work—and in your early career, there's a lot of censorship. Because we haven't matured, we haven't established our sense of identity within a faculty, within a system or within a field of research. But the work I've done has let me accumulate enough experience that I can trust myself to think about any problem and to have a creative thought, even not in my field." That point, where Peter has learned to take the leap and follow his first thought, is Launch.

- What enables you to make the leap on a new project?
- Where do you find the confidence to trust your intuition?

STATION 5. It could be weeks or months after Launch, but eventually there comes a point when the shore you leave behind disappears. If the new shore ahead is not yet visible, then Station 5 appears on your path. It is the period I call Isolation, when you feel completely alone and lost, even despairing. For explorer Christopher Columbus, it was the time when he put away the charts. His men were running out of food, they were talking of mutiny, and there was still no sign of land. In Isolation, the voices of doubt (still inside you) start screaming: "What were you thinking? You should never have left home! This was a huge mistake!" And what are you to do with that? Keep going. Stay vigilant and navigate your way through, even with tiny moves, to keep moving in the direction of your dream.

Louise Rogers always wanted to be an artist but never thought she had what it took, and her high school counselor confirmed her belief. In a telephone interview, Louise said, "I held him in a place of authority, and I thought he knew better than I did what my own heart was telling me. So I went about doing that. I just didn't continue to look for myself." After a year in college, though she performed well in mathematics, she gave up, and chose a two-year certificate program. She got a job as a secretary, got married and had a daughter. Louise was overcome with the despair of Isolation and gave up on herself.

But, that was not Louise's last experience at this station. Years later, while going through a painful divorce, Louise took another opportunity to look for herself. "I had other people supporting me in doing what I wanted to do, and I just decided that I was going to do what I wanted to do. I had more determination then in my life than I ever had and more courage. I don't know if I would have ever come to that point otherwise."

- What are the gifts of aloneness, solitude and loneliness in your life?
- How do you cope with the anxiety there?

STATION 6. Just when you think you can't get any lower, just when you think it can't get any worse, it does. Opposing forces intensify until the Crisis comes, and Station 6 appears. Perhaps you spot what looks like land where what you've been searching for comes into view. Everything in you rallies to get you there. But there are obstacles from outside. In order to get to the land you have seen, you must first pass through the perfect storm. You have no choice but to go into it, and your ship is lost. The feeling here is panic, an overwhelming experience

of instability, imbalance, disorientation and disorder. Any way you look at it, this is a difficult stage.

I came to understand this station several years ago at the seaside. I had been swimming in the sea every day that summer, and I was a strong swimmer. Though the sea was turbulent that day, I was confident. I managed to swim out beyond the waves without difficulty. But when I tried to return to shore, I got into trouble.

I found myself caught in the crashing waves. They were coming so fast and strong that I lost control of my body. I was about to succumb to the waves when, in one moment, everything became clear. I thought of two questions: (1) Which way is up? and (2) When can I take a breath? Those two questions enabled me to find the blue sky and right myself, and then to simply find the moments when my face was above the surface to breathe. They enabled me to focus and find serenity in the midst of the crisis. And, as you might have guessed, I made it to the shore.

- Where do you feel like you're completely out of control?
- Where in the crisis is your clarity?

Launch, Isolation and Crisis are the three stations of the Exploration Quarter, where the work is external and active. These three stations intensify your commitment to the search by throwing up the inevitable obstacles to your enthusiastic pursuit of your vision. It is a time of testing your spirit and strengthening your energy, and it makes you stronger as it moves you forward.

CHAOS. As Crisis takes you to the edge of your personal limits, you find yourself at the next gate, where energy shifts again. Chaos is the far point in the universe, as far from the certainty of Home as you can get. In contrast to the order and stability of Home, here everything is disordered and unstable. Chaos overwhelms you, and it will take you down unless you find a way to let go and surrender to it.

But in the absence of the old, this moment creates an opening in you. If you can take courage and relax, the seed of the New Thing takes root in you.

STATION 7. That moment of surrender shifts you again, this time from the Masculine energy of the hunt to the Feminine, where the new is conceived in the ashes of the old. This first station in the Incubation Quarter is Conception. After passing through the earth-shattering ride of Crisis through the Chaos Gate, here everything settles into stillness. For the first time, you sense that something new has arrived. Station 7 is a sacred moment, a quiet, receptive space where the seed is fertilized, and planted in the waiting soil within you. There are moments at the beginning of every project when you feel vulnerable, and it takes faith just to believe that the seed is there, before it makes itself visible. Being aware that you are in this station enables you to trust the process, and with each turn of the Wheel your faith in it grows.

Peter Fox began his career as a research assistant in his home country of Australia. One of his jobs was to maintain a piece of software that scientists used for graphing their results. In an interview with me, he described how solutions often arise out of chaos. "The program was built in computer language, and the rules of syntax were very precise. So one day someone came into my office and said, 'I really need to do this,' which was to display the number without the decimal point. And this person had been to everybody. And without even thinking, I said, 'Do this.' And the guy stopped in his tracks and said, 'That is absolutely brilliant.'

"It was exactly the right answer. He walked away, and I thought, 'Where did that come from?' I'd never done that before, never thought about it before." Peter describes these most startling of creative thoughts as "out of the blue." In this case, he became a collaborator in the other scientist's creative process, bringing his search through Chaos to Conception, so much so that he sat in wonder of where the idea had come from.

- What methods do you use to get from Chaos to Conception?
- When do you need ideas to come from "out of the blue"?

STATION 8. When you surrender to the hidden work of Conception, you naturally move into Station 8. Gestation is where the seed takes root and begins to grow. The work here is to relax, to allow what is growing beneath the surface and out of sight to do its own work until it is ready to be seen. As time passes, what is happening here becomes clearer. An occasional movement may be felt beneath the surface, but you still cannot see the thing itself. Anticipation and anxiety come hand in hand while you wait for signs of life. But any attempt to push the outcome will prove counterproductive. Taking care of yourself physically, emotionally and spiritually, as the creative channel, will help you develop the capacity to live with this uncertainty until it is time.

Penny Cox is one of the most creative women I have ever known. While efficiency has often been my top priority in life, Penny's life has been an homage to beauty, whether in her artwork, her home or the way she presents a meal. One morning over coffee in her kitchen, Penny said, "Once you've experienced the moment of being a channel, being the means, you keep striving for it. You keep trying to get back to that place. At least part of it is about getting out of the way and just allowing it to flow through. And it does. It's a very specific, identifiable, obvious experience when it happens."

Penny knows intimately the challenges of being receptive and has her tricks for waiting with the process. "It's hard to get the commercial voices out of your head; it's hard getting the judgments out of the way to get clear enough, empty enough, that you can just show up at the drawing board or easel and allow it to tap in. When I am most stressed or overloaded I seem to be able to experience that in the physical doing of the projects, like working on my trailer, or rearranging a room, or making a collage;

whatever it is, somehow there's easier access there than in sitting down at that empty paper or canvas and waiting for that to happen." Penny illustrates how important it is to stay present, even in the most receptive of stations like Gestation, looking for how to meet the process and invite it in.

- How do you deal with periods when it seems nothing is happening?
- What kinds of results are you getting?

STATION 9. Station 9 is a welcome relief; finally the interminable waiting is over. Breakthrough occurs when the baby is finally born or the little green shoot pokes its way through the moist black earth. The moment brings joy, well-being, a sense that all's right with the world. It is the peak experience of the creative journey. This is a moment of appreciation, as you welcome the New Thing into the world. What has been invisible and inaccessible to you now becomes visible again. Now it's time to take a deep breath, relax and celebrate.

Louise Rogers's personal breakthrough came shortly after she graduated with a degree in interior design. "After I got my degree I noticed a really big shift in my confidence. One of the people that I worked with in studio for over three years finally said to me, 'Do it, Louise, because you've got it. Just do it, and be more confident.' And, all of a sudden the switch just happened. Why I needed to achieve that, I don't know, but it seemed like something really important for me."

Today, Louise is an interior designer in Las Vegas, Nevada. "I have no problem now working with clients or other people in the industry and feeling confident that I know what I'm talking about, or at least I'm learning . . . or that I have skills and that I have some intuition to do what needs to be done. Every day I appreciate how much I love what I'm doing and can't believe it could be so pleasurable and still be work, and that I could be earning a living at it." Like all "overnight successes," Louise's epiphany of confidence arrived after three years of diligent

application. Breakthrough always comes at the end of some period of Incubation.

- In what area do you need a breakthrough today?
- What would that breakthrough look like?

Conception, Gestation and Breakthrough are the three stations of the Incubation Quarter. Here the journey turns inward again, where you are called to reconnect action with receiving. You must work with your emotions to trust the process while the work is happening inside you, and sit with your discomfort at having to wait until it is ripe. This requires digging deep, through meditative practices, to find your bedrock in Source.

RETURN. At the end of the third quarter, when the container for internal growth has become too small, another energetic shift occurs. From the cozy inner world of Feminine growth, through the gate called Return, the process turns back to the outward-moving Masculine and the Cultivation Quarter.

STATION 10. Nurturing is the appropriate response for a newborn. In your hands, you hold a fragile new life. It needs unconditional acceptance, love and tenderness to develop. This is the energy of mothering, as you provide for the needs of the New Thing until it can survive on its own. It is a delicate time. If, out of your own ambition or fear, you judge, rather than love, this newborn, you will stall here. Skipping this step, for example, by trying to monetize a product before it is fully developed, is risky. It is too soon for expectations.

Cheryl Coons is a playwright and lyricist based in Chicago. While she has little trouble with earlier stations, Cheryl hits her challenges here, as she shared with me over the phone. "My experience of my reviews in the past has been shattering. The fear of bringing something into the world you've been cherishing as a dream since your twenties is something different and really intense." After years of working on other people's projects, Cheryl finally dared to write and produce a piece of her own. Within three months of the first reading, the show was on stage in Florida. All the reviews but one were glowing, and the play went on to win the Carbonell Award for Best New Work.

But when the show went to Chicago (with the same lead and the same set), the reviews were mixed. "I was so shattered," Cheryl said. "Not that I expected the result to be identical to that in Florida, but I had felt so good and it had sold so well. The reviews in Chicago must have hit some chord in me that I wasn't good enough. I was so identified with this work and shocked by this that I went into an incredible despair. That's the biggest dark night of the soul I've had." Through that experience, Cheryl developed a few simple practices that protect her and her work; she learned how to nurture the New Thing until it is strong enough to take the blows.

- Where do you feel most vulnerable in your creative process?

- What do you do to protect yourself from criticism in the early days of creating?

STATION 11. As the New Thing grows, it begins to spread out and develop its own strength; it needs discipline to assist in this part of the process. This is Pruning, which not only involves cutting from a plant that which drains its life but also involves giving it strength. A creative product must be edited, refined, disciplined to succeed. In the 1984 film *The Karate Kid*, Mr. Miyagi insists that Daniel perform various chores around his house, knowing that the movements required by these chores are the same movements required in karate. Because the process has not been explained to him, Daniel grows irritated with his servitude. Then, one day, Miyagi shows him that the skills he needs to protect himself have become automatic in him.

Stations 10 and 11 actually work hand in hand. While Station 10 was the energy of the Mother, this is the energy of the Father. One informs the other

as the Masculine and Feminine harmonize to move the New Thing to where it can stand confidently on its own.

Even for an accomplished artist like Penny Cox, getting idea into Form is a challenge. "It's one thing to have this full completed image in my head. The real challenge is getting out of the way in terms of the production. Being able to make the hand, the paintbrush and the paints do what is in my head. That's always a challenge. And sometimes it requires a certain letting go, too. That requires a stepping back, just showing up and pushing paint.

"If you're a sculptor and you just sculpt, your access to that is so much more readily available all the time. If you do lots of different things and your head goes off in different directions, it's very hard to channel all that back into one place. And that's a great argument for discipline: showing up every day for 10 minutes, two hours at the easel, the drawing board or the clay, whatever it is, and just doing it." The work of Station 11 is about the daily discipline of doing the work in order to keep your skills sharp and ready when an idea finds you.

- What is the role of discipline in your creative life?

- How do you train yourself in your chosen field?

STATION 12. Harvest is the final station of The Wheel of Creativity, and it appears when the New Thing is mature enough to go its own way. This is easily associated with bringing a product to the marketplace. But it could just as well be sending your child to school or completing the renovation of your home. It is the final step in making the New Thing useful in the world. Not only does it then fill the Hunger you left Home with, it also nourishes the community. It, like you, now has its own creative process as you let go of it and release it into the world. It needs the language of the community to be relevant in your world. You can write a brilliant book, but if readers do not speak your language, it is useless to them. You can create a revolutionary product, but if customers do not understand why they need it, it will fail. Station 12 brings a mixture of feelings: a giddy desire to share what you've created and a sense of loss for the journey at its end. With the Harvest, you have to get through the empty nest, the enormous emptiness that occurs when the process is complete, before you can arrive at the feeling of satisfaction that you have brought the baby home.

For Cheryl Coons, the process of creation is always a collaboration. "There is a line we use in the theater—'You never really finish a musical, you just decide when to abandon it'—because it is just such a complex form. Theater is a very collaborative process. Every time you add another collaborator into the mix, you are diluting the original vision of the creator. My primary collaboration is with myself as a writer, but I am always thinking in terms of the audience. At a certain point I just let go." There is a time to let go of any project and release it to the world; this is the Harvest.

It's a marketing question, too, Cheryl adds. Inevitably, the creator needs to get other people involved in refining and embodying any project. Here it becomes crucial to ensure that everyone involved in the project sees it the same way you do; otherwise it ceases to be your project. At the end of the long road of creation, Harvest can be a very difficult stage, requiring perseverance and inner strength to stay true to your original vision even as you are letting go. The journey that begins with your hunger finds completion when you and your community are nourished through it.

- What is the nourishment you long for now?
- Why does the world need it too?

Nurturing, Pruning and Harvest are the three stages of the Cultivation Quarter. It is an active, external time when you ground your prototype, your New Thing, in the physical world. This is where you produce the result. Here you must engage your body, mind, heart and spirit fully as you bring the energy into form in the world of the five senses. Cultivation requires tools, manpower and consistency to see the project through to completion while it is at its peak.

When at last the Harvest is complete, Home takes on a new meaning, welcoming you back to the stability and calm of the community you knew. Back through the Home Gate once again, it is time for rest and repose. You have completed the cycle of creation.

When you began this journey, you had only a vague restlessness, the feeling that something was wrong. Now you have arrived back where you started with a new creation, and your life has taken on new meaning. You have harnessed the power of your thoughts, strengthened your spirit, calmed your emotions and engaged your body. Through the process of the journey itself, you have been transformed. And now that you have returned Home, you bring with you a New Thing to share with the world and the nourishment you sought when you left.

The journey around The Wheel of Creativity is continual and constant. It occurs in myriad time-frames—from single moments to an entire life-time—with a cycle for every endeavor, activity and experience of your life. For the turning of the Wheel is the unfolding of Life itself.

The Alchemist's Wheel

Every aspect of The Wheel of Creativity is both personal and universal. We receive, we express; we take something in, we put something out. Whatever we touch or write, or produce or react to, is taking its form through us, and we take our form through that process. Through this never-ending cyclical movement, Life turns The Wheel of Creativity in our lives like a great engine of momentum, moving us forward as it moves through us in the world.

The outside of the Wheel is Form, the center of the wheel is Essence, which at depth always rests in Source. Through the course of our lives, we continually cycle between the outside of the wheel, where things are separate, specific and individual, and the center, where everything is one. We continually move Life energy up from Source, through Essence into Form.

This process, of moving between what is within and what is without, is not unlike the processes engaged in by medieval and Renaissance alchemists. At the height of its influence in the world, alchemy functioned on two levels: the mundane and the spiritual. While alchemists worked on the physical level to convert base metals into gold, they understood and used their experiments as reflections of what lay within them. In essence, I suppose, alchemy provides us with a philosophy and inner perspective which keeps the material and the spiritual united.

For centuries, alchemy and science developed hand in hand in response to a single fundamental question: "What is man's relationship to the cosmos?" Alchemists worked in pursuit of what they called the philosopher's stone: a substance that could turn lead into gold, old into young.

By the 16th and 17th centuries, practitioners were splitting into two camps. The first group focused on analysis of chemical elements, which led to modern-day chemistry. The other group, esoteric alchemists, continued to explore the original question using alchemy as a spiritual practice, a meditation on life's elemental processes.

By the 19th century, English spiritual alchemist Mary Anne Atwood described the process: "Alchemy is a universal art of vital chemistry which by fermenting the human spirit purifies and finally dissolves it." Editor, publisher and authority on alchemy texts, Adam McLean adds: "The alchemists reflected and mirrored these outward events into their interior world. They saw the processes in their flasks as an interaction and linking of the spiritual and the material." (Adam McLean, Animal Symbolism in the Alchemical Tradition, The Alchemy Website, http://www.alchemywebsite.com/animal.html)

The alchemists' working process could as easily describe the creative process in your life, when you engage in it as consciously as they did. The forms of your life—people, things, events and circumstances—are intimately connected with your inner creative work; they are the material, and The Wheel of Creativity is the alchemist's flask in which you refine yourself through your interactions with the physical world. Day in and day out, you can move toward enlightenment by deliberately participating in Life's ongoing process of creation, by actively participating in your own life. This is why we are all here.

The Wheel of Creativity unveils the mysterious processes through which creation occurs and invites you to find yourself and take your place within them. The external results you produce in your life begin deep within you and work their way out from there. If you want to change those results, you have to go to the Source and change your relationship to it. You have the power to transform the essential elements of life into the world's most valuable treasure. Take your place and use it!

All Aboard!

I have seen The Wheel of Creativity move me continually forward through my intentions, changes of heart and even mistakes. Unexpected turns of events and happy surprises alike are all pulled into the vortex to create this amazing adventure I call my life. You can enjoy the power and satisfaction of a life well lived if you take your place as the creative force within this process.

In the next 12 chapters, I will take you deeper into each station of the Wheel. I will show you, station by station, how to recognize where you are in the creative process. I will give you tools and practices to get the full benefit of each station and move on when it is time. I will share other people's stories so you can see how they have done it.

The creative process is the rhythm of life. It is no more reserved for artists than dance is reserved for professional ballerinas. It is Life itself always flowing through its fingers—that is, anyone or anything who dares to live according to their truth. It is flowing through you!

Part Two

12 Stations on the Creative Journey

Whatever you can do, or dream you can do,
begin it. Boldness has genius, power and magic
in it. JOHANN WOLFGANG VON GOETHE

1

STATION 1 Hunger

Hunger comes to me on the road like a savage beast,
speaking the truth.
It calls to me from my innermost Self.
It calls me to eat Life, or be eaten by it, to ask
what would nourish me, and then
to go about creating that.
Hunger tempts me with the fruit of the tree
of the knowledge of good and evil.
It tempts me
to be human, to enter the Void
where Fire and Water and Earth and Air can dance
where Form is created
and I, in the creation of it, am nourished.

What are you hungry for? What do you long for? What calls to you from the deepest darkness of your own soul? What's wrong? What's missing? What made you pick up this book, and why are you still reading?

Hunger is the starting point of our connection with Life. It is what brought us here. It is how we survive. In relation to the creative process, I define hunger as the soul's longing for nourishment.

On the Platform in Station 1

Hunger is the first stop on The Wheel of Creativity and the official entry point to the creative process. It is Station 1 in a closed loop of 12 stations that make up the full circle of the creative journey. Inevitably, the journey leads you away from Home and back again. And once the journey's taken, life is never the same again.

Hunger opens the gate to Vision, the first quarter of The Wheel of Creativity, the landscape across which you move away from the comfort of Home. As in all four quarters, you will stop in three stations to reach the other side. When all the tasks are done, you pass through another gate into the next quarter.

You can arrive at your Hunger by choice or by accident, through internal or external forces; but the resulting experience is a deep, inconsolable restlessness. The overall feeling in Station 1 might be boredom, stagnation or a relentless dissatisfaction with the status quo: "This isn't it." The voice of Hunger—the announcer in Station 1—repeats at **43** increasingly regular intervals for anyone to hear, "Something's missing." The graffiti on the wall says, "I want. I do not have." In any case, this stop on the journey is uncomfortable.

If you ignore it, Hunger becomes increasingly painful and eventually all-consuming. When you are blinded by "This isn't it," the beauty of Life all around you—from a simple flower in a vase to the music of the wind or the constantly changing patterns of the sky—becomes invisible to you. When you lose your connection with Life, to a greater or lesser degree, you lose your strength, your confidence and your personal power. When ignored too long, this deep Hunger for Life itself can actually make you sick, as your need for spiritual food drains your personal resources to keep you alive. It is actually possible to starve to death.

Creative Hunger occurs in life transitions as well as creative projects. While Station 1 is commonly associated with midlife, usually called a *crisis*, it also occurs on most of life's thresholds, at any transitional time when the secure shell of the present must crack open for a new future to emerge. It occurs in cultures around the globe as surely as in the privacy of your own heart.

It is the force that initiates new projects, new governments and new lives. It is markedly evident in world news today, as people rise up in one country after another to say, "This is not acceptable to us anymore." But, as we begin to see, now that governments have fallen, the force of Hunger must unravel the status quo. What comes next depends on how well that force is grounded.

Hunger always points to the need for something new; and it often rides in on the wake of loss. It could be a job. It could be a relationship. It could be a government. You could lose your health, your home or your faith. But the loss itself is a gift from Life, to pull you off the security of the shore and cast you into the wild and unpredictable river of Life again.

Sometimes we choose the changes, and sometimes they choose us; but with any inarguable withdrawal from the status quo, The Wheel of Creativity begins to turn.

When we listen and respond to our hearts' desires, Hunger leads us naturally into the creative cycle. But when we are not listening to Life, or fail to respond to its invitation, it gives us a hand, sometimes bringing to an end the very thing to which we cling so tightly.

This is not a recreational ride! More often than not, it can be scary, destabilizing and disconcerting. Most of us would never choose it willingly. But as external circumstances dissolve, they point you to your deeper longing for intimacy with your Self and your Source.

Responding to Hunger requires feeling rather than avoiding the pain. That's why this step takes courage. To live in the gap between what you have and what you want, when you don't have it yet and you don't know where it's coming from or how, is uncomfortable.

It is understandable that people often try to avoid or manage the discomfort of Station 1. Everywhere you look there are plenty of distractions. And we use them as long as we can, acting out in escapism, obsessions or compulsive behaviors like working too much, eating or drinking too much, social media addiction or compulsive spending, reaching in desperation for anything but the here and now.

The longer Hunger remains unattended, the more urgent it becomes, until finally it screams: "I have to have this … now!" You can make huge changes in your life based on this urgency, only to find out down the road, when the honeymoon is over, that things (and you) are still the same. You must stop and feel the void before you act. The only way around this is through it.

The Sacred Voice of Hunger

We are a have-it-all generation. We have so many choices, so many inputs, so many things to fill our time, busy our minds and stuff our bellies with that we have forgotten what real hunger feels like and have lost touch with its value. There are many people in the world, not as materially fortunate as we, who never know what it feels like to not be hungry. Good fortune lies on the middle road.

The gift of Hunger lies in knowing and feeling what you don't want. The stronger the feeling becomes, the more you feel the emptiness. While the void may become very strong, however, it is still unclear, vague, dark, even confusing. And it appears in the very first words of the Bible, in Genesis 1:1–3:

"In the beginning God created the heavens and the earth. And the earth was without form, and void; and darkness was upon the face of the deep. And the Spirit of God moved upon the face of the waters. And God said, 'Let there be light.' And there was light."

The emptiness, the vacuum, the void itself is the beginning of the creative cycle. It may not always feel like it, but it is good. Hunger's discomfort must be endured to get to authentic desire—Appetite. Before you can know what you do want, you must first know what you don't want. This awareness guides you like a machete through the jungle to the clearing of your own mind. If you never let yourself feel it, you'll never have clarity about what's important to you, and what really nourishes you. Appetite moves from inside out, reaching for that nourishment.

In this chapter we will explore what Hunger feels like to you and where it appears in your life today. We will examine your discomfort and what you do with it. We will look at what is required of you to move from Hunger to Appetite, which is Station 2 on the Wheel. And we will look at the reward of trusting the process, through which you come to know what you truly want.

A little reminder: Creativity and art are two different things. When I speak of creativity, I speak of the bigger context of life in which we all live, not the professionalized practice of that force by a few elite talents, and certainly not the trivialization of creativity as a part-time pastime, only indulged in once more important things are done.

Creativity is a way of living by which you take your natural place in Life's creative process. This continual process of creation is one in which we all participate. It is a process through which you connect with and are nourished by the Source of all that is, as you define and experience it.

Life in Station 1

Hunger is a gaping void and it speaks the truth. It acknowledges the Void in the process of creation— the fifth element, required for Earth, Air, Water and Fire to interact and create form. And, when felt, it puts you into the gap between what is now and what is not yet.

We are in this gap in many places in the world today. Japan is recovering from triple disasters in 2011, the outcome of which is still uncertain. The Middle East is rocking as violently, with a crescendo of discontent that crosses borders and defies authority. The West is working frantically to try to repair broken economic systems built on unstable ethics, which are exploding in one industrialized country after another. Hunger's message of "Something's missing!" is going viral around the globe and leaving us spinning with instability.

These crises have shattered the status quo and sent people headlong into bottomless pits of want and need. Part of what has brought us here is that we have collectively ignored the world's Hunger pangs, until now they overwhelm us. Just as the human body can function beyond the initial feeling of hunger, when blood sugar drops too low, the body goes into crisis. Particularly for people with diabetes, this condition can be life-threatening.

The temptation, in vulnerable times, is to stop the hunger we feel, to stuff it down, block it, short-circuit it, make it go away. But the hunger itself is the key to reconstruction. It cannot be ignored and it cannot be appeased—for long. It requires attention, truth and nourishment. And the process cannot be rushed.

There is a growing trend in the New Age movement to suppress our longing. We are told to focus only on the way we want it to be. It is suggested that feeling negative feelings can be dangerous. "We must not complain, keep ourselves positive and ignore the rest."

The Experience of Hunger: Restlessness

Through much of my life, my experience of Hunger's restlessness was fear—of the space, the emptiness, the uncertainty, the longing. But longing is the contrast against which true deep appreciation is revealed. Those who renounce the longing miss the point; the point is not to turn away from those feelings, but to accept them, to welcome them. The voice of Hunger is a sacred voice. To refuse it is to refuse Life itself.

When I was a child, my father always wore a short-sleeved shirt and a pocket protector. My father gave the best hugs—strong, tender, committed. The six or seven different pens he carried in those pocket protectors always poked me. But it was worth it.

Sometimes Life embraces us with strong experiences that are in fact softer and more comforting than you would ever imagine. Even the hard blows have amazing gifts in their pockets; but you have to get close enough to them and let them touch you in order to know the gifts are there.

For exactly six months in 2003, I took antidepressants. I had spent years righteously resisting doing so, in honor of my maternal grandmother. Her life had been lost in psychiatric treatments—from multiple types of shock therapy to a lobotomy in the end—that robbed her of her authentic Self, all because of a questionable diagnosis of schizophrenia. Eventually, exhausted by the mental and emotional storm I now identify as menopause, I listened to my doctor and tried them. I took half the usual dose, and I determined in advance the date when, at four months and two weeks in, I would start reducing the dose. I took them precisely. They helped. And I didn't like them.

I didn't like the way they cut off the highs and lows of my experience of life. I could not reach the high notes I once had; something was missing, and that something was important to me. In the words of the character Zorba the Greek, I want "the full catastrophe" of life. Life may deal hard blows from time to time, but that is part of the experience of being fully alive. For with each experience lived and responded to, I create myself in the world.

I am not demonizing antidepressants, nor do I wish to alienate anyone who is benefiting from them. I value them as a temporary recalibration; I worry about them as a long-term solution. It is not the point of life to be comfortable in every moment, and our dependency on outside substances to take the edge off deprives us of the very thing that will make us whole—our true Selves.

Hunger is an uncomfortable feeling at times, to be sure. But that discomfort changes and diminishes with time. When accepted and received with gratitude, it opens up another world.

The death of a loved one can have this effect. At 5 a.m. on January 16, 1992, my phone rang. I had packed my car the night before to drive from Chicago to Texas for a long visit with my parents, but because of a blizzard on the route, I had delayed my departure. The call came to tell me that my father had died. I got up, dressed, added a black suit to my suitcase and went to the airport. I'll never forget the feeling as I floated through O'Hare International Airport. The world seemed suddenly softer; nothing was all that important; it all seemed pale by comparison to the knowledge that my father was no longer there.

For a few days or weeks, that enormous absence put me in touch with the exquisite precariousness of life in the body.

The Beauty of Hunger

Mystics have known this for millennia, the power of this edge where we are keenly aware of our mortality. Thus, in many of the world's religions, fasting plays a part in spiritual practice. For some, fasting is about denial; for others, purification. For me, it is about making nourishment authentic.

Hunger puts you in touch with the precariousness, and preciousness, of Life at its essence. It puts you in touch with your own Essence.

When you lose touch with your hunger, as occurs in anorexia and other types of eating disorders, you lose your connection with Life, and the ever-flowing current of Life through you. There is nothing more nourishing than that. Yet, there are those who choose this path from a position of power.

The Power of Hunger

For centuries, fasting has been used across societies—including India, Tibet, Europe, the United Kingdom and the Americas—to call for the righting of a wrong or injustice. In early Irish society, fasting was used to call attention to the perceived injustice of a lord; a person who felt he had been wronged would fast on the doorstep of the offender. In India, this custom was practiced from the middle of the first century BC until it was abolished by law in 1861 (just eight years before Mohandas Gandhi was born). The hunger strike, and fasting to death—which has been used by protesters in Ireland, Turkey, Cuba, Sri Lanka and Tibet, among other places—did not come until later.

In the early 1900s, American and British women suffragists used hunger strikes as a form of protest in prison. Rather than make martyrs of them, officials released some of those who became ill, though they were often returned to prison when their health improved. Others were force-fed, a practice still used today, and some of the women died as a result. But, in the end, their sacrifices won the right for women to vote alongside their husbands and brothers.

Probably the most famous of all hunger strikers in the modern era was Mahatma Gandhi. Gandhi, who ignored caste restrictions and devoted his life to fighting racism and injustice within India and outside it, used fasting to speak to the world. Gandhi's first fast, 21 days long, protested the British rule of India in 1932. In 1947, he stopped eating again, in an effort to end the violence between Muslims and Hindus in an India that was splitting in two. Through media coverage of his refusal to eat, he raised worldwide awareness of the cause and gained a mass following among his people.

And these are just a few of the many who have undertaken similar fasts and strikes using their personal hunger to change society.

The Path of Hunger

Biological hunger and the body's need for nourishment are connected but not the same. When a person stops eating, the body goes through a series of stages in its attempts to survive. For the first three days, it uses glucose as its energy source. After three days, ketosis sets in as the liver processes body fat for energy. After three weeks, the body begins siphoning energy from vital organs, muscles and bone marrow; this is the onset of starvation, which can cause death in as few as 50 days.

So why do hunger strikes work? Why does hunger wield so much power? Why did Gandhi achieve so much with his hunger strike?

Hunger is our most fundamental shared physical experience. In it lies our potential for life, and we do not go down the path of life without feeling and reacting to it. So when people deliberately choose hunger, when they decide to risk their survival for a cause, it is a lightning bolt screaming to the world, "This is important." Whether or not you agree with their position, they have your attention.

As I write this, Japan faces radioactive contamination of its food and water supply as a result of its nuclear disaster in 2011. Also in 2011, when floods swept through big sections of Sri Lanka, that country lost 20 percent of its national staple crop, rice. When the supply of food is threatened, its value increases. Life becomes a kind of survival. By contrast, when food is plentiful, we take it for granted. We lose our connection with the Life in our food, and we lose our connection with the sacredness of Life.

The Value of Hunger

It does not take a hunger strike, however, to recognize the positive value of hunger in your own life.

Nonreligious traditions, such as naturopathy, recommend periodic fasting to allow the body to rest and replenish its energy.

In *The Yoga of Discipline*, Gurumayi Chidvilasananda states that the Life Force (what yogis call Kundalini) is not meant to be used only for digestion; rather, its primary purpose is for creation. Her advice is to allow a bit of hunger to remain even at the end of a meal:

"Don't fast. Just eat in moderation. Eat in a disciplined way, and when you're not hungry, don't eat. That is the best fast… . Stop eating when there is still a little hunger left in the stomach. It is actually a longing for/hunger for God. Keep the digestive fire active. It is your hunger for God that sustains you, even more than food." (Gurumayi Chidvilasananda, *The Yoga of Discipline*, SYDA Foundation, 1996)

In the Hindu tradition, physical hunger connects you to your hunger for God. Spiritual hunger puts you in touch with life's deepest questions: Why am I here? What is the meaning of this life? What is my role in it? And there lies Hunger's greatest value. The questions themselves lead us into the creative cycle of Life, in which we have a unique and integral role. And no one can answer them for us; we must do so for ourselves.

Hunger-Defying Habits

In the rush of everyday life, many of us never actually touch our hunger. We eat out of habit. But habits have little to do with authentic hunger, and they interfere with its personalized messages to us. Here are some hunger-defying habits:

Time to eat. Some people eat by the clock. They might eat when they are not hungry just because it's time to eat. Others eat every hour or so just to keep the edge off, so they never feel the real hunger brewing in their bellies. Or they may not eat when they are hungry because it's not mealtime. You can go hours or even all day without eating and feel no hunger at all. Your body still needs refills of fuel, but you have lost touch with the signals.

Must eat right now. Another habit is waiting too long to eat and then, when blood sugar drops, fall-

ing victim to the "I have to eat right now" syndrome. Food preparation becomes urgent, and the quality of eating takes second place to filling up the void.

Too busy to eat. In the best of times, I purchase, prepare and eat lovely food. I relate to it as Life Force given to me with beauty and perfection. At other times, however, usually when I'm too busy to be present, eating slips from urgent to compulsive. I eat more junk food. Rather than having a relationship with my food, I munch. When I get hungry enough, I reach for anything.

Force-feeding. While force-feeding is considered inhumane with prisoners, I have observed it often in free society. You sit down to a lovely meal at home, in a restaurant or even at work. The next thing you know, you look down and your plate is empty, your food is gone, your stomach is full, and you almost cannot remember eating it. The party's over; you were there, but you missed the whole thing.

Craving. You know how to eat, what to eat, when to eat. But you don't do it! Something else kicks in. Why? When hunger is distorted or diverted, it produces craving—an obsession with a particular thing, which could be food, sex, spending, alcohol or anything else. We make all kinds of excuses for it, but at the end of the day, when real nourishment is missing, the urgency of craving sets in.

Eating rotten food. France is famous for its fresh fruit and vegetable markets, and it's a French tradition to buy and eat fresh food every day. My favorite way to spend a Sunday morning in France is to walk over to the market to admire and buy a colorful assortment direct from local farmers. It is a pleasure to bring Nature's beautiful produce home and put it all away. But over the years, I began to notice an unhealthy pattern of waiting until the food was on the edge of edibility before I would eat it. Clearly I had room to grow in honoring the sacredness of Life in my food.

The Belly and the Breath of Life

When I think about my connection with Life itself, it is evident that we all owe our lives to the same force.

We are related not only to other human beings, but also to the animals and plants that sustain us. Native Americans have a simple phrase that expresses it all: "All our relations." If anything cuts its connection from Life to feed me, then the least I can do is to be sure it has not died in vain.

Nature, by its design, fills all my senses with attraction. I look at a beautiful fruit platter and see all the colors and textures, and I realize that all of it is designed for nourishment. Not in the mechanistic percentages of vitamins and minerals, but in living color, taste, fragrance, sound and texture. It is all made to nourish me. It is more than fuel for my body: It is beauty and pleasure and Life itself.

Swami Chidvilasananda referred to the power of hunger's emptiness to connect you to God. For this reason, the breath is also more deeply nourishing than food to the body, mind and spirit. The deep diaphragmatic breathing used by yoga practitioners in meditation relaxes the entire autonomic nervous system. The French words for *wind* and belly are *vent* and *ventre* respectively. When the central cavity of the body we think of as the belly opens to make space for the breath to descend, we make space to receive and transmit directly. This is what the Hindus call Kundalini energy. It is the sacred force of Life itself. Take five slow, deep breaths now and you can feel it.

Yet most of us in modern life find this difficult. We live efficiently, conforming to the institutions we have created. And, losing touch with ourselves, we form unconscious habits of shallow breathing or holding our breath. We begin to deny the free flow of Life Force through us. It is a mechanism of control, and we use it on ourselves.

What if everybody were channeling this energy directly? All the organizations—churches, schools, governments, societies—built on keeping order would be in big trouble. You might call it the ultimate global democracy. What if we taught people, from childhood, how to channel this energy for the good of society? What would be possible then?

This is not about teaching anything; rather it is about helping people remember the most essential truth, so often lost in swells of religious, cultural and personal oppression: We are all connected. We are connected to each other and to all the other life forms with whom we share this great, glorious universe. We are also connected to the Source of it all.

Just like all living things, human beings are designed to be channels for the creative force of Life. Our role here is to receive, transform and create. Life's deepest pleasure comes when we are where we are meant to be, doing what we are meant to do. What then, as we are placed in the world to blossom, could make us sadder or hungrier or more restless than not doing that?

Qualities of Hunger

We are designed to eat. Sometimes hunger is a big round thing, sometimes it is very small, sometimes it is a quiet gnawing, sometimes it is a screaming headache. But I've noticed that the quality of my hunger is very different when I have exerted myself and fatigued my body. Then my body is ready for food.

We are designed to transform energy to create new things in the world. Physically, spiritually, emotionally and mentally. Creation is the counterpoint to inspiration. When you create, you prepare yourself to receive more. When you fail to create, you cannot take more in. Everything begins in emptiness, and the emptiness itself is the invitation to Life for more to be given.

Watching What I Eat

One morning while writing this book, I had a kind of spiritual awakening. Looking down into my bowl of muesli, I saw a tasty mixture of fresh grated apple, chopped almonds, almond butter and lemon juice. And I thought about the origins of each of these foods.

The apples, the almonds and the lemons all grew on trees. I thought about how they all have roots in the earth and stretch their branches to the sky. I imagined the energy of the earth reaching out to me through those roots, through the trees, through the fruit of the trees, rising up from my bowl and into my body.

I felt so much love for what I was eating, for where it came from and for the earth that supports us all. I felt myself in relationship with it, and I felt joy that what I was eating was giving me Life energy. In that moment I was completely nourished, not just physically, but spiritually as well.

Itadakimasu: I Gratefully Receive

Ten years ago, I was having lunch in Villefranche-sur-Mer, in the south of France, with Ikuko Saito, the beautiful young Japanese woman who introduced me to one of Japan's sweetest customs. Ikuko used a word that she told me in Japan is spoken at the beginning of a meal like *bon appétit*. The word, *Itadakimasu*, is literally translated as, "I take your life." More generally, it is understood as "I gratefully receive." And Ikuko described it as a moment of appreciation not only for the food but also for all the hands that contributed to bring it to the table. From the waiter, to the cook, to the person who chopped the vegetables, to the driver who delivered it, to the seller at the market, to the farmer who grew it, everyone is included.

What I love about this word is the way it puts me in relationship with the circle of Life. And it requires me to be responsible for my part in it. Starting with the first bite I put into my mouth, what rises up in my heart is gratitude. Not only to Nature for the food itself, but to all living things for the great collaborative exchange in which we all participate. One person's role is not greater than another's. We are all linked by our common need and our common good, for which we weave the web of Life.

Hunger's Creative Gift

So what does all this talk of Hunger and the avoidance of it have to do with the creative process?

Hunger opens the gate to Vision, the first quarter of The Wheel of Creativity, within which two more stations must be visited on the way to the other side. It is the official entry point to the creative process.

The Task of Hunger: Tell the Truth

The task of Station 1 is to tell the truth, to admit that something is missing, that you long for something more. It is to allow what begins as a vague feeling of restlessness to take root and grow and deepen. It is to give it enough silence to hear what it wants to say. It is to detach from the noisy distractions of the world and the compulsive reactions of your own body/mind long enough to hear the still, small voice within. When you develop the discipline to detach the experience of Hunger from food and eating and all these other things, when you are able to just sit with the feeling, you can learn to value your hunger as a creative impulse rather than as a sensation you have to get rid of.

It is in the emptiness of Hunger where the oneness can be felt. Hunger is open space, receptivity and possibility before form. Hunger brings you into contact with the Life Force, in what you eat and in what your body does with it.

Your body breaks food down to release essential elements, and then your body replenishes the cells that build your tissues. When you eat the nourishing, natural food designed for the human body, you empower yourself with Life Force. By contrast, when you eat nonfoods (processed things that come in boxes, with very little Life in them), you become less alive.

The same is true for the creative process. We are the bodies of Life. We take the existing forms of our lives, break them down to their raw essential materials and build new lives with them. Every single day.

The moment of Hunger, which often endures, is an opportunity to detach from your reaction to or anticipation of what is not in this present moment. It is an opportunity to practice presence with what is happening right here and right now in a way that you choose.

Hunger is the starting point in your connection to Life. It is the starting point of the Wheel. It is the starting point of your experience of yourself as a channel of Life and the creative Life Force.

When you finally settle down into Hunger, there's a very tender energy there. On the other side of this station, past the screaming body and tangled mind, is a softer touch to life. Through the sadness, an exquisite beauty emerges; a finer kind of energy, as opposed to the thick and heavy energy of fullness. It is a fine-tuning of the receptor that your body is.

The Reward of Hunger: Awareness

When the truth is told, Hunger's reward is awareness. It is awareness of what you do not want, awareness of what needs to be filled and the faint glimmer of the light of desire on the distant horizon. And that awareness puts you on the train to Station 2: Appetite.

A STORY OF HUNGER

Kim Lambert, Truancy Prevention Specialist
Current City: Hayward, Wisconsin

> "I'm a believer that the more confusing and mysterious it is, the greater the learning I have in store, if I'm open to the possibility."

I have never met Kim face-to-face, though we have had a few powerful conversations via Skype. A mutual friend, whom I met by chance in Colorado, connected us two years ago. Even without knowing me well, he knew that our meeting would bear fruit.

Kim's story illustrates the value of honoring the longing within and staying with it as Life leads you through seemingly unrelated experiences to discover something that truly nourishes you.

KATHERINE ROBERTSON-PILLING: Could you tell me a little about your job?

KIM LAMBERT: I work in a grant-funded position at the Boys & Girls Club in the Lac Courte Oreilles Band of Lake Superior Chippewa Indians, part of the Ojibwa Tribe. I serve students who are showing up as truant, which means that they are missing all or part of a certain number of school days. In my work, truancy is a symptom of a bigger problem in Indian child welfare.

KRP: Why did you take this job?

KL: I did not grow up on the reservation or spending much time with my many relatives who live here. But I've always wanted to serve the community here in some way. So, when I got my training as a life coach in 2005, I approached a couple of people with the tribe; but the timing wasn't right. I maintained my own business in Madison [Wisconsin], until five years later when I was approached by the executive director of the Boys & Girls Club. Within a month after applying, I took a leap of faith and moved up here to build a new life. Soon after that, I met Dr. Lane Lasater, and now I recommend students to attend his Social Responsibility Training program, which we call Mastering the Journey.

My theme with the kids is, "I not only want you to succeed, but I want you to want to succeed." I want them to want more for their lives, their future and eventually their community. And I don't think they've ever really heard that before.

I tell the kids I'm working with, "If you're going to play video games, then figure out a way to be the best that you can be; whether that means designing games, or helping others be more productive in their lives through games." I'm not a big promoter of kids sitting around playing video games, but if they can do it in a positive way that serves the world, then I'm for it."

KRP: It seems to me that the principles of community, along with connection with the earth and sustainable living, were originally all there in tribal culture.

KL: You're very right in that they were there. Before reservations, Indians were on their own land. They all worked together to take care of the unit, and everyone had to do their part. They had to be the best gatherer, the best hunter, the best fire tender that they could be; and that served the greater whole. But what I think is unfortunate in today's life—and it's global—is we have an expectation that somebody should be taking care of things for us.

The good news is that we're making a lot of progress toward making the overall culture of our reservation much more positive. We have an immersion school at our tribal school—grades K–4 right now—where they only speak Ojibwa language in the building. We have a two-year college, and are in the process of getting accredited for four. We have a new tribal council in place, whose theme is "Mission Possible."

We still have regular powwows, and there is a lot of participation by our young people. Our tribal school still has a dress-up powwow, meaning our kids wear all their regalia and dance along with the staff. And they have their own student drum group, where they sit around a large drum and sing. No drugs or alcohol are allowed on powwow grounds. It is considered a sacred time.

KRP: What do you think has been lost in the Native American community?

KL: A lot of what we suffer from is historical trauma. There are some people who practice very traditional ways of living the best they can. But many are forced by the ways the world is evolving to practice more contemporary ways, and a lot of the traditional ways, I think, are getting lost.

Unfortunately, there's a sense of settling on the reservations: "This is the way it's always been. This is who we are." With any value, be it love, humor, even creativity, if we don't feel worthy of it, we're not going to experience it. And when people grow up without something that they feel they should have had—a father or mother, or a true home—worthiness issues arise. If they feel helpless and unable to provide for themselves at any level, they're going to resort to others to take care of that for them.

KRP: And how is this showing up in the community?

KL: The kids are looking for a place to feel safe, to have an identity, to be accepted and wanted. And unfortunately, they look to gangs. So we've hired a gang-prevention specialist, and we're adding services that allow our youth to be more involved in positive activities.

The gang is in it for the gang and not the people involved. The tribe, when it's working together and organized, is in it for the people involved. I've recently been asked to become more involved in expanding our youth council. We're helping the kids—ages 13 to 19—develop a charter and a set of bylaws, conduct their meetings in business fashion, and raise funds to benefit service to the community. The idea is that they will be seasoned in tribal government and understand the importance of service to our

community and hopefully take on a leadership role. The enthusiasm is there; and once the other youth see this atmosphere of leadership, they'll want to be part of it as well.

KRP: I hear a lot about leadership in what you're doing.

KL: From a personal and professional standpoint, the foundation of the work I do is empowering youth. Helping them understand leadership—government, council, a sovereign nation and how treaties have protected our rights—helps them see that they have personal power to accomplish whatever they want. For some that's a completely new principle in life.

KRP: What is your experience of Great Mystery (a Native American term for the creative energy present in all things)?

KL: In my personal experience, it is the adventure of life. I try to practice that in every aspect of my life, whether it's a hike, a new relationship or even an acquaintance. To me, everything is part of the mystery of my life. I always work to embrace the unknown, appreciate the unknown, and try never to take anything for granted. I'm a believer that the more confusing and mysterious it is, the greater the learning I have in store, if I'm open to the possibility.

KRP: How would you define creativity?

KL: Wow, Katherine. I guess first of all, it's a willingness to accept who I am by my own definition. And then it's a willingness to always expand upon that definition, to move beyond it. Every day is a new and exciting definition. Whatever I focus on, I want to learn to expand upon it and make it better. And if I make it better for myself, I know I make it better for the world. That's how I get creative.

KRP: How do you experience a greater force?

KL: It starts with love of myself always.

KRP: How did you discover that?

KL: Probably dealing with my own worthiness issues. I grew up without a father, and to believe that somebody chose a different life than living with me, raising me and being part of my life built an underlying worthiness issue. So I didn't like myself. I didn't want to be alone with myself; and no matter how many friends I had, I was lonely. But I came to grips with all that through my own life coach, spiritual advisers and study of Native American spirituality. Once I got to appreciate who I am, my creativity just blossomed.

KRP: Because of that, are you better able to work with your students?

KL: Exactly. If I want to help the youth who are most challenged and at risk, I need to be able to look them in the eye and tell them that I've been through difficult times. The challenges were not the same, but I made it. And I do get vulnerable with the kids. I stayed behind strong protective walls for so many years that to get vulnerable with anybody is one of my biggest challenges. But when the kids see that in an adult, a whole new relationship develops. Then they're willing to put their walls down and do their work.

2

STATION 2
Appetite

It doesn't interest me what you do for a living.
I want to know what you ache for
And if you dare to dream of meeting your heart's longing.
ORIAH

On the Platform in Station 2

Appetite is the second stop on The Wheel of Creativity. It is Station 2 in the 12-station loop that moves you around the creative journey and home again. Appetite is the place where your longing must be named, your vision clarified, your desire refined and your resolve reinforced in order to move what-could-be out of thought and into the physical world.

The experience of Appetite is desire. Its task is to pay attention. And its reward is direction.

While Hunger was a feeling of restlessness, Appetite takes that restlessness to the next level. The voice of Appetite is "You're all I want." With Appetite, you move from the vague feeling of Hunger into the specific awareness of what you desire.

What is the relationship of Appetite to Hunger? In the Hunger Station, by telling the truth about the emptiness in you, you begin to gain awareness of what you're hungry for, what you long for. That awareness—of what attracts you and what nourishes you—moves you to Appetite

As you become clearer, you feel what you desire more strongly. But knowing what you want is just the light going on. That strengthening of your desire makes the light grow brighter. What you do—or don't do—with the desire comes later. Appetite and the action of reaching for what you desire are two different things.

In the creative process, Appetite refines desire. It evolves Hunger from an internal emptiness into a particularly definitive vision. It makes it specific. It is beginning to reconnect with what you are attracted to, what you feel strongly about and what you feel called to, perhaps for the first time in your life.

Defining Appetite

The Oxford Dictionaries define *appetite* in two ways: (1) "a natural desire to satisfy a bodily need, especially for food" and (2) "a strong desire or liking for something." It originates with the Latin words *appetitus* (desire for) and *appetere* (to seek after).

Hunger is the physiological drive to find and eat food. Appetite is the psychological desire to eat specific foods. Appetite aids digestion by stimulating the secretion of saliva and other digestive juices. **55**

In fact, you need only see a food you like to begin the process. Giving your attention to foods leads to appreciation of them, and that starts the digestive juices flowing.

Appetite also stimulates the desire to eat enough food to nourish your body with the elements needed to rebuild it and supply it with enough energy to sustain itself continuously. When enough food has been eaten, the brain registers this and flips the off switch on appetite.

Mind and Body

When Aristotle talked about desire, he described it as the craving for pleasure. And he referred to two types: rational and irrational (or natural).

Rational desires are born in the mind. They are given to us, in a sense, because they have been described to us in positive terms, and we have believed in them. This could describe the cause of many of the uprisings occurring around the world today. The fight for democracy may be founded for many in what they have heard from others. And today, the media play a huge role in this. Advertising and marketing have their roots in rational desire, as advertisers lead us to believe their products and services are the solutions for our natural desires.

Natural desires, according to Aristotle, are not based in the mind, but are connected with our senses and originate in the body. Through our bodies, we experience the desire for nourishment; that is, we are hungry and thirsty. Natural desires are awakened in us through our senses as they connect us to the outside world.

Balance and Wholeness

The purpose of physical appetite is to create and sustain wholeness and balance with true nourishment for the body, mind and spirit. The body is not separate from the mind and spirit. Our bodies are chemical manufacturing facilities, producing finely balanced electrochemical processes that keep us alive and ticking.

Our bodies are designed to take physical matter (Form), break it down to release energy (Essence) and rebuild it again as new tissues. If our bodies cannot digest our food—that is, break it down and extract the energy from it to rebuild our tissues—then we are not nourished.

This is what happened to me when I developed algodystrophy after breaking my hip. For whatever reason (they say it is often associated with Type A personalities), my body was breaking down the bone tissue in my leg but not rebuilding it. My entire right leg decalcified to the point that I broke my heel just by putting my weight on it. With proper nutritional support, within six months my leg had recalcified, and the complete break of my femur had mended itself. This is not unusual; this is what the body does.

Fear and Control

Appetite is an experience of desire, but it's more than that. It also involves the will. The natural response to appetite is to eat what will nourish our bodies, but we do not always respond this way. And when we ask our bodies to break down what is not truly nourishing, then those things become toxic to us.

Google the word *appetite* and you'll find Internet links to an array of appetite suppressants and stimulants. There is big business in developing elaborate (and often harmful) ways to control the appetite, ranging from diet aids to drugs to surgery. And we still never get to the core of what we're really hungry for or what we really need to live.

Eating disorders—compulsive overeating, anorexia and bulimia (or binging and purging)—are distortions of true physical appetite, and they are on the rise. According to a 2011 study conducted by the Imperial College in London, obesity rates have doubled in the past 30 years, and not just in the West. By 2008, 205 million men and 297 million women around the world were obese, and 1.5 billion more were overweight. Since 1990, the US rates of bulimia and binge eating have almost doubled, while the rate of compulsive undereating—anorexia nervosa—has been stable at 0.3 percent.

Either way you approach it, eating disorders are a distortion of the body's natural desire to eat what nourishes it. They stem from a disconnection from true hunger, which has at its core a disconnection from the nonphysical, spiritual Hunger within. Anorexia is just saying no to whatever nourishes you, spiritually and emotionally. We will visit this again in Station 3.

Pity the Hungry Ghost

Many forms of Buddhism talk about the idea of Hungry Ghosts. These pitiful creatures wander between worlds, starving and unable to eat. They are often portrayed as teardrop shapes, their tiny throats and huge bellies rendering them perpetually victimized by their own hunger.

Mark Epstein, in his book *Thoughts Without a Thinker*, describes them this way.

> Phantomlike creatures with withered limbs, grossly bloated bellies, and long thin necks, the Hungry Ghosts in many ways represent a fusion of rage and desire. Tormented by unfulfilled cravings and insatiably demanding of impossible satisfactions, the Hungry Ghosts are searching for gratification for old unfulfilled needs. They are beings who have uncovered a terrible emptiness within themselves, who cannot see the impossibility of correcting something that has already happened. (Mark Epstein, *Thoughts Without a Thinker: Psychotherapy from a Buddhist Perspective*. New York: Basic Books. 1995)

Hungry Ghosts are completely attached to physical form. Trapped in the past, they find no satisfaction in the present moment. We all know people like this, who can see only what is not, and never what is.

But the longings within ourselves are the harbingers of possibility, if only we acknowledge them. They are the messengers of the creative process, pushing us to move from Form on the spinning perimeter of the Wheel (the things we believe we must have), to Essence, to the center, where, in stillness, we know completely what authentic nourishment is for us. But we get caught up in the external world, and the return to ourselves is a process.

The Hungry Ghost's problem with the throat has to do with the silent voice, the habitual failure to own our own appetites, to want what we want. The only antidote is to find our voice and speak. To express what we want, opening up the space in our throat to be heard, even by ourselves. Throughout centuries, Buddhists have practiced rituals for Hungry Ghosts, which include praying and chanting and offering food, out of compassion for their suffering.

What Defiles a Person

In response to the stringent laws of food preparation among the Jews of his day, Jesus said, "What goes into a man's mouth does not make him 'unclean,' but what comes out of his mouth, that is what makes him unclean'" (Matthew 15:10–11). He was saying that it is not the circumstances of life but our responses to life—our thoughts, words, emotions and actions—that determine the quality of our lives.

Today we can still become righteous about personal nourishment. We demand fat-free, gluten-free, high-protein, low-carb. Things have to be a certain way for us. We have this luxury in the Western world. But nourishment begins beyond that. It is what occurs within us as we mine the circumstances of our lives for treasure.

Most of the industrialized modern world is caught in a cycle of insatiable consumption. We devote our lives to making more money, accumulating more things, saving for the future, surrounding ourselves with possessions that we are sure will bring us satisfaction, security and serenity. But they never do. Because what we long for, what will truly satisfy us, will never come from outside. We may drive world economies with our appetites, but the things we produce and accumulate will never fill the emptiness within us. And we are destroying the very source of our life in the process.

So how do we nourish ourselves?

Principles of Eating

What, if any, principles do you eat by? Appetites come in two flavors: natural and unnatural. In an industrialized world of processed substances officially labeled "food," our appetites have lost touch with Life. But preindustrial appetites looked to Nature for nourishment and found the very things designed to fuel the human body. Naturopathy, ayurveda and yoga are traditions offering sound principles for eating in harmony with Nature.

NATUROPATHY. Food may be the most common and overlooked miracle of our daily lives. From the moment we are born, Nature instantly provides us with the perfect food. That which even moments before did not exist suddenly begins to flow from our mother's breasts.

The holistic tradition of naturopathic medicine views the human being as a part of Nature. It offers perhaps the simplest, most sensible principles for eating my American mind has ever encountered. Just be sure that what you eat fits these criteria:

- It is whole. Nature provides whole foods with their own wrappers. In the name of progress, we process them for convenience, shelf life and durability. But their value to us is lost in equal measure.

- It is clean. Food is not a transport system for sauces, seasonings and texturizers. These tasty extras distort our tastes. We enjoy our food less, and our bodies react with allergies and cravings.

- It is alive. No other animal eats cooked food. Cooking destroys not only harmful bacteria but vital nutrients as well. The less we cook our food, the more aliveness it carries to our bodies.

- It is simple. Animals consume only one food at a time, and this is how our bodies are designed to digest. We would have far less need for digestive assistance from drugs if we simply ate one food at a time or combined them effectively.

- It is natural. Eat from the hand of Nature. Eat foods that Nature gives us; they are the foods designed for our bodies, and our bodies are designed for them.

What beautiful evidence of the perfection in the design of the Universe: The earth is a living system that balances and sustains itself through complementary processes. We are a part of this system, and food is our daily miracle.

The more we eat what is natural to us, the more we connect ourselves to the world we are part of. Yes, our bodies digest physical matter for the energy to make new cells. But eating also provides us with intimate moments throughout the day to connect with the Life Force flowing through us. When we do that and consider ourselves one among many, it eases the loneliness we feel in the face of increasing alienation from our fellow human beings. We are nourished, senses and spirit, as we eat of the Tree of Life.

Perhaps this is what the Lakota people of North America mean when they utter the simple prayer *Mitakuye Oyasin*, meaning, "All my relations," or "We are all related." Like *Itadakimasu* in Japan, it is a simple recognition of the connectedness of all that is, within which we have a place and a responsibility. We are connected there, and our place means something.

AYURVEDA. In the ancient Hindu system of ayurvedic medicine, foods are classified into six tastes (*rasas*)—sweet, sour, salty, bitter, pungent and astringent—that are combined in many foods. Each taste has a balancing effect, and all are used together for natural healing. Including some of each provides complete nutrition, minimizes cravings and balances the appetite and digestion.

- Sweet (*madhura*): milk, butter, sweet cream, wheat, ghee (clarified butter), rice, honey, raw sugar, ripe fruits of many kinds

- Sour (*amla*): citrus fruits, many immature fruits, yogurt, pomegranate seeds, tamarind

- Salty (*lavana*): salt (ayurveda recommends rock salt), salty pretzels or pickles

- Bitter (*katu*): bitter gourd, greens of many kinds, turmeric, fenugreek

- Pungent (*tikta*): chili peppers, ginger, black pepper, clove, mustard, radish, white daikon

- Astringent (*kashaya*): beans, lentils (*dhals*), turmeric, cruciferous vegetables such as cauliflower and cabbage, cilantro

Ayurveda recommends that you have all six tastes in every meal. And it's a delicious way to eat. This is where the idea of chutney originated, incorporating all six tastes; a little goes a long way at every meal.

YOGA. In *The Yoga of Discipline,* Swami Chidvilasananda speaks of food as something sacred. "When you recognize food as scintillating Consciousness," she says, "your whole relationship with it is altered." She describes simple practices used throughout India to follow this way of life:

- Combine foods properly.

- Do not overeat. Food digestion powers the body. When we overeat, we lose energy and power.

- Leave a tiny bit of hunger in the belly when you eat.

- Keep the digestive fire active in you, for creation as well as digestion.

- Find balance, harmony, moderation and poise around food through discipline.

This discipline creates a smoothly operating, functional, open channel, energized as a vehicle in the world for the spirit. That is the perfect and right use of the body in the world.

Appreciating Appetite

Rene Descartes, in "Meditation 6" of his *Meditations on First Philosophy*, described sensations like hunger as teachers on the road at their intersections with thought, that the body and mind are not separate but one:

"Nature likewise teaches me by these sensations of pain, hunger, thirst, etc., that I am not only lodged in my body as a pilot in a vessel, but that I am besides so intimately conjoined, and as it were intermixed with it, that my mind and body compose a certain unity."

For many of us in the "civilized" world, hunger has become a dirty word. It is a message we prefer not to hear. It is something to be kept at bay, whether by eating too much, or continuously, or by starving ourselves to the point where we don't even feel the signals anymore. Appetite tells us what we're hungry for. So, as hunger's messenger, it is equally rejected.

Theodore Roosevelt once counseled, "Keep your eyes on the stars and your feet on the ground." Appetite is about doing that—connecting the distant object of our hunger with our place in the here and now. Taking our place in Life. Eating life, breaking it down and using the energy released to build something new. It is the secret to happiness, in our personal lives and in our relationship to our world.

Life in Station 2
The Experience of Appetite: Desire

The experience in Station 2 is desire. Desire is not hope. It is not wishing for something. It is not craving or longing or fantasy. It is not a frilly feeling.

Desire is the line you put up between your heart and reality in the physical world. When you throw a line out from your heart to Life, it requires that you grow up, that you acknowledge the gap between your inner life and your outer life, and that you step into the role of resolving those. From the unnamable restlessness when the status quo of Home no longer fits to the exhilarating moment when you decide to let go of the shore, the entire first quarter of The Wheel of Creativity asks you to take on this task. The journey is not always a direct route either, and it may require that you revisit this station a few times before you're ready to move on. The process requires honesty, attention and love.

The Task of Appetite: Pay Attention

The task of Station 2 is to pay attention. From the experience of Hunger in Station 1 as something happening to you, here you come to know what you want. Hunger is transformed into something you claim and own within you. Through the process you transform yourself from the object of your Hunger to the subject of your desire. You are at cause for it, and you take responsibility for it.

Appetite is the process of coming to know and define your authentic desires while you detach from external cues, which can pull you out of your center and distract you:

- Denial. You stop wanting what you want because it's too painful to live in the gap, and you make up a poor, less confronting substitute.

- Busy-ness. You cram your life so full that you never have time to experience the hunger inside. I call this spiritual gluttony.

- Compulsive behaviors. You learn effective avoidance methods—workaholism, shopping, overeating, doing anything unconsciously—to not be present with your truth.

In his classic 1937 success book, *Think and Grow Rich*, Napoleon Hill reminds his readers that as the world evolves, it is always looking for new ideas, new processes and all kinds of new products. No matter what your new idea is, fulfilling the needs of the world, says Hill, is the path to riches. So what creates the link between the idea person and the world around her? According to Hill, "Back of all this demand for new and better things, there is one quality which one must possess to win, and that is

definitiveness of purpose, the knowledge of what one wants, and a burning *desire* to possess it." (Napoleon Hill, *Think and Grow Rich*, Chicago, Illinois: Combined Registry Company, 1937)

That is the other side of this station. From a vague sense of "Something's missing" to really feeling the emptiness, you move through this station to gain a clear sense of what you want. The work of Station 2 connects your Essence with your presence in the world. You see how your life can be useful and meaningful. It could be the world at home, with your family, or the world at large, as your influence grows and expands.

Practicing Station 2 is about paying attention, consciously and deliberately. And doing that fans the flame of desire and makes it stronger. That's all there is here. There is nothing to do yet but listen. Make space. Feel the attraction.

The Reward of Appetite: Direction

The reward of Station 2 is direction, moving from here to there. You have transformed your Hunger from a vague inner feeling to intention, to a definitiveness of desire. You have taken responsibility for what you want.

Defining your Appetite in the context of reality empowers you to live an authentic and meaningful life from the inside out, whatever your circumstances are on the outside. Without completing the work of Station 2, you would jump from Hunger to Go, not guided by your authentic awareness, not connected to your personal spiritual purpose. Awareness without direction creates the world of the Hungry Ghosts. Here you learn what nourishes you so that in the next station you can choose it.

This is the Gayatri Mantra:

> Om bhur bhuvah svah
> Tat savitur varen(i)yam
> Bhargo devasya dhimahi
> Dhiyo ya nah prachodayat

Your Life's True Purpose

For Hindus, one of the best known ancient Sanskrit mantras is the Gayatri Mantra, which means "May the Almighty God illuminate our intellect to lead us along the righteous path."

Gayatri is a five-faced goddess with dominion over the five senses *(pranas)* or life forces. The mantra incorporates singing, meditation and prayer in an invocation for her protection.

But Hindus also believe that the syllables themselves enhance the chakras, or energy centers, of the human body by their sound alone. *Om*, the first syllable of the Gayatri Mantra, is considered to be the primordial sound of the universe. It is present in all universal elements—Earth, Water, Fire and Air—plus ether, intelligence and consciousness. Hindus believe that chanting the Gayatri Mantra removes the obstacles to wisdom and spiritual growth. By it, we can ask the goddess to "illuminate our path toward our higher consciousness and lead us to our true purpose in life." It is the invitation to the Feminine principle to give us what we are finally open to receive.

In the Vision Quarter, in this station and the next one, we learn to make choices that express our value. We know there are no guarantees. You can't know the consequences of your choices until you live them out. You may need to change your course of action when you're halfway there, but you learn about yourself by bringing up from the deep dark places of yourself what needs to be transformed.

Not choosing, which is a common response, is to stay stuck. It is to refuse to be nourished. And that puts you on the train to Station 3: Anorexia.

A STORY OF APPETITE

Ben Hollis, Television Host and Producer
Current City: Chicago

"If you do not bring forth that which is within you, that which is within you will destroy you."
(The Gospel of Thomas)

I met Ben Hollis in an improv class in Chicago in 1988. He was the teacher. We went on to become friends and then partners for several years. Ben introduced me to some of the most powerful spiritual practices of my life, through which I first caught a glimpse of my life as a process, and to a community of creative people I shall never forget.

KATHERINE ROBERTSON-PILLING: What first made you want to perform?

BEN HOLLIS: In childhood I was really turned on by seeing performers on *The Ed Sullivan Show*, *Shindig* and comedy shows like Johnny Carson, Dean Martin and the Three Stooges. I loved comedy and music. I wanted to be a rock star. I discovered that I could be funny and entertain people, and I became known as the funny guy. In high school, we formed a group called the Help Me's, doing performance art before it was recognized as performance art. And in college, I got into improv, which I continued with Second City, when I came back to Chicago.

When I got married the first time, I started getting some influence from my first wife and her family, and I decided that I needed to get a so-called straight job, with a regular paycheck for a change. I chose advertising, and I worked really hard to get a job as a copywriter. Even though I had aspirations of showbiz and having my own show, I was willing to give that up. It gave me a nice exit, relieving me of the responsibility to look after my own talent. It was self-sabotage, really. So, after a year and a half of copywriting and corporate video-making, I got laid off.

Almost the first thing I did with my severance pay was to go to LA and try to get a job in advertising, with the ultimate goal to migrate over to showbiz. I

did two three-week stints in LA, working harder than ever looking for work.

I did not get a single job offer. But there was a lot of interest in a novelty tape I had done, called *Rent-A-Friend*. Creative directors and senior copywriters would ask me, "Why do you want to be in advertising? You should be on TV." One guy suggested I get in touch with John Davies, a guy back in Chicago at WTTW, the most watched PBS station in the country. So I did, and he liked it. And he said, "How would you like to make a pilot for a TV show." I was stunned, but I dropped everything and made the pilot. And *Wild Chicago* became a multi-Emmy-winning show and perhaps one of the first reality shows before reality TV became *de rigueur*. The dream never died. I just had a limited idea about how it should unfold.

KRP: If the creative process is a journey, how would you describe yours?

BH: It is a journey, and my journey is multitentacled and multipathed. But fundamentally it's to know God's will for me and to have the courage to do it.

About four years ago, I became interested in public speaking. I wanted to use my experience and innate talents of speaking and presenting to inspire others. So I did some training and got out there and did it. And the material was my life.

Throughout my whole career, I've been interested in people's stories and giving them space to shine by telling their stories, and doing that in a fun, playful way that's entertaining.

I used to think of *Wild Chicago* as a piece of fluff. But over the years, people have told me how much joy I brought them. And through my reading and spiritual life, I began to realize this is a gift, and the opportunity to tell you about it now is moving.

I think that the real payoff for all involved comes by me getting more and more out of the way and less attached to the whole bit, even letting go of this thing I would call personality and ego—who I think I am—and just take the direction and do it. And be a conduit. I'll give you an example.

While I was on vacation recently, I had a dream that gave me an entire TV show idea, wrapped up around the *Wild Chicago* concept. If it comes in a dream, I pretty much accept that it's God working, because my conscious mind is not doing it. And I told my wife about it, and she said, "Why don't you just try doing God's will? Take that dream as an order, and fill the order."

KRP: What experiences have taught you the most about the creative power of Life?

BH: The story that comes up for me is how I met my wife Julia. My relationship history was really about having an instant attraction to somebody, like an adrenaline rush. And the first time I met Julia, I had no physical attraction to her, nor she to me. She thought I was a sad sack, and I thought she was poor white trash, because of her expensive asymmetrical haircut, which I thought was do-it-yourself. But in the process of getting to know her, I actually found her interesting and funny, and I liked her. But it wasn't a zingo bingo type thing.

As I got to know her, looking back, I know that the Universe and Life were laying groundwork that I couldn't even see. So on this particular day in December of '94, we had lunch at this Mexican place, and she was going to go away for Christmas with her kids to visit their grandmother. And instantly I saw her differently: Wow! Julia! She's really cute. I'd like to put my arm around her.

And from that moment over the next few weeks, God was inviting me to something I had no control over. And I was willing to be led. I never thought I'd want to be involved with somebody with two small children, but that's what Julia was all about. I knew very early on that I wanted to marry her and be a family with them, which was again a very big surprise. It was definitely Life pulling me.

Then plenty of passion and attraction showed up. All the pieces traditionally associated with falling in love were being laid without me seeing them.

KRP: What in your life is the relationship between creativity and purpose?

BH: I'm definitely being called to a bigger life of expressing the gifts that I have to offer. But I'm still nagged by the fear of leaving the status quo. Over the last 20 years, I came to realize that perhaps my greatest Higher Power is comfort. And that's not where the gifts lie. That's a big theme in Unity [Church], where I get a lot of spiritual support. And there's this statement in the Gospel of Thomas: "If you do not bring forth that which is within you, that which is within you will destroy you."

KRP: How do you define creativity?

BH: I think creativity is a lifelong process, and it has to do with identifying my gifts to the world and then sculpting a life out of that, forging the willingness, the courage, the ability to carry them out, to be of greatest use to humanity.

In my talks, I talk about the flow of good or the flow of God, and the concept of W.I.L.D., being What I Love Doing. Do what you love doing. I'm grateful for the people who do continually bring that forth. The artists who inspire me, I find they're not that different. Most of them just do stuff.

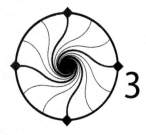

3

STATION 3
Anorexia

Our deepest fear is not that we are inadequate.
Our deepest fear is that we are powerful beyond measure.
It is our light, not our darkness that most frightens us.
MARIANNE WILLIAMSON

On the Platform in Station 3

Anorexia is the third station in The Wheel of Creativity and the third station in the Vision Quarter.

The term *anorexia nervosa* refers to an eating disorder characterized by the compulsive refusal to eat. I call this station Anorexia because here, in response to the clear desire of Appetite, appears the automatic refusal of what you find nourishing. It could include physical self-deprivation, but I use the term primarily as a metaphor. Here you say no to what you know nourishes you spiritually, mentally, emotionally or physically. It is, at its simplest, saying "No" to Life.

Why would anyone say "No" to Life? How could we refuse the flow of Life through us? We do it through social conditioning. We do it because it gives us the illusion of control. When life delivers the uncomfortable, the painful, the intolerable, then the illusion that we can control those things makes us feel secure. But in reality, while there are many things in our lives that we can change, we cannot control the flow of Life itself.

The voice of this station repeats some version of "Don't you dare." It could be milder: "You re-

ally shouldn't do that." Or it could be harsh indeed: "Don't you ever let me catch you doing that again, or else … ." We all have different voices in our heads, and we have emotions in response. If we can identify when we first remember that feeling, that voice coming in, it can give us some clues as to how we learned it. One thing is certain: We are not born with Anorexia; rather its responses are learned.

Out of Your Mind

The purpose of Station 3 is to move you out of your mind. The Vision Quarter is the quarter of the mind—thoughts, ideas—and its element is Air. The next quarter, Exploration, is the quarter of the spirit and energy, and its element is Fire. To move from the internal experience of the mind to the external experience of the spirit requires energy, power and momentum.

The avoidance experienced in this station helps create that power, just because it has to be overcome. However, we cannot overcome it with control. It helps us to identify the "Nos" that stop us, to count their costs and to choose another way.

The resistance to something, the avoidance of it,

65

keeps you attached to it. You're every bit as attached to what you hate as you are to what you love. You're hooked, you're locked to it, and your resistance keeps you in relationship to it.

If we try to skip this station we continue to recycle through the first three stations: the restlessness, the desire, the "No"; the restlessness, the desire, the "No." This repetition can be brutal—something like being banged around inside a washing machine. It is in this endless loop where we feel stuck, sometimes in fear (which is the avoidance), sometimes in anger (which is resistance), sometimes in procrastination (a kind of clinging to the status quo). All of these can be experiences of Anorexia.

Nipped in the Bud

I have a lovely gardenia plant that has been traumatized by some kind of insect. It has small deposits of what looks like white fuzz on some of its branches. Otherwise, it looks healthy: Its leaves are green and growing, and it is budding. But the buds are paralyzed at what looks like a closed-fist stage. They are still green and just about ready to open, but they never do. That is the experience of the Anorexia Station, being stuck at the bud and unable to flower, unable to blossom into what you're meant to be or want to be in the world.

In The Wheel of Creativity, Anorexia follows Appetite. You feel your desire in Appetite, and it gives you direction. That direction starts to push you, and pressure builds to get moving. But the movement itself then brings you into contact with obstacles; it brings up things in the path that might stop you.

These obstacles can be internal or external. If you want to launch a business, some will say it will never work. If you want to make a sale, you have to overcome your customers' objections. If you want to produce different results of any kind, you have to disempower the negative voices.

Obstacles are a natural part of the process of moving out into the world. But when they are internalized, they can easily take on an automatic, unconscious quality that seems to give you no choice

in the moment. You do not respond to something, you react. And very often you don't know why.

The experience of Anorexia can be simple—holding your breath or clenching your jaw—or it can be as dramatic as a phobic feeling, like a deer paralyzed in the headlights of a car. Anorexia can also appear in very subtle ways, like going shopping but not allowing yourself to buy even the smallest thing. It can be manageable or it can lead to panic attacks and anxiety disorders. But when the "No" becomes habitual, eventually a kind of spiritual paralysis ensues.

Two examples of the manifestations of Anorexia are:

- I know exactly what I need to do and don't do it.
- I know exactly what I need not to do, and I do it anyway.

This station reveals your blocks, the places you get stuck and what stops you from within. It is an opportunity to make conscious your automatic unconscious reactions, to bring them into awareness. And with awareness, you have a choice.

While Anorexia offers you the illusion of control, Appetite demands its antidote. It requires that you choose. It requires that you make a commitment to your desire, even though you don't know how it's going to turn out. It requires that you meet it and give yourself to it.

Surrender to Life

Surrendering to the energy that wants to flow through you is the surrender to Life, with your desire as Life's bud. It is challenging, because you cannot control Life's response to you. That makes you feel vulnerable, and it triggers all the stored reserves of vulnerability you have not resolved from the past.

So Station 3 asks you to deal with the inner conflicts, old hesitancies and residual fears you learned along the way. In order to experience this surrender and move forward, you have to deal with those things inside. Do not imagine that this is an instantaneous process or a decision you make once and forever: "Okay, that's the last coffee I will ever need to have." It is a lifelong process, just like physical fitness. Just like building a muscle, the more times you go all the way through this station, the more comfortable you become with it, and the more you will trust the process.

You will come to know deep within that what's coming on the other side, even though It might scare you, is good. What you're surrendering to is your own life, and it is *for* you, not *against* you. Welcome it. Appreciate its gifts.

On the Wheel, Anorexia leads you through the gate called Go. Each gate is like a solstice or an equinox. Each is a change in season, where the energy changes. And at this gate, Go, the energy shifts from internal to external. It takes a lot of power to get off the ground, a lot of energy to get to that next station, Launch. Overcoming the obstacles you meet here—avoidance, resistance, clinging—creates that power.

Honor the Resistance

The automatic "No" can show up in intimate relationships or in everyday routine. One of my clients, a highly competent corporate project manager, describes this perfectly when she says she will see the beautiful new apples in a bowl in the kitchen and never take one for herself, always leaving the nice things for the children. Another recognizes it when she goes shopping and sees things she likes and wants but consistently passes by. Some of them cost less than $1, so it's not about the money. It's a habitual pattern.

For most of my life, I had a mysterious habit of dating men I was not attracted to. The ones who really attracted me scared me to death. I was afraid of the power of what I felt inside, afraid of wanting it too much, afraid of the pain of the void when it was gone. I was not going to surrender, even if it meant consistently saying no to the men who spoke to my heart.

Anorexia is this automatic "No." It's really about not trusting yourself, not trusting the attraction you feel for Life, and even more painful than that, not trusting Life itself. In the moment of choice, you are in conflict, and the "No" has become your habit.

Where in your life are your "Nos"? We all have them. Just identifying your habitual "No" moments gives you a mirror to see more clearly how you treat yourself. And it gives you a choice in the matter.

Fast or Slow … Coming to Know

One of the goals to be achieved in the Anorexia station is getting to the point of taking action, even if it's not the right action. There is a kind of perfectionism that is part of Anorexia—an illusion of control that will keep you from acting until you are entirely certain.

My husband is a naval captain, in command of a large ship. He has trained himself to make big decisions that affect the safety of the ship and crew in a matter of seconds when it's required. It's a skill that works for him, one he has developed like a muscle.

I'm the opposite. I will wait and wait and look at all the sides of a situation before making a decision. I like to describe it this way: "I don't know, and I don't know and I don't know. And then one day, I know."

There is a process that must be respected of waiting until something feels right. The process can be fast or slow. But when the "No" becomes habitual, then the organic process is replaced with a destructive pattern. Waiting for something is open and receptive; it is a "Yes." But the habitual "No" of Anorexia is closed, controlling and repelling. The challenge comes in learning to recognize the difference.

Life in Station 3
The Experience of Anorexia: Paralysis

The experience of this station is paralysis or inertia, the inability to move. The feeling is a kind of frozenness, numbness or deadness. It is the loss of feeling that comes from blocking the energy of Life.

Anorexia has different qualities and comes in different flavors. It can appear as procrastination, which arises from clinging to the past. It can be avoidance, which arises out of fear. It can be resistance, which arises out of anger. If Life were your parent, in Anorexia you would be a spiritual toddler, blindly engaged in a power struggle with it.

Anorexia can come from different sources, but it is the Life Force of the Universe to which we are saying "No." It gives us life and nourishes us, and we say "No" to it. The Anorexic "No" always creates suffering because it is a futile exercise. Life will always come through. If we don't learn to allow it to flow, we develop symptoms and side effects. We get tense or we get sick, because we're fighting against reality.

The core issue of this "No" is our attachment to Form, our attachment to our expectations: "It has to look like this." "It can't look like that." When we get too attached to what we have in mind, we lose touch with Life itself.

What is called for here, as it is throughout The Wheel of Creativity, is the return to Essence from Form, to intimacy with who we are as living beings. The creative process moves continually between the two, between Form and Essence. As we engage in that process, we weave our lives in the world.

Echoes of Childhood Trauma

The pattern of Anorexia often takes root in us as a response to some kind of trauma. When we are children, this sometimes has to do with bullying. It could have been our parents who bullied us, teachers, ministers; or it could have been other children. Even a perception of bullying, like low self-esteem, is enough to create the trauma and trigger the anorexic response.

As a child, I projected my low self-esteem onto other people's reactions to me, gathering evidence that I was unworthy or defective in some way. The most memorable of these occasions happened when I was nine years old. I had a serious crush on

Jimmy Henry, the 11-year-old boy down the street. I had written him a "secret admirer" letter, and a friend of mine had offered to give it to him. I waited on the curb in front of our house for her to round the corner with his answer. When she returned, the note was torn in half, and his response to me was, "You tell that son-of-a-bitch that I'm not her secret admirer, never have been and never will be." I asked my mother what a "bitch" was and struggled to make sense of his remark. I was devastated. Then I decided I must be repulsive, and avoided the boys I liked as much as possible for decades thereafter. There lay the roots of my Anorexia around men.

We all have stories like this one. We make decisions about ourselves and live our lives based on them. Then, under the illusion of control, we begin to bully and terrorize ourselves, believing that if we preempt what we fear from the outside world, we will be safe. But nothing is more painful than being abandoned by yourself.

Think about concrete examples or situations in your life where you automatically say "No." Where is the "No" so deeply ingrained in you that you are no longer conscious of it? This is where you begin to look to reclaim your authentic Self, your Essence, and your role in life.

The Body's Wisdom

If you need clues about how this works in your life, your body will show you the way, for there are physical consequences to these decisions as well. When we try to control the flow of energy, our bodies become rigid. Where we withhold energy, our cells are not nourished.

Digestion, which we talked about in Stations 1 and 2, is a problem of epidemic proportions for many Western societies today. As habitual and unconscious eating has increased (a highly effective method for "stuffing" feelings), digestive problems like heartburn and acid reflux are increasingly common. In 2010, the American Gastroenterological Association estimated that 33 percent of people in the

United States have acid reflux disease; its cumulative costs approach $10 billion per year.

Clenching the jaw and grinding teeth are also related to unconscious attempts to control the Life Force. Estimates vary about how many people are affected by this condition, but they range from 50 to 95 percent of the population, including 15 percent of our children. And in many cases, people are not aware they are doing it, because it occurs primarily when they are asleep.

Breathing is one of the most fundamental processes of the body, and yet when we lose touch with ourselves, the natural rhythm of the breath can be blocked. Blocking your breath also blocks energy and is an equally effective way to stop feelings from surfacing. The breath makes energy physical in our bodies, taming it to feed our cells with the oxygen they need for life. When we hold our breath, that energy remains untamed, ungrounded, wild; and the far reaches of our body are deprived of life-giving oxygen. For this reason meditation, and the deep breathing associated with it, is a powerful antidote for a multitude of psychophysiological imbalances, including anxiety, preoccupation and jitters.

I have experienced all these conditions at some point in my life. Some of them were deeply rooted in my psyche as well as my body. And medical treatments could only address the symptoms; resolving the problems that caused them had to come from within.

I have been studying singing off and on for most of my life, and during the past five years I have reached a new level in my training. Part of the training required me to take a more serious look at how my jaw and my breath affect not only my singing voice but also my life.

Good singing technique is an extremely physical endeavor. It requires that the body create a strong and consistent column of air, grounded in the diaphragm. When it is well-grounded, the breath rises up through a relaxed throat in which vocal chords vibrate freely to form the sound and carry it up and out through the mouth cavity. When the breath is not grounded in the diaphragm, the jaw and throat contract to try to *produce* the sound the mind wants to hear. The quality of sound of the former is completely different than that of the latter. One is infused with spirit; the other is not.

Life produced from the mechanics of control does not nourish us, because it does not flow through us on the breath of Life. Life lived as an organic process, created in collaboration with the breath of Life, can be very hard work. But at the end of the day, it is being alive rather than just imitating it. This is work that we have to do throughout the course of our lives, to open up to Life flowing, in its Essence and all its Forms.

All these conditions can be treated at the level of symptoms with medications, stress-reduction techniques, prostheses, etc. But treating symptoms and curing the source of the problems are two very different things. If you view them as evidence of long-forgotten decisions that prevent this big, powerful Life energy from coming through us, the entire focus shifts. "The full catastrophe" of life is frightening sometimes. We are not in control.

All these conditions follow the energetic channel through the center of the body, for this is where our energy centers lie. According to ancient Hindu texts, applied in methods from Tantra to yoga, energy flows through the human through the chakra system. Seven chakras sit strategically along our vertebral column, from the base of our spine to the crown of our head. Each aligns with a physical element, and each governs an aspect of our human experience.

1. Root. At the base of the spine. Earth. Governs security and belonging.

2. Sacral. Below the naval. Water. Governs health, pleasure, sexuality.

3. Solar Plexus. At the solar plexus. Fire. Governs our sense of personal power.

4. Heart. Middle of the breastbone. Air. Governs our ability to understand.

5. Throat. At the throat. Sound (Aether). Governs communication.

6. Third Eye. Between the eyebrows and slightly above. Light. Governs our intuition.

7. Crown. At the top of the head. Space. Governs our ability to live authentically.

As these controls become automatic and unconscious, the life we're living starts not to feel like ours anymore, because we're just living out a pattern. We might know something, but then we stop knowing it, because it's not okay. We don't feel what we feel, we don't want what we want. This kind of life eventually becomes intolerable, and we begin to live lives of quiet desperation.

"Don't you dare ... enjoy your life."

When I was 23, I realized that I had a deep-seated belief that happiness and significance were mutually exclusive. I had split the two ingredients to a purposeful life—passion and contribution—which in fact must be reintegrated for meaning to emerge. But authentic significance comes only by being who we truly are and then doing what flows naturally from our Essence into the world. Authentic happiness is the byproduct of this flow. There is nothing more important to do.

Station 3 brings us to the futility of resisting or trying to control the creative process of our life. We wear ourselves out with it, like a child who cries herself to sleep. We fight and fight and fight against Life until we exhaust ourselves. When we are finally willing to surrender and say, "Okay," then Life starts to flow again.

It is not an either/or choice, though that is often all you can see at the time. In any decision, when it seems either this or that, creativity always allows for a third option. But you have to awaken from the sleep of unconscious behavior to look for a third option

and see it. And you have to have a good enough reason to do the inner work that it takes. That is the purpose of the suffering produced by blocking.

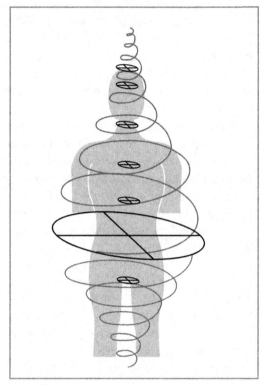

Seven Chakras, Seven Wheels of Creativity

The Task of Anorexia: Choose Love

The good news is that you don't have to stay stuck in this cycle. There is a choice. Someone once defined insanity as doing the same things over and over again and expecting different results. The value of this station is that it brings you to the end of your illusion of control. Coming to the end of what isn't working gives you freedom, gives you the choice, gives you the option of doing it differently.

The task of Station 3 is to choose love. The Sanskrit term *Nirvana*, when it is translated literally, means *blowing out*, which you could understand as exhaling or letting go. The surrender of Station 3 is just that, exhaling. You are willing to let go of your breath because you trust that the next breath will be there.

What does it mean to choose love? In this context, it means to choose Life in the here and now. And there are three variations on this theme.

First, choosing love means choosing to love what is. It means to love what is happening right now, even though it might not please you. Before you can move on and create something new with the raw materials of your life, you have to know what you're working with. And you have to be willing to pick them up and use them to create something else. Choosing love means, simply, responding to the moment with, "This is reality, and I accept it."

Second, choosing love means choosing to love the process of your life. The choice is to breathe the air around you, to take it and use it and enjoy it. Watching birds glide on thermals is a beautiful example of this. They wait and watch and feel, and then all of a sudden, they open their wings and dive in, reaching out and allowing the air to carry them. They trust and relax and play. To choose Life is to eat Life, to take it in and digest it and use it to sustain you, like a fish opens its gills as it swims and the oxygen just flows right through.

Third, choosing love means choosing to love yourself. It is holding the vision of what is possible for you. It is choosing to have compassion for yourself, as a work in progress, patient with what stands between the small, wounded you and the one you are intended to be.

Only when we are willing to eat Life, to eat of the Tree of Life, do we really take our place on the planet. We have to be willing to take something that exists and crush it between our teeth. We have to be willing to take Life in, digest it, gain strength and use it to form ourselves in the world.

Several years ago, on a secluded piece of fertile land in Provence, France, I awakened to this reality. I was there to participate in a Sweat Lodge ceremony. Our guide was an elder French man named Bison Noir (Black Buffalo), and he had been trained for decades by Native American elders in Arizona. Part of the ritual was to gather small offerings from Nature for the altar at the entrance of the lodge. We were taught to do this with awareness, appreciation and respect for the land, to take only a small amount of any single plant and pass six more before taking another.

As I ventured out into the vibrant green jungle around the lodge, I realized for the first time that I could not take one step without crushing something beneath my foot. All the tiny plants I saw, and the things I could not see that crawled within them, were vulnerable to my footstep. This grieved me. I felt my impact on the earth. Between one step and the next, I was deeply humbled. But this is part of what it means to be alive.

The Way of Acceptance

Buddhists talk about the Middle Way, the way between the opposites, the way that integrates them both. This is the way of acceptance.

The first two stations of The Wheel of Creativity offer you awareness about what you *don't* do and what you *do* do. Acceptance is the next step, and it must come before action. If you try to skip it and go straight to action, you will end up making decisions in reaction, based on *not that, so this*.

When we take time to move through the period of acceptance in this station, we have the opportunity to work through our blocks so we don't keep acting them out. The value of Anorexia is to identify your conflicts, define your boundaries, define your authentic "Yes" as well as your "No."

The Reward of Anorexia: Torque

What is created in Station 3 is torque, and this is its reward. In physics, torque is the tendency of a force to rotate an object about an axis. It measures an object's turning force. When an outside force is applied to an object it creates energy. Until there is an outlet for that energy, pressure builds.

When you engage yourself in response to the forces you feel, whether outside or inside yourself, energy is created. Until that energy has an outlet, pressure builds. And that pressure creates torque: the power, the force to move you into the next quarter. It starts the Wheel turning. From there, each choice you make focuses and channels the energy of the Universe through you. It expresses and defines your vision in the world. It is a lifelong journey of awakening.

Just as it takes time for a rocket to build enough power to defy the laws of gravity and achieve launch, going through this process has a timing all its own. But go through it you must for energy to flow again.

Gridlock: Blocking Traffic

The choices we make are transpersonal as well as personal. Their impact extends beyond our individual lives, beyond the here and now into a world beyond space and time that touches all that is. Life is more than all of us in our little sacks of skin distinguishing ourselves from each other; at its essence, life is the opportunity to participate in the full process of all that is expressing itself in the world.

Everything is made of energy. This is a well-accepted scientific fact. Everything that exists—living and not living—is in a continual process of creation and dissolution. Life uses energy to create new forms and dissolves those forms to release more energy. Everything is grounded in Nature by this force.

All matter, including a human being, gives off an energetic (electromagnetic) force. The world's oldest philosophies give this force names like Prana and Chi, and we have modern names as well, like Life Force and Aura. As a human being, you are at the center of many energetic fields, from your circulatory and nervous systems, to organs, muscles, glands, cells, molecules, right down to the electrons and protons of which they are all made.

The interconnectedness of all things is wonderfully represented in a Buddhist concept called Indra's Net, described by Timothy Brook in his book *Vermeer's Hat*:

> When Indra fashioned the world, he made it as a web, and at every knot in the web is tied a pearl. Everything that

exists, or has ever existed, every idea that can be thought about, every datum that is true—every dharma, in the language of Indian philosophy—is a pearl in Indra's net. Not only is every pearl tied to every other pearl by virtue of the web on which they hang, but on the surface of every pearl is reflected every other jewel on the net. Everything that exists in Indra's web implies all else that exists. (Timothy Book, *Vermeer's Hat: The Seventeenth Century and the Dawn of the Global World*. New York: Bloomsbury; Toronto: Penguin; London: Profile, 2008)

In his podcast "Following the Middle Way," the late Asian scholar Alan Watts describes it this way:

> "Imagine a multidimensional spider's web in the early morning covered with dew drops. And every dewdrop contains the reflection of all the other dew drops. And, in each reflected dewdrop, the reflections of all the other dew drops in that reflection. And so ad infinitum. That is the Buddhist conception of the universe in an image." (Alan Watts, *Buddhism: The Religion of No-Religion*, ed. Mark Watts, edited transcripts, Tuttle Publishing, 1999)

I call this the Field of Wheels.

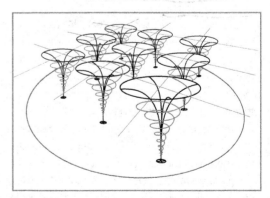

The Field of Wheels

Every one of us with our Wheel of Creativity is connected to the web of life in Source, from which we all bring something into the world that is essential for the fullness of Life to exist. Each of us is a species unto ourselves; when we do not take our place, there is a vacancy in the web of life.

The role you play in Life's unfolding has less to do with what you do for a living than it does with how you do it. You could be a Nobel Prize winner or you could be a seamstress. You take your place in the adventure of life by how you live, how you move between Form and Essence, how you connect the nonphysical potential of Life itself with its manifestation in the physical world.

In this Field of Wheels, we are all connected to each other as expressions of all that is. We do not source creative energy ourselves, but it flows through us. It not only gives us our ideas but the power to realize them.

We dream the dream of separation so that we can create harmony within diversity. Think of the poverty of music if all voices sang the same notes. Rather, the separation itself creates the harmony, and the depth and texture of the music is magnified many times over.

In this world, we experience ourselves as separate, but we weave the fabric of the universe together. We can either develop our skills to receive and use Life's generous gifts, or we can keep trying to do it on our own and miss out on the transformative power of everything we do.

With every thought we think, every word we speak, every feeling we feel, every action we take, we are expressing the energy of Life flowing to us in the world. When we fail to express it, when we block it, as we do in the Anorexia Station, we create a traffic jam, which I call gridlock. The energy that wants to move through us to someone else in the world can't.

It could be that you refuse to smile because you're having a bad day. It could be that you haven't called your father. But a smile can change someone's life. Your father may not be there the next day.

The will of the river of Life is stronger than us; it will continue to flow. If we say "No," it will go somewhere else. But we are the greatest losers because we block the Life that nourishes us.

The Creative Way

In the turning of The Wheel of Creativity, all these elements of life are harmonized together, as we progress through the individual stations on the way. Each aspect of how we express our Essence in the world is developed in one of the four quarters of the Wheel. In Vision, we make conscious every thought we think. In Exploration, we own every word we speak. In Incubation, we sit with every feeling we feel. And in Cultivation, we take responsibility for every action we take.

With all these creative building blocks, we weave our way between Form and Essence, between potential and physical reality. As we do this in our individual lives, we weave the fabric of reality in the world. We are all doing this all the time. And what we are creating, with our children, with our businesses, on our own little spots, where our feet stand on the earth, is crucial to the whole. Whether we like it or not, choose it or not, is another matter. We are responsible.

In order to take our place in this adventure we call life, we must overcome our Anorexic "No." When we do, our smallness disappears, dissolved in the landscape of all that is. Our return to our Essence, which is initiated by our own Hunger, restores us to ourselves, because we surrender the way we think things are supposed to be to a flow of energy that is bigger than us.

To surrender to what is, is to accept your life as it is today, with all its external forms. From there, the next step is to return from Form to Essence, to remember what is true beyond the Form. And that is the return to the flow of Life through you into Form. When you come to the end and are brought to your readiness to choose love, then you move through the gate of Go and catch the train for a new quarter (Exploration) and Station 4.

A STORY OF ANOREXIA

Cal Harris: Musician
Current City: Phoenix, Arizona

"There's always a market for love; that's the biggest market there is."

Cal Harris Jr. has worked in the music industry all his adult life, supporting artists like Earth, Wind and Fire, Whitney Houston, and Mariah Carey on tour and in the studio. But it wasn't until three years ago that he manifested his dream by making a CD of his own. That first CD, *Inside Out*, went to the top of radio playlists and charts around the world. His story illustrates how choosing what you love connects you with Life and the world.

KATHERINE ROBERTSON-PILLING: What was going on for you in the years when you wanted to do a CD but you couldn't bring yourself to do it?

CAL HARRIS: I'd write another song, or go out and take piano lessons or get a voice teacher. There were so many competing ideas, I wasn't sure of what I wanted to do, or how I wanted to do it. There was definitely a point where I realized that the smooth-jazz-type format was a place that might be receptive to what I do naturally.

But over time, I started to find limitations. Am I a good enough player? Is the format even viable? I think more of my fear came around what would happen if it *was* successful and how people would respond. It was paralysis.

KRP: What has your experience been now that you've had the success you've had with the CD, compared to what you were projecting?

CH: Well, I wasn't completely wrong about that. Very few people responded the way I expected they would. I found support in places I didn't expect it, and I didn't get support in places that I thought for sure I would.

KRP: So there's some level of associating the cre-ation of something and going public with it with gain and loss of love?

CH: Yes. There is this thought out there that the only things worth doing are the things that can make millions, and you're not going to make millions with a smooth jazz record. "Why would you do a smooth jazz record, when you could get the software and do this thing that such-and-such a person did, and be right there?"

KRP: This "there" would be a commercial success, like giving people what they want rather than following your own vision?

CH: Right. For most of my life, that's always been the Holy Grail. You get a hit song, and everything gets good. You get the girl; you get the house; you get the life; you get self-respect; and you get all these things. As long as you have an idea in your mind, you always have hope that at least it could come… if you just do the right thing.

I've always believed that artists end up having trouble when they do get that and it doesn't measure up. And it's like, "So now what? What's going to do it for me now?" And to top it off, everyone's looking at you like, well, of course, you're there. We're all just trying to get what you have.

KRP: That's the isolation that you feared.

CH: Exactly. At least before you make it, you can commiserate with other people who haven't made it, and talk about how great it'll be if you make it.

KRP: They're both addictive processes. One is the addiction of commiseration—feeling bad because I don't have what I think is going to make everything perfect. And the other is getting the thing that I thought was going to make everything perfect, and then it doesn't, and I have to have more.

CH: Absolutely.

KRP: So how do you experience your creative process differently, having produced the CD?

CH: Before the record was done, everything was still in question as to whether I could actually put out a professional product. And now that that's out of the way, I can get deeper into refining the product itself. I know who I'll call to play guitar or lay down drum tracks or engineer.

I'm also aware of mistakes I made on the first record: "I really wish I could've turned that down, or turned that up." And yet I still get feedback from people who got what I was trying to say. Perfection is no guarantee that your message gets through, and getting too caught up with how you're saying something becomes the obscuring factor.

KRP: So, if message is more important than perfection, what is that message made of?

CH: It's really a snapshot of where I was at that moment. For me the creative process is like being struck by lightning. For many years, I was just happy to know that I could still be struck, and that was enough a lot of the time. Now it's becoming more important for me to follow through and to capture that moment. I'll hum a melody to myself and record it, and when I listen to it, the whole thing will come back.

That's a moment where you're touched by God. You can be struck, and you suddenly connect to this source of abundance of love and peace and whatnot. And that's something very worthy of sharing. The art, whatever form it takes, expresses the contrast between the fact that the source is there and that most of the time we're not connected with it. You put those two things together, and it's beauty in contrast.

KRP: What do you see coming next? What brink are you on now in your creative process? And what are your challenges?

CH: Now that I've broken the ice, I really have a lot more to say. And I'm anxious to say it. It's like, you know, you show someone a poem, and they're like, "Oh, this is really nice." And it's like, "Oh really, you like

that?" And then you pull out the box! So what's next for me is pulling out the box.

Even in my life. A big part of my survival growing up was how well I could keep things in, but it doesn't work like it used to. In this process of trying to bring stuff out, it's a lot more difficult for me to keep stuff in.

KRP: Yes, you create the thing, and the thing creates you. Do you see your creative process as a path of personal transformation? Now that you have created this, and put it out to the world, and gotten feedback, is that changing you as a person?

CH: I'm definitely becoming more open. It's become a lot more important to show up because that's the difference between whether you reach people or not. Music was something I could hide behind. If you look at my album cover, I'm in the shadow. Everything is dark and black. It might not even be me behind those sunglasses. The video was almost harder to do than the CD, because it's the visual me. And with this next project, I really want to be more open.

KRP: So the fear that you talked about initially is not just an internal fear. It's a process you have seen?

CH: Absolutely. Working for so many artists, I know what's being said about them behind the scenes. It's within all of us—being moved to do something. And I think the way that we manage the fact that we're not doing it is to point out all the problems or how stupid it is.

KRP: So what about this dilemma, "Do I do the work that I want to do, this sacred mission to bring forth into the world? Or do I do the work that is going to have a market? How do you feel about that?

CH: Learning to deal with that is a continuous process. But I think it's largely a myth that if you do what you love, there won't be a market for it. Because there's always a market for love; that's the biggest market there is.

What we consider to be marketable versus non-marketable is really just a matter of what's been seen versus what hasn't. Everything that is now pop, or popular, was at one point obscure until people started to accept it as an expression they could relate to; then it became popular. When rap came out, it used to be something that guys on the street did; it was this obscure thing, until it became a vehicle of anger for a lot of angry people.

You know, art is so often more a vehicle than a tangible thing. It's what comes through the vehicle that counts. You can get a bunch of guys in a room who play very skillfully, and when you open up the doors there's nothing in there. I think it's more important to make sure that there's something in there when people open the doors than how big or fancy the package it comes in is.

People are often disappointed because, "Hey, you know that last truck was full of televisions and iPods." And then the next truck shows up, and it's empty. I think that's why the pop phenomenon is always in flux, because people get attached to the last vehicle.

KRP: The Form without the Essence.

CH: Exactly. But if there's any love in it, people will pick it up.

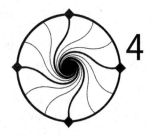

4

STATION 4 Launch

Come to the edge, he said.
They said: We are afraid.
Come to the edge, he said.
They came. He pushed them,
And they flew.
GUILLAUME APOLLINAIRE

Launch is the first station in the second quarter, Exploration.

When we come to this place in The Wheel of Creativity, we often come with the feeling, "No, not yet. I'm not ready. I want to be ready, but I am not." The echoes of our Anorexia still ring in our ears. But arriving at Launch is not about being ready. It is the process of becoming ready.

You arrive here from the Vision Quarter, where you paid attention and saw what you do not want, what you do want and what comes up inside you to keep it away. Vision is the foundation for willingness to step away from what is known in pursuit of what has not yet been found. The three stops in Quarter 1 take you through the process of building power, developing the energy within you to break free from the inertia of the status quo and make the move.

The First Gate: Go

The move from Vision to Exploration requires a decision. The first part of that decision is to choose love, which is the task in Anorexia: to choose to love your-self where you are, to love what is and to flow with your life into the next place which you can't yet see.

That decision takes you to the first gate, which I call Go. Go is the threshold between Air and Fire, which is the element of the Exploration Quarter. The work of the first three stations in the Vision Quarter creates the energy to make the crossing, the torque to change direction, the power to get off the ground. This is where you choose to get on board your own life. Once you begin to move out of the paralysis of Anorexia, you begin to feel the twinges of energy returning.

There is the energy born of cycling between resistance and desire, and the energy that comes to meet us, from beyond us, as we allow old forms to slip away. The energy created by resistance is equivalent to tense and nervous energy. But the flowing energy we feel when we are grounded in doing what we love is the true energy of life. And it comes in surrendering and letting go and choosing love. As we become willing to let old forms go, those forms become our launch pad.

Changing Quarters

TS Eliot describes the necessity of Station 4 in his poem *East Coker*:

> In order to arrive at what you do not know
>> You must go by a way which is the way
>> of ignorance.
> In order to possess what you do not possess
>> You must go by the way of
>> dispossession.
> In order to arrive at what you are not
>> You must go through the way in which
>> you are not.

(TS ELIOT, *FOUR QUARTETS*, HARCOURT, 1943)

Exploration is defined as the act of traveling for the purpose of discovery. Not everyone travels for this purpose. In the 1988 film *The Accidental Tourist*, William Hurt plays a travel writer whose main agenda is to keep things as familiar as possible. Whether we travel this way or not, many of us find ourselves living this way out of sheer habit and convenience.

In order to learn something new, we have to be willing not to know. It is what Japanese martial arts such as aikido call beginner's mind, referring to an attitude of openness and teachability, no matter what our level of study. In contemporary Western culture, we have a lot invested in knowing. We will do just about anything to prove that we do know. And we find it quite shameful when we are shown to be wrong. But the only way we can move beyond the past to discover something new is to go through a period when we do not know.

Exploration is the practical investigation and analysis of what we don't know that leads to knowledge, skills and understanding—things we can actually use. We can set out to explore because our situation requires it of us, or just because we're curious. But a true exploration, if undertaken with curiosity and open-mindedness, almost always results in unexpected, unusual or innovative outcomes.

On the Platform in Station 4

Launch is the first of three stations in the Exploration Quarter, as we begin to move away from what we know. The word Launch comes from the Middle English and French, meaning *to wield a lance*. It brings a number of usages to our topic:

- To set or thrust (a rocket)
- To put into the water in readiness for use (a boat)
- To initiate (a career or business venture)
- To introduce to the public or to a market (a product)
- To give (someone) a start in a career or vocation
- To begin a new venture or phase
- To enter enthusiastically into something; to plunge

The ultimate experience in this station is enthusiasm, but it can be both frightening and exhilarating. Exhilaration typically occurs at the point of liftoff; the work of Station 4 is to bring you to that point. You may enter this station fearful and hesitant, but you reach the other side prepared and ready to go. Sometimes you are more ready than others!

I find it personally empowering to realize that fear and excitement are flip sides of the same physiological coin: Both produce adrenaline in the body. When fear is made conscious, you have a choice; you can use the power of that adrenaline rather than be its victim.

One of my clearest lessons in this was performing. I always had terrible stage fright as a singer/songwriter, feeling so nervous that it's a wonder my fingers actually moved on the guitar strings at all! In my 20s, a gentle performance teacher in Chicago taught me that I could use my nerves to give me an edge. Just like my voice, I could learn to channel their energy. I learned to launch myself.

There is a great deal of preparation to do before launch occurs. The challenges that lead up to that moment of truth require effort, time and attention to ensure that we are prepared for it. The feeling of exhilaration comes right at the point of departure, when the rocket leaves the launch pad, when the boat pulls away from the shore, when the spear is released from the hand.

Many of us, women especially, are accustomed to seeing ourselves as the objects of our lives, rather than the subjects of them. We see our circumstances as outside our sphere of influence, and our experience of life as something that happens to us. When we arrive at this station, we may feel that it is something we are being compelled to do, rather than something we are choosing. But we are in this station because we have chosen.

The voice in Station 4 repeats: "Into the wild!" Moving through the station involves two distinct phases: preparing for departure and then setting off. No matter how much you prepare, you will encounter the unexpected, because the information from where you sit is limited. Prepare for all eventualities, and equip yourself for the ones you can't anticipate. But eventually you have to set off.

Getting Ideas off the Ground

In the Exploration Quarter, Launch is the first step from the potential of a thing to the actual thing, from the dream of something to the reality. The "No" of Anorexia keeps the New Thing frozen in potential, and the dream is safer and less demanding than the reality.

The most striking current example of this precariousness is what has been named the Arab Spring: the underground spring of everyday folk flooding the Arab world with a long-suppressed dream of democracy. It is an ennobling act to resist oppression. But for an entire generation of young people who have never experienced it, it is the long-term work required to bring that dream to life in their everyday world that will determine their true nobility.

In my flat in Nice, I have large French doors on two sides of the living room with a view of distant hills and several old villas nearby. In typical Mediterranean style, the rooftops of these villas are red clay tiles. Every spring the seagulls build their nests up there, and every year, I watch their newborns grow. I have learned a lot about Launch by watching them.

I had always assumed that baby birds just jumped out of the nest, tried their wings and instinctively knew what to do. But on two memorable occasions, the neighborhood gulls taught me that it is not easy to learn to fly. The signal for lesson time is squawking.

Lesson 1. One day, I stepped outside to find a young gull pacing on a large flat rooftop across the way. His (or her) mother, perched on a different building, called, and he answered. His attention was fixed on her. He moved toward her, but only so far. She tried a number of different approaches to lure him from his spot—farther away and closer, higher and lower—but he did not fly. Eventually, when I looked again, they were gone. But I could see it was not an easy task for either of them.

Lesson 2. Another day, there was so much squawking that I stepped out onto my balcony to see what was going on. I saw that a larger bird was walking around on the street below. She was making so much noise that the neighbor across the way was watching too. This time there was no mother in sight. The poor bird really struggled to gain altitude. Finally she managed to get enough lift to make it from the street to the roof of a parked car. From there she took off toward the villa across the street but was flying so low that she hit the utility wires and crashed in my neighbor's garden. Half-running, half-flying, she tried her hardest, skimming along the ground beside the house. The neighbor's cat took off after her, and the neighbor pursued her cat.

It was heartbreaking, but it showed me just how much courage it takes to leave the solid ground of life as we know it and set off in pursuit of something new. But Life is change itself, and if we do not flow with it, it becomes harder, not easier, to overcome the inertia.

In 2001, I left the United States on a six-week walkabout, never imagining I would be gone for more than 10 years. Something inside me knew the change would shatter the world as I knew it, and my terror was marked. It took me three months longer to leave than I had planned. But eventually I left, and I was right; it changed my life forever. So many people have called me courageous for this, but what I have learned about courage is that it feels exactly the same as fear; it just keeps moving.

The Launch Station offers both a blessing and a curse. The blessing: You are unique in all the world, and the gift you have been given to share is one only you can share. The curse: You must go alone. People may share your vision, support you, and assist you, but the journey is yours alone. No one knows the way, not even you yet. Still, you have a sense that there is something out there for you. It is a way that must be discovered in the journeying.

Becoming Ready

Whether or not you agree with his mission, Christopher Columbus was a master explorer. Still, the very nature of his voyage was based in not knowing; that was the whole point. So he did a lot of preparation. He raised money. He built three ships. He hired his crews. They sewed the sails. They bought supplies. And they set out.

In preparing for Station 4, we anticipate all the eventualities we can, and we equip ourselves with the tools to respond to the ones we can't anticipate. Boats and ships are stocked with everything they might need to handle problems that come up at sea. Some things are solutions, and others can be used to create solutions. The unanticipated problems on the way call upon us to be creative, and they require that we trust our creativity, our ingenuity and our ability to meet what comes. And that, perhaps, is what scares us most. Good preparation not only reduces the risk, it also increases our confidence in the journey.

One of the television series I worked on in Hollywood was about stunt men. There I learned that, contrary to popular opinion, stunt men are not big risk takers. Their jobs require them to perform highly dangerous acts and then be able to get up and do it again the next day. They are meticulously scientific about it. They study, research and use all the latest technologies. Daredevils, on the other hand, are out to prove something, love the risk and are by definition reckless. This is not what is required in Launch.

Checklist for a Successful Launch

The most graphic human illustration of the Launch process is outer space exploration, where we can see the key elements of a successful launch.

The first thing you need for launch is a stable platform. In rocketry, the ground platform includes enormous service and umbilical structures flanking the rocket. These structures are less about stabilizing the rocket than servicing it with supplies and feeding it resources right up until the last few minutes before ignition. What stabilizes the rocket until liftoff is a set of bolts that hold it to the platform when ignition occurs. The base for your launch platform is the world as you know it, the status quo, Home. The platform is built here and now, taking into account the real lay of the land of your life.

Second, you need a firing control system. The power or thrust required for Launch must be greater than the gravitational field of the status quo. The Fire of Quarter 2 is the powerful force of creative Life energy and what yogis call the divine fire of Kundalini, which we talked about with regard to Appetite. That power must be ignited, controlled, channeled and focused in order to get the rocket (i.e., you) off the platform.

Third, you need ground control, where your progress is monitored. You are out there on your own, but someone back home knows you're there and can support you if you get into trouble. For me, it is primarily my husband and my closest friends who staff my ground control. It is crucial for a successful launch and a safe recovery to have a community of people you know you can trust to give you honest feedback if you're getting off course.

The first part of the Launch Station is getting to the point where you can say, "All systems go!" This does not always mean you are personally ready, but the window of opportunity is closing.

The 13th century Persian poet Rumi said it beautifully:

"Load the ship and set out. No one knows for certain whether the vessel will sink or reach the harbor. Cautious people say, 'I'll do nothing until I can be sure.' Merchants know better. If you do nothing, you lose. Don't be one of the merchants who won't risk the ocean."

Many of us at this point must confront our addiction to perfection—that in us which would rather keep preparing until everything is perfect. Unless we do, we end up never living our lives. And we never go, we never launch, we never set off. It's never good enough. It's never the right time. We're never comfortable. And then we end up, like my mother on her deathbed, saying she never got her turn. Finally, whether or not your preparation is complete, like my squawking neighborhood gull chicks, you must leap. You must decide at some point to set out.

Life in Station 4
The Experience of Launch: Enthusiasm

Leaving the platform or the shore is sometimes an act of faith, and at other times an act of desperation or sheer exhaustion. In any case, there is a great release of energy at the start. It is the moment of enthusiasm you've been preparing for.

The word *enthusiasm* comes from the Greek *enthousiasmos,* which comes from *enthousiaszein* (to be inspired). It is the combination of *en* with *theos* (god). It has evolved to mean keen interest and intense enjoyment, but its original meaning was to be "in god," that is, inspired or possessed by the divine. Socrates taught that the inspiration of poets is a form of enthusiasm.

Throughout history, while the East has built its philosophies on this direct connection, Western religious and political institutions have used the term to invalidate individual inspiration as religious hysteria. No doubt it sometimes was; but this is the typical response of a centralized system of control that needs to prevent the individual from finding his or her personal power in direct connection with Source.

Enthusiasm and excitement are different things. It's easy to be excited about something—it is a reaction, an emotional and then a physical response. But enthusiasm is grounded in something deeper, grounded in something beyond you, grounded in Source. It is a real respect for the power, the energy, the fire and the force with which you are engaged.

Knowing You're Ready

To the one who asks how to know when you're ready, I answer, look to your heart. The only antidote to the shame of our addiction to perfection is love. Life is not a process of perfection. It is a process of experience and learning. The whole idea of Exploration is setting off for the purpose of discovery, and part of what we're discovering is ourselves.

Only when we go around in the washing machine enough times do we finally return to ourselves, to our Essence and to love. It's one spin after another until we build the muscles to grow stronger. The antidote is forgiving yourself and accepting where you are, rather than looking for your circumstances to change before you let go. This is how you build a stable platform for your Launch in the context of your life here and now. Wherever you are, stay with it. Listen. Forgive yourself for being there.

When you feel great urgency, when you feel you must do something immediately, wait. You know the feeling when you get an email, one to which you have a strong reaction, and you just want to shoot one back? That kind of situation is a "No" for me. I have come to learn from experience that it would be better if I sit with it while I work out an answer. Then I continue to sit with it until I feel calm in my heart. Then I'm ready. Do I always do the right thing? No, but I'm out of the reaction phase. In detaching from the external form (and my reaction to it), I can return to the center of the Wheel, to Essence, and then a new form can come from that.

On the other hand, sometimes Life says, "Now," and there is no time to wait. You see it in Nature: The seagull pushes its baby out of the nest. We discover whether we're prepared or not when we get out there. And each time we go and we're not as prepared as we would have liked, we learn something for the next time.

One year before I started dating my lovely husband, I was invited by my future sister-in-law to go on a 10-day Mediterranean cruise with her. We set off together on a gorgeous, 170-passenger sailing ship. During the course of the cruise, I fell in love with a gorgeous Croatian man 18 years my junior. I had not set out to do this, but I was open.

When I made the decision to say "Yes" to this man, I weighed the choice. It was spontaneous, but not frivolous. Because of our age and cultural differences, I knew it would not be permanent (though at the time I would have been happy to be wrong). I knew there would be pain at the end if I gave my heart.

I can remember seeing myself standing on the precipice, and I recognized that I had to choose. I could either be the woman who said, "No, this is doomed to cause me pain, so I'm going to hold back and take care of myself." Or I could be the woman who jumped, who took the risk. I didn't want to choose from fear again; I wanted to be the woman who jumped, who dared, who took the chance. And I made the conscious choice to do so.

It was a huge and beautiful experience in my life. It was painful, as week after week I had to confront my insecurity and self-doubt, all my demons around loving. But it was that very process that opened my heart, for the first time in 25 years, and prepared me, as the relationship finally ended, to meet my husband. Station 4 is that moment when we finally jump.

Here, again, Station 4 calls us to move our awareness from Form, on the periphery of the wheel, to Essence, deep at its center. It calls us to inform the forms of our lives with the deeper truth of who we are, what they are, and the truth of our relationship with each other.

We are nothing if not channels for the energy of Life to flow through. It flows through everything that exists. We get attached to our bodies and our personalities because we have come here for the human experience. But in our attachment to the forms, we block Life, becoming unconscious of who we really are. All there is to do is to become conscious of our blocks so that we can choose. And then we simply surrender and say, "Yes, I want this energy, I want Life to flow through me. And I'm willing to commit, no matter what, to that." This is the opportunity, the privilege of being alive. This is what spiritual awakening is: awakening to the spirit inside the body, which all too often we forget completely.

Whatever the external forms in our lives, our work with them is always internal. And we are called to move back and forth between the two—Form and Essence—to approach them and work with them creatively.

What's Out There Is in Here

No matter what we have going on in the outside world, our inner world is much more amazing. There is as much fire inside us as there is in the world outside. It is right there in our neurology.

There are 100 billion neurons in the brain, firing (launching) all the time. Each hooks up with 50,000 other neurons to send and receive messages for every action we take. Imagination, inspiration and new ideas all come from these connections. The connections are electrical and chemical. It is our ability to make these connections that allows us to see things in new ways, to produce new things with old elements, and to progress.

Imagine if our brains were conditioned by our habitual patterns to always say "No," say "No," say "No." Now imagine what could be if we could stay open, stay open, stay open. And this is the internal experience of Life as a creative process happening within us all the time.

The Task of Launch: Leave Home

The task of Station 4 is to leave home, which requires overcoming the inertia of the status quo in order to form the new connections that lead to new things in the world.

In general, the law of inertia states that an object tends to resist a change in its current state of motion. If it is still, it resists moving; if it is moving, it resists becoming still. Newton expanded the principle in his First Law of Motion by stating that a change in velocity only occurs as a result of some external force, primarily friction or gravity.

Friction occurs when surfaces in contact with each other move relative to each other. The friction between the two surfaces, because of the electromagnetic forces in their particles, creates kinetic energy and converts that energy into heat. This heat can be considerable; all but the most urban of us know that you can actually start a fire by rubbing two pieces of wood together.

Gravity is one of the four fundamental interactions of Nature, along with electromagnetism and the nuclear strong force and weak force. It is a natural phenomenon by which physical bodies attract other bodies. The force of the attraction of each body is proportional to its mass. We are kept on the earth because the mass of the earth so far exceeds ours. Gravitation is responsible for keeping celestial bodies in their orbits.

In our lives, the law of inertia would state that we tend to stay with what we have rather than change to something else. And yet, Life asks us continually to move and grow and change all the time. Friction describes the obstacles we encounter when we change our relationship to the people, places and things we are in contact with. Gravity is the force that keeps us in our current orbits; the larger the "bodies" around us, the greater the force they will exert on us when we try to leave their sphere.

We become entrained with the people, the institutions and the systems around us. We must do this as children, but most of us in Western culture gradually slip away from our own creative weight—our "mass" in the world—and the paths we are best suited to lead. This return to ourselves, this recovery of our fullness, requires us to Launch away from these systems. And the systems don't always want to release us.

Again, we see the dramatic effects of this being played out in world events. Right now in Syria, the fight for governmental control is ruthless. The established system is deeply threatened when individuals rise up and speak with their own voices. Swiss psychologist and psychiatrist Carl Jung said, "Whatever you resist persists." And it applies as surely in the world out there as in our psyches. Once the first spark of passion catches, external resistance ignites it. Managing that fire is the key to a successful Launch.

There are always obstacles inside us, as we come up against our own internal reactions, like fear, panic, resistance. These are best overcome before the Launch, but it is more common that they are refined during the journey. Launch is the process of moving beyond what's holding you back, in order to let go. Even as you are lifting off, you have to dig deep to ground yourself in your Self and in Source.

Prepare to Succeed or Prepare to Fail

Wild Survival was another television show I worked on. It was a documentary series about people who went off into remote places for pleasure and got into trouble. Sometimes they had gone out in one kind of weather, ill-prepared for when the weather unexpectedly changed. Other times they had failed to let anyone know they were going, and when an injury prevented them from returning, they had to wait for days to be found. Often they just didn't do their homework to understand the realities of where they were headed. Whatever caused their trouble, most times their vulnerability to it was due to a lack of preparation. And good preparation is required to move safely through this station.

Enthusiasm arrives in a whoosh when you are finally on your way. Then you must be able to navigate the change. Your desire—your longing, your vision—is your true north. You have to have systems in place that support your body, mind, spirit and emotions throughout the journey. Too often we rely on teams that are inadequate or outdated. We keep going back to people who are not changing with us, who cannot support us in leaving.

When I left the United States in 2001 on my walkabout, I had still not reached the point where I felt prepared. I had postponed my departing flight 10 times, and I could not change it again. And so, reluctantly, nervously, I got on the plane and set off. I was scared, but somewhere deep inside me I knew I could trust the process. People look at my daring adventure and call me courageous. But I know a secret: Courage is fear that just keeps moving. Enthusiasm was always there, and though I did not always feel it, through one experience after another, I came to own it as my natural state.

The Reward of Launch: Freedom

The reward of Station 4 is freedom—the joy of being alive and a renewed experience of the powerful simplicity of pleasure in the moment. You've worked hard to get there, and when you let go, you can do so with confidence. It is not a blind leap, but a leap of faith—in yourself, in your intuition to let go and in your life's creative process.

As you let go of the here and now, a new here and now appears, and another. This freedom is won by your own hand, as you break free from the chains that bind you to your past. With it, you set out to explore the unimagined possibilities of your life; you learn to trust your intuition to guide you, and you experience a new kind of power, born of your connection with what flows, rather than from your investment in the way it's always been.

The reward is not assured, however, until the task is complete. If you do not commit to the Launch and let go, you are left with two options. Either you leave the launch pad and move toward the promise of your original vision, or, still attached to the systems around you, you continue to generate heat until you are consumed by the destructive force of this incredibly creative power.

But if you do move through Station 4 all the way to Launch, the energy generated takes your vision, your ideas, your thoughts and begins to move them through your spirit into the world. The moment of Launch is a moment to be savored, because sooner or later it gives way to Exploration's challenges, coming next in Station 5: Isolation.

A STORY OF LAUNCH

Nall Hollis, Artist
Current Cities: Vence, France, and Fairhope, Alabama

> "There are many poems that will not be written, and many paintings that will not be painted, because of spiritual lethargy."

I met Nall Hollis a few years ago at The N.A.L.L. Art Association in the south of France. I was smitten with his wrenching, visionary transmutation of experiences I had also lived growing up in the American South. Seeing his studio, I was awed by the scale of his commitment to his entire life as a creative expression. And in interviewing him, I was touched by his unconditional transparency as a human being. He creates what he lives. Nall's story illustrates how leaving the shore of what you know opens doors to discovery that never existed before.

KATHERINE ROBERTSON-PILLING: You have been quoted as saying you are "inspired by the material and encouraged by the spiritual." What does that mean to you?

NALL HOLLIS: I came from a banking family, and for my father, God was money. America is a materialistic society. So it's natural that I've been inspired by the material. But the spiritual side of life encourages me to look deeper. And you can't be forced to be spiritual; I had to be encouraged.

KRP: Absolutely. As human beings, I think we bridge the spiritual and the material, and the work that you do just screams that. There's so much Life Force in your work, even though at times it's quite obscured. How do you manage the energy of that?

NH: Well, I get up at three or four o'clock in the morning. I do computer work. I clean after my apprentices. I water the plants and garden a little bit, and then I walk and do yoga with the apprentices at 7:30. Then we work. It's a continuous thing. When I'm awake, I have to be doing something. I cannot sit in a chair without going to sleep. 'Cause I've got to be active; I've got to be up; I've got to be moving, whether it's drawing, or cutting paper or painting... .

KRP: What would you say to an ordinary person about creativity?

NH: Well, what I say to my apprentices is, "You're supposed to be artists, poets. There are many poets and many painters, but few poems and paintings because of spiritual lethargy." Now fire up that lethargy into action. If you don't do anything about it, you can have all the talent in the world and never get it out.

I tell everybody everything in my paintings. I say, "Yeah, I lived these." "Oh, they're suicidal!" "Yes, I've lived that." And it comes out, every feeling. That's one of the secrets—I don't edit. I don't hide. I'm transparent... .

All people have talents; they all have something they can contribute to the process of society. It can be a destructive force or a constructive force. If they get into the positive cycle, it will lead into a production of activity of their talent. If they get into the negative cycle, they can also be led into a production of the activity, but of their negative traits. You've got to be really vigilant in choosing. You have a choice.

KRP: Is that why you created the art association and foundation?

NH: I started the foundation to help young artists sober up. A friend of mine in Alabama, an actress, had a son who was in a rehab clinic in Birmingham. And she said, "Now look, I have a son with double suicide bracelets, and he's sworn that the minute he gets out of here, he's going to commit suicide. And he admires your work. You don't know him, but he's been to your shows, and you're the only person I can think of that can help him." . . .

So I worked with him, and I told him if he wanted to come to France, he had to stay sober for six months, which he did. He was my first apprentice.

And I gave him a show of his work. Once the word got out to my friends, I had all these phone calls, "Would you take so-and-so? Would you take so-and-so?" So I did that for five years.

It gave me a cause. After 20 or 30 years of painting, one exhibition after the other, do you think I'm doing this just to make money so I can pay the electricity? Working with students gave me another cause. I don't mind working 24 hours a day, because when I see one of these kids get sober and get it, wow!

KRP: Do you ever wish for a simpler life?

NH: Oh yeah. I think you spend the first 50 years of your life accumulating this material stuff. And the last 50 years, you get rid of things. I'd like to reduce everything before I go out. I'm an orphan. I don't have kids. My family of friends is my real family.

KRP: The family you choose for yourself.

NH: Yeah. When I left the States at 21, I realized that my work and my life is more important to me than following somebody else's recipe for what I should be. And that was a head start.

If you're born an artist, you can't do anything else. You're a target in every field, except in art. I can create in the kitchen; I can create in the garden; I can create in the painting studio; I can create when it comes to decoration and doing anything that has art or aesthetics involved. I could be an artist-writer. I can create a foundation, but I don't like to manage it. I'm certainly a hands-on person.

KRP: What I hear you describing is the full circle of The Wheel of Creativity. You leave home with a hunger. You go to the far side of the world, where you don't know, where the seed of the new is created. And then you come back with the harvest that nourishes you and nourishes the community as well.

NH: That's what I've done. I lost everything. I gave up family, friends, money, a job, the ownership of my father's businesses. I said, "I prefer to be a starving artist." That's what I've had to do. I had no fear. I was young, nice-looking, and had everything given to me, so I didn't know what *no* meant. But I wanted

to merit something, and I knew my only field of possibility was art. So I'd pray, "Please let me live from my art. I could be a teacher, I could do anything; but please let me live from my art."

KRP: Who were you asking?

NH: Well, I had denounced God. I was having a war with God. I was horrified with the concept of what people had done to Christ and with his teachings in what I saw around me in the Bible Belt. But they were just human, and I was the worst example of anybody. I had to leave or be a hypocrite. So I fled. Then I realized that I had taken myself with me, and that I had to work on myself, which I chose to do first through Hinduism, rather than, "Believe in Jesus, and everything is cool."

KRP: Is your art a part of that? Does it heal?

NH: The art is a tool to keep me sane. It's therapy. It's like reading meditative books. It's like doing yoga. It's like walking into a cathedral and praying. It's like going into Nature. It's like adopting dogs, cats and students. My art is just another thing to keep me on the right path. I'm using God's gift. He gave me a little talent, and I'm using it. I have to use it.

KRP: Is there an energy that goes through you, that passes through your art, which ends up with somebody else? Is something shared?

NH: I think that people can see it in my work…. They realize that it's not decoration. They realize that there's something going on. And they're attracted to the mystery or to the spirituality. I like to say, "If art is not spiritual, to me it's decoration." Even if it's negative spirituality, it's still spirituality.

KRP: Where does it come from?

NH: Where everything comes from. Who is responsible? The God-energies, the Higher Power has put everyone on earth. Everyone has a purpose. It is not a very important purpose, whatever it is, because we're just little drops in the ocean of humanity. But, for ourselves and our egos, it's important that we make progress, for the spirit of the soul to progress toward perfection, which will never be attained, but we progress.

5

STATION 5
Isolation

To navigate you must be brave . . .
and to be brave you must remember.
MAU PIAILUG

When Christopher Columbus set out on his first voyage to the Americas, he was in his 40s. He was a navigator and colonialist. Atlantic voyages in the 1490s opened the door to exploration and colonization of the New World by Europe, and it changed the balance of economic power for the European continent. But the journey to discover the Americas was not a straight shot to glory. Christopher Columbus made many mistakes, and when he reached the edge of his charts, he and his three ships found themselves in Station 5 of The Wheel of Creativity: Isolation.

Station 5 is the inevitable moment when hope is lost and the journey itself seems a big mistake. It might occur weeks or months after Launch, but eventually there comes a point when the shore you left behind disappears; no shore behind, no shore ahead. The experience of open sea with nothing else around can be a glorious feeling, but usually it is not.

Isolation is the midpoint of the Exploration Quarter. From the Vision Quarter—the domain of the mind and thinking—you passed through the gate of Go into Exploration—the domain of the spirit. Here a new aspect of the human experience is developed.

You arrive at Station 5 from Launch, where you attained a big enough surge of energy to get you off

the ground, out of the box, and away from Home. But with your goal not yet in sight, in Isolation, your experience is being out there. A completely different set of skills is required.

On the Platform in Station 5

Isolation has many subtle definitions, but the basis of them all has to do with being set apart. Other meanings relevant to our story include:

- Solitude or lack of contact with other people
- The state of enforced physical, social or mental distance from the environment that is usual or desired—most often one's family or community
- Separation of a person with a communicable disease from those who are healthy
- The act of separating one substance from another in order to obtain a pure or free state
- Moving individual parts of the body independent of others

87

In every case, there is value in the separation, as something is made distinct through it.

You set out on this journey because you longed for something authentic and true. But what comes now is not easy. From the thrill of Launch you descend to Isolation, where you feel completely alone and lost, even despairing. If you had known what you would find here, you might not have set out at all. But now it's too late to turn back.

When Columbus reached the point where he thought the Americas should be, his ships were running out of food, his crews were talking of mutiny, and there was still no sign of land. In Isolation, the voices of disappointment, doubt and despair scream: "What were you thinking? There's nothing out there. You should never have left home! This was a huge mistake!" What are you to do with that?

When the external cues are not what you think they should be, a deeper vigilance is required. Move from the Form of it to the Essence, move to the center, own the experience, know that it is part of your own life and that you can find the incredible beauty in it.

This moment of feeling lost can be frightening, but it is always an opportunity for deeper awareness. Keep going. Stay vigilant and navigate your way through, even with tiny moves, to keep going in the direction of your dream. If you can take a breath and settle a bit deeper, it can also be glorious.

The Value of Getting Lost

Across most of the Western world today, our top priorities are productivity, competitiveness and results. But in our drive to get ahead of the rest, our lives are so busy that we have lost touch with ourselves. Our corporate cultures reject the very essence of this station, which is irreplaceable in the discovery of the authentically new. And we, of course, have created these cultures.

Rarely do we take the opportunity to be truly alone, to drop down into ourselves and hear the still, small voice within us. That is one of the functions of this station. By being separated from the rest, we hear something inside ourselves that we can't hear in the noise of everyday life.

One of the many visits I have made to this station occurred in 1997, in the backcountry of Colorado. I had been living in Los Angeles for several years and working in television. In television in Los Angeles, there is a collective thought that you're only as good as your last project. I was doing interesting work on respectable shows with good ratings and good reviews. There was something missing for me in my work, but it paid the bills. And I could not allow myself to leave the treadmill of productivity.

Then my mother died. I continued to work, but my heart was not in it. I visited a friend in Colorado for a few days to sit and stare into space. He had a log home on 100 acres of land surrounded by a national park, a national forest and a national wilderness. Days became years as I deepened my relationship with this friend. I left Los Angeles and its notorious rush hour for this isolated valley, where the only traffic was the migration of the elk. Without my noisy L.A. life, Nature's silence confronted me with my own emptiness. But the longer I stayed, the more comfortable I became with the Life in the silence of the place, and I began to hear that still, small, creative voice I had been ignoring. My creative work matured, and my life took a different course.

Life Beyond the Grid

Isolation is the station where you unplug from the grid. It is where you train yourself to always know where you are.

Here, in Isolation, you must sink your keel deeper to listen to the voice of your own spirit, which speaks to you through intuition, which can be developed through contemplation and looking within. Men have shortchanged themselves for millennia by limiting intuitive knowledge to a box called "women's intuition." Rather, it is a depth of knowledge and understanding available to all human beings who cultivate their receptive nature.

Our greatest longing is not for the ideal man or woman, or the right job, or the perfect friend. Our greatest longing is for ourselves and for our deeply intimate connection with what lies beyond us. Our longing is for what is there all the time, at our side, waiting to feed us and nourish us and make us whole. And usually we must remove ourselves from the external forms of our lives in order to hear the voice within us. Sometimes Life does it for us.

Station 5 offers you one of Life's greatest gifts, because to live your life and never hear what is inside you needing to be expressed is possibly life's greatest tragedy. It is a loss not only to yourself but also to society, as all your creative contributions, great and small, go unmade.

But only when we detach from the external forms of our lives—the tyranny of the urgent and the need to compete—do we have the opportunity to hear the tender cry of the New Thing from beyond the horizon. Thus, Life brings us to this station, to offer us the opportunity to commune with ourselves and give birth to something new.

Practice. Practice. Practice.

The practice of creativity in the arts offers wonderful training in this process, especially if you are not an artist, or if you think you are not creative.

More than anywhere else in my life, my training in navigating this edge has come from singing. I've studied singing off and on for most of my life, but quite seriously for the past six years, working with two opera singers developing my vocal technique. Good singing technique is an extremely physical endeavor. When I am trained, and the technique is there, there are those magic moments when I just get out of the way and something flows through me.

When I am conscious of it, singing is the pinnacle of everything I do. Even though I do not, and probably never will, make my living through singing, the discipline of all these years has familiarized my body with the habits and patterns that harmonize strength and relaxation within me. Every time I try to manufacture the sound that my mind tells me I should be making, the authentic sound of my voice is blocked. As time goes by, the blocks become more

evident. It is a mystery understood not with the mind but with the spirit.

This principle is true in all fields of endeavor, from cooking to business and beyond. Whatever the field, this training is aimed at staying open to receive and transmit the truth beyond what you already know. Trial and error is the process of testing the boundaries of knowledge; failure does not exist here.

Knowing the Way

In modern culture, we don't get much training in listening to the voice within. Perhaps that's why singing is such a powerful practice. In so-called civilized society, amid our ever-quickening worship of progress, we are losing our connections with the wisdom of our ancestors, and even the skill to tap into it. But this wisdom and our interpretation of it are what guide us through our lives when we cross the limits of what we know.

Like the aboriginal tradition of walkabout, we reach the Isolation Station when we leave our community in answer to a spiritual call. The journey is ours alone, but the unseen tracks we follow are the tracks of our ancestors. For the Aborigines, the original deities who first walked the earth were ancestors who laid down the songlines in chants and stories handed down from generation to generation. Embedded in the traditional songs they sang on the journey were the directions—from rock to stream to bush—to follow, to find their way. It's how they always knew where they were, even though they were in the middle of the desert.

For oceanic cultures, these traditions took place on the sea. Ancient Polynesian navigators also relied on traditional knowledge passed down from generation to generation to show them how to read the signs embedded in Nature. With ancient knowledge and present-moment vigilance, they navigated thousands of miles on open seas in double-hulled canoes without instruments.

Our lineage and our history, what is written deep within us in our cells and in our DNA, shows us where we are. We just have to remember what we know.

This station is about learning to use our knowledge to navigate through our lives. It is what allows us to enter the void without getting lost, and to find our way to our destiny, guided from within.

Life in Station 5
The Experience of Isolation: Despair

Station 5 always requires something of us to find our connection. It is here we learn to deal with the negative voices inside us, because when things get tough they will start to scream and wail. The overall experience in the Isolation Station is despair. We feel alone, out there, separated, secluded and withdrawn. Without knowing our connections, without training, without the wisdom of our ancestors, we are lost indeed.

Discovery lies beyond the charted waters. Without good navigation, the farther the distance traveled, the greater the doubt. But the greater the discovery to be made, the farther you must go alone. With no shore in sight, the old skills don't work.

Not All Who Wander Are Lost

What is new exists just beyond the border between the known and the unknown. You must be willing to go to the edge of the world if you want to discover it and bring it back as a new creation. Even if it is the synthesis of two existing things into one, you have to separate from the past; you must be able to see beyond what they have always been before in order to find their potential for something new. You must see beyond their Forms to their Essences.

In this stage, you navigate out of known waters to the unknown. It is more active than a blind leap into the void. You must do your homework to get this far, or you truly will be lost. Using your tools, skills and the knowledge of the modern world, you piece together a map. And you must be vigilant.

The Task of Isolation: Stay Vigilant

Western culture has forfeited, or perhaps we never had, the relationship with Nature and the sophisti-cated spiritual technologies that connected ancient cultures to the land and sea. We have developed all kinds of instruments to do the job for us, but we have lost the skill of navigation, our ability to know where we are in the world. And we suffer for it.

The task of Station 5 is to stay vigilant. This journey is not a straight line, and there will certainly be points where you may think you are off track, when you are not where you thought you would be. But maintaining your course, even when you think you are lost, and finding the tools within yourself to do that, is what this station teaches you.

Navigation Lessons

The first and simplest method of navigation at sea has been to follow the coast, lining up landmarks, always keeping the thread back home in sight. Leaving the coast for farther shores, however, requires a deeper relationship with Nature to understand its particular language of location. Since ancient times, seafaring navigators have worked with natural forces to find their way from one shore to the next.

You can be sure that Columbus used the latest navigational methods for his explorations. Beyond the land covered by his charts, he could use verbal descriptions of trade routes made by those who had gone before to piece the sea together. Of course, he used instruments like the compass and sextant. But Columbus also benefitted from sophisticated navigational knowledge and experience developed by global cultures before him.

The Greeks had navigated their archipelagos by paying heed to clouds and odors. The Phoenicians navigated by the heavens, following the movements of the sun through the day and positions of constellations at night through the Mediterranean skies above them. Norse navigators, or Vikings, watched the patterns of birds in flight and of currents, as their skies were not always as clear as those in the Mediterranean.

While all these cultures used the navigational methods best suited to their environments, the undisputed masters of navigation were the ancient

Polynesians of the Pacific Ocean. These masters of navigation traveled among 1,000 islands, covering 16 million square miles of ocean, using all the methods above, plus observation of winds and clouds. They too were colonizers, in a sense. They carried animals and plants from home to set up new homes on new islands, with no plans to ever return to their origins. And they held a very high status in their societies.

Ancient Polynesian navigators found their locations and determined their courses by watching sea and sky for patterns that told them where they were, what land masses were near or far, and where they were in relation to home and their destination. The pattern of the currents revealed shores miles away. The faintest glint of color on the belly of the clouds told them the weather for the days ahead. They sculpted charts out of palm fronds and shells. And they turned their boats into instruments by carving niches in the wood to mark degrees of direction.

Similar to the songlines of the Aborigines on land, the poetry and chants of Polynesian navigators contain the mysteries, hidden to the rest of us, that guided their people from one place to another. Their ancestors empowered them with this skill, handing down the knowledge from one generation to another.

But the art of Polynesian navigation was almost lost as the elders who kept the traditions passed away. Since the early 1970s, Polynesians have taken up the task of keeping the art alive. In 1973, a group of Hawaiians calling themselves the Polynesian Voyaging Society built a copy of the original double-hulled canoes used by the original navigators. Rekindling the ancient methods, learned from the last of the ancient navigators, such as Mau Piailug, they have completed numerous voyages without instruments, from Hawaii to Tahiti and farther. They navigate by observation alone.

As human beings, we have the ability to navigate through life with what is inside us. But in Western culture, we are alienated from that. Perhaps our parents and their parents lost their connections; perhaps we have refused to hear them. These mariners remind the rest of us that our connection with Nature as human beings still holds mysteries far beyond those that most of us will ever explore.

According to Bruce Blankenfeld, a member of the Polynesian Voyaging Society, "Once you learn to find your way, you can never be truly lost—no matter where you go."

How Do You Navigate From Within?

Station 5 is about learning to find your way. It is a process. In order to stay present with the voices of ancient wisdom within us, we must learn to manage the three greatest enemies of seafaring: drifting, distractions and despair.

With your crew in mutiny, it is time to become the leader of this voyage. It is when the voices come up that we are called to leadership. Most of us do not fully step into that role until we get lost. Only when the crew begins to mutiny do we hear what's inside of us and see it; until then, it operates unconsciously. We do not see how our lives are the consequences of our choices, and we feel like victims.

1. Set and maintain your course.

In order to keep from drifting, you have to navigate. You navigate using what you have at your disposal at the time. Navigators typically use three points to steer by: current location, destination as a point on the horizon and the heavens.

- The heavens. For all celestial bodies—stars, sun, planets, moon—the farther away your reference point is, the more accurate you will be in plotting your position.

- Your destination. This is your vision, which you began clarifying in the first quarter of the Wheel.

- Your current location. This is the point deep in your center where you just know. You must know where you are in order to navigate.

As captains of our ships, we are responsible for those ships. We may want to avoid this reality, but we cannot. No one else is or ever will be the leader of our lives but us. Not only does responsibility mean we are accountable for our safety in the world, it also tells us that only when we take our role as captain are we able to respond to conditions outside us. When we reach the end of our days, the credit or the blame will be ours alone.

As I was writing this chapter, early one morning I woke startled from a dream. I was in a car with a woman I did not know well but had met through a friend. She was driving through a gorgeous countryside that resembled northern Scotland, with vast, green rolling hills whose rocky peaks scratched a dark and ominous sky. I was content to let her drive me. Then we approached a large body of water the color of a swimming pool. As she drove the car into the water, I turned to her with a questioning glance. She smiled wryly and said, "It's okay." I was uneasy, but I said nothing, expecting that the water was shallow and we would cross to the other side soon enough. But we did not, and the next thing I knew, the car was submerged under 100 feet of water, and there was nothing I could do. I could not breathe.

All of us, but particularly women, have a tendency to go along in one circumstance or another. We are taught that others are the experts about our lives. We are taught to pick our battles, minimize conflict, settle rather than fight. In the continual use of "outside instrumentation" to help us navigate through life, we lose the skill most fundamental to being human. We look to someone else to tell us where we are, where we're going, what to do, and how to get out of this mess. But all the while we hold the map. We hold the key, and until we put it in the lock and start our own engine, we are lost. No matter how many good advisers we have around us, it is someone else's journey we are making, not our own.

2. Keep clear of distractions.

In Greek mythology, the Sirens were beautiful women who seduced passing mariners with song, luring them off course to crash on the rocks of their island. Avoiding distractions is a very important aspect of navigation. If you do not remain vigilant, you cannot know where you are.

Modern life is busy. We are enslaved to our computers; clearing emails, managing a wealth of resources on the Internet, staying in touch. We lose track of our boundaries and relinquish our ability to choose. We feel pushed around, bullied by these things. Station 5 is an opportunity to pull back and ask, "What's really important here?"

We get distracted by the past—what we should have done, and by the future—how things are going to turn out, or how we thought they were going to look. And we grow weary and fall asleep.

Navigators always know where home is. They always know where they are in relation to it. In that way, they are never truly lost. If we leave home in a violent way, cutting our connection with it, we cannot know where we are. Polynesian navigators joke that you can always tell the navigator on a boat by his eyes: They are always red. They are always alert.

3. Manage the screaming meemies.

It is not until the baby bird is kicked out of the nest that it can ever know if its wings will carry it or not. You can see the babies walking around on the rooftops stretching their wings, even stretching their wings and running; but this is not flying. Perhaps it is mechanically similar, but the experience itself is a completely different thing. And this you cannot know until you step off the roof.

There is a time in every creative process when you reach this stage. "What were you thinking?!" Supplies may get thin, your sense of time may become distorted, all your references are gone. The crew inside your head decides to mutiny, and the voices within and around you tell you it was all a big mistake. They may well be the same voices you hear when you're meditating or when you have space in your schedule. While uncomfortable to hear, this crew reveals your hidden weaknesses and gives you the opportunity to address them.

Managing the screaming meemies, the cries of the crew, again requires leadership. When you're out there on your own, survival depends on choosing, on rising to the occasion. It requires knowing what to do when the place where you thought you would find land yields nothing.

When we see ourselves as the victim of this station, this station is extremely challenging. Our experience of the solitude is negative. We feel lost. We despair. We feel like we are in exile. Something is wrong.

When we move out of the frightened victim role, we feel the spaciousness and exquisite beauty of being at sea. We are alone with the enormous but intimate force that's keeping it all happening. In the darkness we can see the stars, and we can hear our own still, small voice.

The Reward of Isolation: Discovery

When you do learn to stay vigilant, the reward of Isolation is discovery. You cannot know, when you set out, what you will find waiting for you. Discovery most often comes with a surprise. And it is so much more than the new thing you thought you were after. This station offers other, perhaps more important discoveries: what's out there waiting for you beyond the horizon, what's inside you and what you're called to be part of.

Something's out There

Here in Station 5, the new world you were hoping to reach is still not within grasp. You may have sighted it; you may have a clearer picture of what you're looking for. But you have not yet reached the other shore. There is more journey to make before you do.

Station 5 offers you the chance to discover what's out there waiting for you. The wild, unbounded energy of Life flowing—the storms within and the storms around us—needs to be grounded in us in order for us to use its power.

Something's Inside You

Station 5 demands that you discover what you're made of, what you have inside you. As your experiences teach you to trust, the voices of your fears grow softer. Station 5 invites you to move out of the victim mentality as you see yourself weather the storm. And finally, when all the other noise is out of the way, you come to hear the still, small voice within.

As you discover who you are in relation to the great mystery of Life, you see yourself in the context of something larger than you. And that brings you face to face with what you're called to be part of. From your limited view of the picture, you come to see the truth…you are a part of Life, in all its magnitude, as opposed to seeing only a fragment of it.

We cannot know ourselves without knowing this bigger, transpersonal context in which we play but a part. It is deeply exciting to know you're directly connected to the Source of Life, apart from everyone else you think you need to survive.

All these new discoveries along the way enable you to stay on course and keep from turning back. They are the antidotes to your despair.

It is said that a Polynesian navigator always knows what the land looks like on the other side of the horizon because he knows the stars and signs so well.

When I left the United States in 2001, all I knew was that I was setting out on a walkabout. I looked ahead on my path, and I could see the edge of my flat world. I could see the horizon, and I could see myself going over it. But I could not see beyond it, and I could not see myself coming back. As far as I could see, I just disappeared, and I was terrified. I had no experience of this. And if my ancestors did, which I imagine they did because of their life experiences, they did not teach me. Perhaps they tried, but in the arrogance of my youth, I would not listen.

With training, and as I go through this process

again and again, I learn what I have inside me to navigate with, and I begin to know that what waits for me on the other side of the horizon is also navigable. I may not always know this in my mind, but I know it intuitively.

So, this new skill gives us the ability to take on bigger journeys, bigger projects and deeper explorations into ourselves. At the end of the day, the journey out there is always about the journey inside. Our bodies are our ships, and our ships are our instruments. These are the vehicles that carry us through Life. And not only is the sea all around us, it is in us too. Even in Isolation, we are at home.

Leaving Your Box

We know now that Columbus was not the first to discover the Americas, as was once believed. In fact, he was quite wrong about many of his calculations, such as the earth's circumference, which had been proven long before. He found many unexpected islands, from the Bahamas to Cuba, before he found America on his third voyage. He exaggerated claims about his discoveries. His crews mutinied, settlers rebelled, and he was even arrested for a period of time.

However, even though he was wrong, Columbus was willing to leave the box, to set out into the unknown. By doing so, he dispelled the belief held by most Europeans at the time that there was no land between Europe and Asia, which had made a sailing voyage impossible up until then. He put a new continent on the map in the middle of the vast ocean between Europe and Asia. Not only did Europe get its trade route, but the world had a whole new playground.

Columbus's errors as well as his vision allowed him to enter the void, to go into uncharted territory and discover something where it was not supposed to be. This place where we leave our charts is a very important part of our discovery of the new things "out there" as well as a crucial part of the process of self-discovery and self-definition.

Are You Exploring or Are You Lost?

How did Columbus find the New World? He had to use all the navigational tools at his disposal, make his own interpretations and keep moving into the void. Despite his other flaws, Columbus was a man of vision, leadership and vigilance.

The thing that keeps you from getting lost is your navigational skill. And in The Wheel of Creativity, the task is learning to navigate from within. Columbus had enough faith in his vision to not turn back, no matter what. It is this tenacity that produces the reward:

- Looking for signs of land and persevering
- Finding awe in conjunction with the trepidation
- Learning to manage your mind (your "crew") and stay on course

But so many of us feel alienated, adrift, because we have lost touch with our place in Nature, our connection with the natural forces that speak to us with reliable voices. We have lost our ability to read the signs. So we feel cut off from the natural world of which we are a part. We are not dominators of this world, but players in it. We have objectified the natural world by our alienation from it; we have alienated it by our objectifications.

We no longer have a connection to the respectful, honoring tradition of our elders, through which we can learn how to make our way in the world. This station comes to remind us.

This journey is an outside voyage with circumstances and demands and objectives and needs. And it is an inside voyage with the desires, thoughts, intuitions, feelings, sensations and dreams that are ours. They are our gifts, and we are their caretakers.

Supporting Yourself in Station 5

According to Hawaiian navigator Bruce Blankenfeld, "From a Polynesian perspective the canoe is a spiritual entity; it is the embodiment of an ancestral spirit.

It is a mental, physical and spiritual—a full body experience. You're not sailing on the canoe, you are sailing with the canoe."

This is my experience of my life and why I see it as a creative adventure. I am not living my life as much as I am collaborating with it. Each time I come to this station and go through it, I know that what's out there in the midst of the sea is part of my journey. I trust the process a little bit more because I've experienced it so many times.

My parents, in their loving wish to protect me from the dangers of the world, passed on to me their best navigational tools. But filtered through their unconscious fears, their tools were not always accurate. Twenty years ago, someone taught me that the process of the journey can be trusted, and how to trust it. And that gave me a new skill that I've used and developed.

With each journey, technique, training and experience are gained. With each journey, the despair moves closer to excitement, as less and less often do you feel lost. When Polynesian navigators lose track of where home is, of how they got to their current location, they stop the boat. Even the best of them can get lost. But you are never lost forever. Nature is always there, giving clues that bring awareness out of despair, through renewed vigilance.

Isolation is the station where knowledge and intuition meet. Knowledge and training inform your connection with the natural world, giving you the language to hear and understand its clues. The skill you have already attained in your life is put to use here, as you synthesize that knowledge in new ways to meet the unique challenges of each encounter. The Forms of your life become the seas you sail, and the journey is your creative process. Your task is to observe the external Forms of your life, to read their waves for the Essence in them, and use those clues to maintain your course toward your destination, your vision.

A STORY OF ISOLATION

Diane Lydon, Events Producer
Current City: Nice, France

"Everybody wants a quick fix to everything . . . me included. But after years of searching, I've found that it really doesn't exist. I think we have cycles in life, and for me, meeting you and learning about The Wheel of Creativity is a point for me of returning to somewhere that I've been before."

I met Diane Lydon in Nice a couple of years ago. I was struck by her strength and at the same time her willingness to acknowledge that something she once had got left behind along the way. More than 10 years earlier, she had gone on vacation to Bali and returned home to the United States pregnant with her now-10-year-old son. She made a choice to change her life in response to Life's call. Her story illustrates the power of staying vigilant and continuing to watch for signs of land.

KATHERINE ROBERTSON-PILLING: What in your life have you returned to through The Wheel of Creativity?
DIANE LYNDON: If you want to get to the true essence, for me it was a rekindled hope and to refind my hope and my faith. Faith is a lot of different things to different people. But I think faith and hope are what keep us motivated, what keep us working with our strength. It's that kind of internal flame that burns inside us. So, it was a rediscovery and a rekindling of those two things for me, as well as a touchstone, going back to somewhere inside myself.
KRP: How have you created that in your life before?
DL: One is through competitive sports. I swam competitively with the same team that produced Mark Spitz and Debbie Myers. And when you train, and compete and finish something, it gives you this sense of well-being inside. Confidence, hope, faith, or trust, I find that well-being there. I don't compete anymore, but I do like sports for what they give me.
    Now, I also find it in a spiritual practice, like The Wheel of Creativity. I think we've all put a lot of faith

in something else, and we think something else is going to do it for us. It could be God, or your community, or your family. But really, it's a matter of having your faith and hope inside and internal to yourself. For me, The Wheel of Creativity showed me that, "Wait a second, this is where you need to be. And keep along that, and then from there things will work."
    Life is super tough, but that's just what it is. I'm a very strong woman, but strong women don't always have the answers, and they never ask for help. And The Wheel of Creativity is a way to look at things where you can feel comfortable with asking for help. And it's given me an ability to share, actually giving of myself to other people. I have something to give and I can give it. I don't have to hoard it, because if I do then I won't have anything.
KRP: Do you see a guiding thread through the course of your life, or something that is at work beyond you?
DL: For me, the constant is my intuition and my sensitivity to that intuition. I noticed it when I was about 11 or 12 years old. I would be in a group, and I would think something someone was going to say, and then they'd say it.
    And it's been with me throughout my life. I can be thinking of someone, and they call. It could be as simple as knowing when not to do something. I remember when the US invaded Iraq the first time, it's almost like I felt a crack in the earth inside my body.
    If I am attuned to it and I listen to it, then life seems to work out. And if I don't hear it or see it, if I don't pay attention to it, then things don't go so well.

It comes in a lot of different forms. But it is always in the form of thought and it does manifest in creativity. It's a deep sense of connection; you don't know where it comes from, but you know it's there. So that's the constant in my life, through which I move to create my life and manifest my own destiny.

KRP: What would you say is your primary creative work?

DL: I've struggled with this question for 15 years. My initial thought is my work with people, service to people. But I don't see that as being creative. If I could have worked in the Peace Corps, that would've been awesome and it would have been creative.

I guess my primary creative work would be the direction in my life that I want to take. For example, I've always loved the Olympics. I'm really a sports fan, and I did reports on the Olympics. I watched all the Olympics. And eventually I was able to manifest that into actually working in the domain of the Olympics. That is my creativity.

KRP: In what ways, other than what you do, do you see a creative force or energy at work in your life?

DL: I see it in my son. I see a lot of creativity there, in his expression of himself, in dance, and song and humor. I'm so proud of him, and I'm proud to be his mother. I can't tell you how many times people compliment me on my son. He is definitely one of my creative processes. Probably from the point of birth, from the point of conception.

I see creativity when I'm walking in Nature. Sometimes just walking down the street, you can look at architecture and then it all of a sudden gives you an idea to do something, something that has nothing to do with the architecture.

KRP: So creativity lives in your response?

DL: It doesn't move me to go home and paint a picture. Sometimes it moves me to come home and dance, or call somebody on the phone, or move something. That's the point I need to get that going. It's the missing link to get somewhere else, the missing step on the stairs. It helps to put the puzzle pieces together. I think my creativity is very practical.

KRP: Knowing that the process is at work, even when a product is not visible, does that make a difference for you?

DL: Absolutely, because I wouldn't be moving through my life if that wasn't the case. That creative process gives you confidence, the willingness to move through difficult things.

KRP: Are there any steps you regret taking or not taking in your life?

DL: Where I am now, it's almost like I don't know where my career went. I had a path, and I was moving in a direction, and I was successful, and things were great. And all of a sudden I had my child, and it pretty much stopped. I took 10 years off my career to raise my child. And I've done well at that. It's not necessarily been to my benefit careerwise, though things were flowing financially up until about 2007. But, as I said, everything comes around in cycles.

I have had to readdress my career. I've had to readdress my femininity and my sexuality. I've had to readdress my inner consciousness, through The Wheel of Creativity, meditation and my whole process of being. Can I create a new business? Can I have a sense of self-worth through money? At the same time, can I share my life with a partner? And provide the stability, love and sharing with my son, so he can continue to grow? Those things are really at work right now. How they'll come together, I'm not really sure.

KRP: To me the most creative thing we do is create a life—our own life—and most of us don't take responsibility for that. It's a lot easier to feel, "I've just been handed this life. Life happens, and I don't control it." And the things that happen to us are also the stuff with which we create our lives. You got pregnant, and you chose to create a life with that, and a son and a relationship.

DL: It's funny. I see that as the direction I wanted to go, even though it wasn't planned. For example, I wanted to move to Europe long before I got pregnant. From the first time I visited, I was like, "This is me. This is home. I feel better, my health is better." But I couldn't see how to do it. There were all these obstacles, all these excuses.

And then I got pregnant, and then there were absolutely no obstacles. All the obstacles faded away for me to move here, because I wouldn't raise a child in the US. So my son got me here, so to speak. Life came, I got pregnant. And yes, I made a life of it. But the thing that came was already created. It was the point that I needed to take the other step forward.

6

STATION 6 Crisis

There is a moment in any kind of struggle when one feels
 in full bloom . . . vivid . . . alive.
One might be blown to bits in such a moment
and still be at peace.
To be such a person or to witness anyone
at this moment of transcendent presence
is to know that what is human is linked
by a daring compassion
to what is divine.
ALICE WALKER

Station 6 on The Wheel of Creativity is Crisis. The word *crisis* has its origins in the Greek word *krisis*, from *krīnein* (to separate, judge). At a social level, crises are usually deemed to be negative changes in some aspect of life, such as economic, political, societal or environmental affairs, especially when they occur with little or no warning. We talk about a midlife crisis, a medical crisis, a suicidal crisis, a crisis hotline, crisis intervention, crisis management. We have read about the US financial crisis, and now we have a world economic crisis.

A crisis is a turning point. Its adjectival form, *critical*, describes a decisive point or situation where the status quo must change. How does that play out in life? Here are a few interpretations:

- In political, social or economic affairs, it is an unstable condition involving an abrupt or decisive change, especially when there is a distinct possibility that the outcome will be unfavorable.

- In medicine, it is a sudden change in the course of a disease or fever, toward either improvement or deterioration. It can be a paroxysmal attack of pain, distress or disordered function.

- Personally, it is an emotionally stressful event or traumatic change in a person's life.

- In literature and filmmaking, it is a point in a story or drama when a conflict reaches its highest tension and must be resolved.

The Character of Crisis

Crisis can look and feel like failure if change doesn't come on the other side of it. And many times, if we are not connected with the absolute necessity to change, we will not. We will stop. And we will fail, when successful change lies right on the other side. In our case, what's on the other side is the entire second half of The Wheel of Creativity.

Crisis takes something that once felt certain and stable and shakes it up. It is usually seen as an obstacle or a threat to your goal and your vision. We generally view a crisis as negative because it disrupts our lives as we know them.

In fact, Crisis is the turning point alone. In the creative process, as dramatic as it may be, it is not negative but neutral and malleable.

We go along, as long as things are comfortable. It's human nature. You may not be happy, but you're not willing to change. And then your partner threatens to leave you, or you are put on probation at work, or you get sick. Life does it for you. In so many areas of our lives, we may see a problem, want to change, even work on it, but we don't change until we're forced to. It is a core aspect of being human, because change is uncomfortable.

Crisis also offers an opportunity for something good to emerge from instability. But that opportunity does not occur in this station; it occurs after you make the turn. You must harness and channel the power that is generated in times of crisis in order to seize the opportunity and effect your desired outcome.

On the Platform in Station 6

Station 6 is the third stop in the Exploration Quarter. From Home we've moved through Vision—Hunger, Appetite and Anorexia—building enough momentum to overcome the inertia, leave the status quo and move through the gate of Go. We have launched and left the shore, we've passed through Isolation, where we had to dig deep and learn to navigate, stay vigilant and stay on course. We also learned the value of knowing where Home is and having a crew that can support us in the journey. Even if in Isolation we sighted land, that wasn't enough. Sighting land and being there are two different things.

Even though we may see what we want in the distance, we still have to overcome obstacles to get there. Life puts in our way the obstacles that refine us and purify us. This is the value of being in

Crisis: It is where Life eliminates the aspects of our character that would prevent us from being good stewards to the idea that wants to come through us into the world.

This final station of Exploration puts you fully in the Fire, the element of the Exploration Quarter, the element of purification. From the ignition of Launch to the crucible of Crisis, you have to engage with this element in order to move through the quarter to the other side. Station 6 is where everything that is not essential to bring forth the New Thing is burned away.

This brings you to the end of the first half of the Wheel, all of which is about letting go of the old form so that energy can be released with which you create the New Thing. We move from what is comfortable and stable and known to the very opposite.

Launch, Isolation and Crisis are the three stations of the Exploration Quarter, where the work is external and active. To work with what appears out there as an obstacle, you must come down into your center. You must find the essence of who you are in relationship with the world and the essence of the world in relationship with you. This enables you to get grounded and do the work of this station, which is to move through the panic and to focus.

Life in Station 6

These three stations work to intensify your commitment to the search by throwing up the inevitable obstacles to your enthusiastic pursuit of your vision. And Station 6 tests your spirit, strengthens your energy and makes you stronger as it moves you forward.

Just when you think you can't get any lower, just when you think it can't get any worse, it does. Opposing forces intensify until the Crisis comes, and Station 6 appears. Perhaps you spot what you've been searching for. Perhaps what looks like land comes into view. Everything in you rallies to get you there, but you are not there yet.

This does not happen just once in life. We cycle through this station many times in many areas of our lives. And we're the same people, so we have the same issues. Going through this process in different aspects of our lives enables us to work on those issues from many different angles.

Here you face the storms of life, the earthquakes, the tsunamis, the hurricanes and the tornadoes. They require you to turn inward, throwing your keel down in the water as deeply as you can to stabilize yourself in order to survive. Here the external circumstances can be so strong that you cannot right yourself. Here the forces of destruction overwhelm you.

The Experience of Crisis: Panic

You can prepare for life's storms to a point, but beyond that you are totally vulnerable. And you know it. Life shakes us to our core, taking us beyond the point to which we're prepared to go in order to transform us. If the despair of Station 5 reminded you to stay vigilant, the panic of Station 6 demands absolute surrender to what is.

When the earthquake hit Japan in 2011, the people were as prepared as they could be. Most skyscrapers survived because they were designed and built to withstand such tremors. But the tsunami that followed the earthquake devastated the country's infrastructure, and the effects rippled around the planet for months.

The experience in Station 6 is panic, the task here is to focus, and the reward is capture. The focus here is finding the single-pointed focus deep within that produces effective results in the external world. This is a point where all our planning and fighting just don't work. That is this station's greatest gift, because then we surrender. Then we open ourselves again.

In order to get to the land you have seen, you must first pass through the perfect storm—perfectly designed to test and refine your character and prepare you to receive and bring up the New Thing. What you know as your ship will be lost, and you just have to go into the storm and through it. There is no choice. If you didn't, then the work that needs to be done to transform you would not be, and you would just recycle back through the places you've

always been before. The work of the Crisis Station is to find the stillness in the eye of the storm.

"Catch Me If You Can!"

The voice here is saying, "Catch me if you can!" We've spotted land. We're moving toward it. And the storms come up between it and us; this is a natural rhythm of life.

In the animal kingdom, both in hunting and in mating, this process can clearly be seen in action. The target is sighted. This is followed by a covert, quiet stalking, almost imperceptible but very active nonetheless. Then, in an instant, everything changes; things become very focused. In a wild stampede of energy, everything that is not the prey ceases to exist. From the stillness at the center of the confusion, you capture the result.

This process occurs in the hunt for food or for procreation; in both instances, it is the Life Force. It is the survival instinct of Life itself. University of Pennsylvania professor Victor H. Mair speaks of Crisis not as opportunity but as focused completely on survival, whatever it takes. Crisis is the turning point in the hunt, which is again the work of the Exploration Quarter.

Which Way Is Up?

In my crisis experience in the Mediterranean Sea in the south of France, the storm of water around me left me powerless to control my body. But the panic of that moment pushed me to reach deeper than I ever had for a new solution. Without the intensity of that experience, I would not have come so quickly to crystal clarity.

1. Which way is up? "There's that little patch of blue light there."

2. When can I take a breath? "It's coming, it's coming. Right there. Now!"

Those two questions led me to a kind of focus that is very rare in life. I was instantly yanked from total disorientation and confusion and shown the way through, back to the surface, and safely back to shore. The questions themselves were the reward; that was the capture.

Anything but . . .

What do you typically do in this station? Looking back at the phrases most commonly associated with the word *crisis*—crisis management, crisis intervention—we see that we try to intervene; we try to manage the crisis; we try to control the circumstances. We do anything but surrender to what is and allow things to turn. But trying to control often causes harm. Sometimes taking control is appropriate, but sometimes, by intervening, we reject the seed of the New Thing.

In the moment of surrender, it's as if everything goes into slow motion, because, in fact, we have disengaged our awareness from the drama of time and space, and returned to the center, to stillness. For me, that day in the sea (and it is typical of so many life experiences), things had to get that bad before I would surrender. If I could have, I would have continued to try to fight it. But it's only when we really let go that the clarity comes.

The phrase *hitting bottom* is often associated with addictions and compulsive behaviors, which sheds a bit of light on this station as well. It is widely accepted that recovery cannot begin until addicts have hit bottom—that is, reached the end of their illusion that they can control their addiction. This is the admission so many people try to avoid at all costs. But think about this with me for a moment.

When I was a teenager, I did a lot of diving at the local swimming pool. When my form was really good, the splash I caused was almost imperceptible. With little resistance, I would penetrate the water to quite a depth. I always liked the feeling of getting deep enough that I could touch the bottom of the pool. It gave me the leverage I needed to spring up to the surface again; without hitting bottom, I had to swim up under my own power.

When moments of Crisis appear before you, they are opportunities for you to find your center, and for Life to pour its clarity into you when you become open.

The Task of Crisis: Focus

The task of Station 6 is to focus. Earlier we noted that, in general, the law of inertia states that an object tends to resist a change in its current state of motion. If something is in motion, it doesn't want to stop. If it's still, it doesn't want to move. Crisis is the flip side of the inertia of Home, and here there is as strong a pull to change as there was to stay still at Home.

By giving all our attention to the present moment, we learn to choose, to focus while staying open. We're not fighting; we're not rigidifying. We're open to all that's there, and we're choosing.

This process links Form and Essence for us. Even as we move out into the world, we're moving deeper down into ourselves. So what's required of you is to know when to stop fighting long enough to become present.

The Exploration Quarter is the quarter of research, and this is the experiment of our lives. Each time we try something, what transforms it from failure to opportunity is how we respond to it. Are we present to capture the tiny seed of hope from which to grow the future? What needs to be changed to move to the next place?

All the work that's come before, all that you've been doing up to this point, enters into the process here. Over time you develop the skill to stay present, no matter what's going on around you. And it becomes more natural to you each time you practice it. One day, surprised by an unexpected sea, you find you automatically know what to do.

The Reward of Crisis: Capture

In Station 6, you must consciously disengage and let the old form dissolve in order to move to the creative side of the Wheel, out of the first half, which is all about dissolution, into the second half, which is all about creation.

The reward of Station 6 is capture. And I liken this to the process of making love. Crisis is that point just before orgasm where there is nothing else; you are in pursuit. Chaos is orgasm, the moment of oneness and union; it is the place where you leave your awareness of yourself as a physical being and find oneness only attainable at the spiritual level, in Essence.

The French call orgasm *la petite morte*—the little death. It is surrender, truly allowing yourself to be "taken." To be penetrated by the divine Masculine, which is complete focus, pointed and directed. To allow the explosion of yourself in service of the birth of something greater, something new, something that just wants to come through you.

Crisis brings us to the Gate of Chaos, which is the counterpoint, the very opposite of Home, where nothing is known. If Crisis is the peak of the hunt, Chaos is the bliss on the other side. On the other side of Chaos is Conception, and a new quarter, and the birth of the New Thing. But not yet.

The Second Gate: Chaos

We cannot talk about Crisis without talking about where it is leading, and Station 6 leads you into definitive transformation on the far side of the Wheel. Crisis is the ultimate turning point, where old forms dissolve. The station of Crisis cannot be completed until the old form gives way, releasing energy. Chaos is the pure and formless energy that remains.

As Crisis takes you to the edge of your personal limits, you find yourself at the next gate, where energy shifts again like the season. Chaos is the far point in your world, as far from the certainty of Home as you can get. In contrast to the order and stability of Home, here everything is disordered and unstable. When we allow ourselves to get to this point, we are totally open and receptive beings for the Universe to create through us, with us.

What we know of Chaos today has been constructed from concepts and ideas passed down for millennia, forming the mythologies of cultures around the globe and through thousands of years.

The Ancient Greeks

Chaos was a predominant theme in Greek mythology. In Greek, the word is *Xaoç*, pronounced *ch-a-oss*. It means *gaping void*. For the Greeks, Chaos was the primeval state of existence from which the first gods appeared. The ancient Greek poet Hesiod spoke of *Chaos* as a yawning chasm or void, one of four primal entities from which the universe evolved.

Ancient Greeks saw Chaos as a mixture of the four elements: Earth, Air, Water and Fire. According to the Greeks, Chaos was (1) a bottomless gulf where anything fell endlessly, (2) a place without any possible orientation, where anything fell in every direction, and (3) a space that separated and divided things (such as the earth and the sky).

Judaism and Christianity

In the Old Testament, the void of Chaos is referenced in the first verses of Genesis: "The earth was without form and void." It is from the absence of form that God created the world and everything in it. That emptiness (formlessness) is Chaos.

In Judaism, the Kabbalah contemplates Chaos as a period of repose and absence of physical manifestation, when the Negative reigned supreme. Negative here could be understood not in the judgmental sense but as the emptiness that surrounds a form. Negative is also often associated with the Feminine, receptive aspect of creation.

Native American Teaching

Native Americans use the term *Great Mystery* when referring to the Life Force, the creative energy that is both the void and is present in all things. Everything comes into existence out of Great Mystery. It is also that from which Great Spirit emerged, the directive force that moves that energy into form.

These two energies—the void and the directive force that moves energy into form—are distinct, complete and necessary to the creation of all things.

Hinduism

In Hindu philosophy, Chaos is linked with the term *Pralaya*, which is Sanskrit for "dissolution." Everything that appears to exist is subject to dissolution, a very different thing from destruction, as dissolution leads to recreation. As a period of rest, dissolution is the opposite of *Manvantara*, the period of full activity. It is the difference between death and life, whether of a person, a planet or the whole universe.

Pralaya is identified with *Mahapralaya*, the great dissolution at the end of a cosmic cycle, during which all things are consumed with fire and dissolved in the formless waters of procreation. Hindus see this as the process by which the Soul moves from higher planes and projects its consciousness downward in order to take incarnation as a human being. *Pralaya* is an energetic pause during which the individual soul rests in the Heart of God before becoming active again on the vibrational plane that corresponds to it.

On The Wheel of Creativity, Chaos is the point of dissolution of life as you've known it. It is the point of separation, a break in your attachment to all that is known. The feeling during Chaos is instability, loss of control, the inability to force something; everything as you have known it is gone.

You are in the void between worlds, between projects, between relationships, between lives. This is literal and it is metaphorical. In these moments of true loneliness, you are cut off, even from yourself. It is a pregnant pause, the beginning of something else that can't yet be known. That something else comes next; but until it does, all you can feel is the void.

The Crisis Station cannot be completed without moving into Chaos. And the willingness to move into Chaos is the need to change, which makes a success out of this loss of something huge, something we've known before.

So the opportunity, which the scholar Victor Mair says does not exist in Crisis, does exist in Chaos. Chaos is nothing but opportunity, and it comes at the end of this station.

A STORY OF CRISIS

Peter Fox, Tetherless World Constellation Chair and Professor of Earth and Environmental Science and Computer Science at Rensselaer Polytechnic Institute
Current City: Troy, New York

> "Trying to rush or force the creative processes is futile, and . . . a great deal of trust is required in connecting to any greater force. It always means I get exactly what I need exactly when I need it. No more and no less."

I met Peter Fox about 15 years ago when we were both living in Boulder, Colorado. I interviewed him in 2002, and was delighted to have the opportunity to do so again 10 years later. Fox was awarded the 2012 Martha Maiden Lifetime Achievement Award for service to the earth science information community, and he has been awarded the 2012 Ian McHarg/Earth and Space Science Informatics Medal by the European Geoscience Union. I can personally verify that he is as impressive a human being as he is a scientist.

KATHERINE ROBERTSON-PILLING: Peter, would you please describe your work to me?
PETER FOX: My work today, which has evolved a lot over the last 5 to 10 years, centers on application of mathematical and computer science techniques to address a variety of problems, largely in environmental science. For example, the focus is on the health of marine and terrestrial ecosystems—water quality, air quality and related topics—with a midrange focus on the effects of climate change on regional environments. We're trying to harness very large amounts of U.S. environmental data from diverse information sources that exist today. The range and diversity of data is overwhelming, and the data infrastructure has not kept pace with our ability to produce it. So many of our science questions are not answerable simply because we don't have the tools available to us.

In turn that stimulates a lot of interesting research work: in mathematics, how to develop algorithms to analyze very large amounts of data; in computer science, how we represent knowledge, and how we

choose the terminology that describes the data, so that scientists who analyze it can converse with each other about it.
KRP: What needs have you recognized? And what innovations have you created in response to those?
PF: The first area of innovation is the encoding of knowledge-based information within our data systems. For a very long time, a lot of human intuition and expertise was required for people to make sense of the data or information sources they were looking at, particularly through the Internet and Web. Over the last eight years, we have brought semantic encoding—the semantic web—to science systems, first to solar terrestrial physics, and now to ecology, hydrology, oceanography and geochemistry, and a very wide variety of areas.

The second area is the development and formation of knowledge networks. These are networks of people, somewhat inspired by the advent of social networks but applied to science. We started with existing networks, which were recognized as very important in collaborative endeavors. But no one had analyzed what those collaborations were. They could tell when they were working and when they weren't working, but they couldn't say how or why. So, we've applied information modeling to understand the relationships in these networks, so that we can design them rather than letting them form accidentally.
KRP: How is this making a difference for people?
PF: You can only find patterns that you're looking for. You can't find patterns that you don't know exist. So the real attraction here is to do true knowledge discovery, finding the needle in the haystack. These new

tools and techniques reduce the burden on the user to have to understand all the things in front of them. They can use the computer for some automated reasoning and inferencing on the data, to follow the multitude of all possible parts through the graph, and to offer up potential relationships. Scientists can then sort through those, rather than going through all the possible combinations themselves.

A lot of the work I'm interested in is what we call heroic science. It's the place where all the new discoveries are made. But it takes two years, five years, 10 years; and with the very rapid advance of climate change, we don't have two years or five years or 10 years. The current rate of species loss, the loss of sea-level rise and habitat change, means that we have to solve some of these problems on timescales of months rather than years. So we are working to turn the routine part of heroic science into something that's automated, so that scientists (myself included) can devote their time to analyzing the important part of the data, rather than the mundane and uninteresting parts of it.

KRP: Yes. I believe that reaching the limits of knowledge is very important. The Wheel of Creativity traces in everyday life what has been called the Hero's Journey, in which you must leave Home, where everything is known, and move around the Wheel to the far side, where nothing is known. The second half of the Wheel, the return, is the creation process. From your experience, does that strike any chords for you?

PF: Yes, there's a lot of resonance there, especially the far-flung stage where you are basically lost. I've experienced exactly what you describe; and a lot of my current work is focused on moving more deliberately through those stages with good tools to use. I think a lot of scientific work, a lot of research work, never is brought to fruition because you can't fully understand whether you are or aren't finding something new. Negative results are as important as positive results.

When an artist wants to paint but doesn't have the technique, they develop the technique. People develop their ability to move through a creative process—whether it's intrinsic to them or they've been given certain knowledge and skill. Then their creative process is much more fluid and much more rapid. What I'm trying to do, in scientific creativity settings, in the face of most people being overwhelmed and underprepared for conducting science, is to make that scientific exploration process more fluid.

KRP: How do you see the creative process in your life?

PF: Having moved to a university, I see it every day, especially in the teaching work that I do. Part of my work has been to create new courses—graduate courses—to teach much of the material I've been talking about. So we've developed three brand new courses that have never been taught anywhere else in the world. And it turns out that, to translate sophisticated research methodologies and ideas into a form that graduate students can learn, and where I can evaluate whether my objectives can actually be achieved, is a highly creative process. Interestingly, students are not motivated by learning but by grades. And it's challenging to stimulate their curiosity so that they actually learn something, versus just repeating something to get a grade.

The other area is with the graduate students in the lab. They're all doing PhDs, and they're all doing research work. So I need to carve out a large number of research problems to push them way beyond what they already know. That means I have to think about topics for which I don't necessarily know the answer. And that is a highly creative process.

A lot of our incoming students are conditioned to come in and talk to their professors every week, having solved a problem the professor gave them the week before. So the first thing I do with all the students is to get them to do something I know they cannot possibly solve by the next week. And they're all nervous, and they cancel the appointment, and finally they come back in and admit, "Well, I didn't solve the problem that you gave me." And I look at them and say, "That's good." And then their heads fall off and their eyes roll. And I say, "The object was for you to get lost. That's what research is about!" It is not an assignment. It is research. You don't know what you're doing. You're lost. And they learn their own way to get *unlost*.

KRP: Do you have any experience in all of this of a power greater than yourself?

PF: Largely based on my personal experiences with the world, I think there are a couple of things. First, my intellect was my most powerful enemy. In the past, it was very clear to me that all situations could be reasoned upon and understood and moved past. And that's not correct. My intellect was getting in the way, and my lack of acceptance that there were forces that I didn't need to understand. Some of the things I learned from that are that I'll know something when it's time for me to know it, that trying to rush or force the creative processes is futile, and that a great deal of trust is required in connecting to any greater force. It always means I get exactly what I need exactly when I need it. No more and no less.

7

STATION 7 Conception

But little by little,
as you left their voices behind,
the stars began to burn
through the sheets of clouds,
and there was a new voice,
which you slowly recognized as your own,
that kept you company
as you strode deeper and deeper
into the world . . .
MARY OLIVER

The Big Bang theory is science's current explanation for the origins and early development of our universe. It states that around 13.7 billion years ago, the universe formed suddenly from a cosmic expansion (or explosion) of previously existing hot and dense matter. The theory's author, Georges Lemaître, who was a Catholic priest, astronomer and physics professor, called his 1931 theory the "hypothesis of the primeval atom." It is what is today called "the God particle."

Hindus have, for far longer than Lemaître, described this Big Bang as the moment when all the souls of the Universe could not contain themselves and exploded, traveling at extreme speeds in all directions. The explosion produced fragments of Creation, each of which contains all of Creation in it. At the same time, each fragment exists to express Creation in a unique way.

Changing Quarters

Conception is the first station in the Incubation Quarter. From the turning point of Crisis, we arrive at Station 7 by passing through the Gate of Chaos. Chaos is the Big Bang of the creative process, where old forms are dissolved. It is free-floating opportunity, whether we choose to take it or not.

As Quarter 1 relates to the element of Air and Quarter 2 to the element of Fire, Quarter 3 relates to the element of Water. In The Wheel of Creativity, Incubation is the domain of the heart and the emotions, and the Jungian function of feeling.

In our context, Conception refers to both physical conception and to the conception of new things. It has various definitions:

- In procreation: the act of conceiving in the womb; the initiation of an embryonic animal **109** life, the onset of pregnancy, usually marked by the implantation of an embryo into the uterine lining; the state of being conceived

- In cognition: the formation in the mind of an image, idea or notion
- In creation: the event that occurs at the beginning of something
- In invention: the creation of something in the mind; creation in the inventor's mind of a useful way to solve a problem; the act of visualizing an invention, complete in all essential detail

In Conception, the Fire of the spirit penetrates the Water of the heart. The process we create with is the same process we are created by. The fragments of Creation are the seeds of the new, all of us and everything else that exists, inseminated by Fire in the moment of Conception. Now they are transferred to Water in order to grow. The flame is extinguished, but the Fire continues, permeating the Water as heat. Each fragment then begins its own creative journey through Life.

The work here is to move what has been developing from the mind through the spirit into the heart. It involves being present with what is and taking your place in the creative process. It means taking responsibility for what you have as your medium to create with and staying with it until both you and your world are transformed.

Here we return to the Feminine energy of Water after three stations in the Masculine energy of Fire, and we must shift our relationship with what is being created through us. We are now again allowing Life to penetrate us and create through us in the process.

If Ideas Had Souls

What if ideas had souls? What if the Universe sows ideas in the world like seeds?

Hindus define God as the sum total of all purified souls in the cosmos at a given moment. At the moment of the Big Bang, they say, these souls were scattered through the cosmos. Every soul requires a body to work out its karma on its cosmic journey. What they call the divine fire within us is the Hunger of Station 1, the spark of Life wanting to come into form through us.

As we take our place as creators in the world, we receive ideas from the resting state looking for form. And they look to us to help them do that. Those who are most receptive to these seeds of Life—who are willing to commit to them to help them grow—are the ones who will bring those ideas into the world. If you don't do it, someone else will. But the adventure is in the doing.

In the dissolution of what was, as one world is dying, we naturally resist. Then finally, when we let go and get quiet, energy starts to build again. It builds and builds until the will of the elements (souls) grows to its full capacity, and something new is ushered in with a bang.

The process is continuous and ongoing. We build one thing, which grows and grows, and then that thing gives way. This is life. You are the plant, not the flower; don't attach to what flows from you. Stay grounded and grow your flowers, one after the other, each different and perfect in its own way.

Conception is the result of the big bang of Chaos, where everything scatters to the winds. The seeds are scattered in Chaos, to be planted in the ground here, where they germinate. It is the sowing of the seeds in the universe and in you.

We are always moving between the outside of the Wheel (Form) and the center (Essence). The experience of Station 7 is both intimate and universal.

We do not plant the seed; Life does. It is an experience of being loved by Life completely and unconditionally, being made love to by Life. At the same time that the process occurs at the universal level, it occurs personally as well.

Just as Jesus said in his parable, some seeds fall on rock, some fall on fallow ground, some fall on fertile ground and take root and grow. It is the same with us and the creative process. The same principles are described across cultures, from the mystical texts of the Kabbalah to the founding precepts of Hinduism and Buddhism. The souls of ideas come to humans to take root in us. And we offer different types of ground.

Each of us is more receptive to certain things than others. Some are the ground for science, other for art, and still others are fertile soil for business and money. We each have our specialties. And here we either love Life back for its bounty or we reject it in fear and self-protection. But in the end, it is how we meet this gift of Life that matters most. To tend the soil of your own being and become receptive for what you are here to give birth to is your human right, privilege and duty in your lifetime.

If all ideas have souls, then each thing that wants to be born has its own vision. We are cooperating—human forms and idea forms—in creating the universe we share. When the seed takes root in us, it continues expanding. It lives to grow. It grows to the point where it must change form or change containers in order to continue growing, and then that old form dies. It is a continual death and rebirth; although the Form is changing in the material world, the Essence remains unchanged in the stillness of Source.

On the Platform in Station 7

Station 7 is where we become the container for Life to inseminate us with the seed of the New Thing. However, this alchemical process is not just about what is being created "out there," but more importantly, about how we are creating ourselves through the process. It is not about doing, but being. This requires us to shift from the active back to the receptive principle.

While Exploration was external and outward moving, Masculine and active, this is a very internal time, receptive, Feminine and always moving inward. From here we travel deeper into the realms of the heart and the emotions, into Station 8, Gestation. But the work of this station must be done first, certainly before we see any external indication of a New Thing in the world.

Evolution on the Wheel

The Hindus and the Buddhists hold the Wheel as a symbol of karma and reincarnation—a succession of births, deaths and rebirths moving continuously toward spiritual liberation.

Your Wheel of Creativity is the chakra of Life, where energy flowing in various patterns meets. It sits in the center of a massive web of highways where there are others like you with their own intersections. If you do not open up personally, then you block the energy in that place on the grid. This is not just a loss on a personal level, but for the entire human community on a universal level; the entire expression of the energy in all that is suffers.

The conception of a new thing is the material expression of the spiritual conception within, produced by the union with the Divine. The creative energy of Life is a neutral force; it is indiscriminate rather than elitist. It does not require a highly evolved being to create with. It is just the way of spirit: It will express itself in whatever way it can through anyone or anything it finds.

But the opportunity always exists, when engaging with Life in this way, to be transformed in the process. In order to create something big, I need to begin with something small—to be more open and available for the bigger thing. It's like practicing scales; doing, but always in balance with becoming. All of Life, everything we do, is the equivalent of practicing scales.

To develop your skill with the creative process is to increase your ability to conceive. The more you create, the more fertile you become. And the more your power of conception develops as you come to know the secrets of the Universe through your own experience.

Some people, such as shamans and artists, are here to go to the edge and, like Prometheus, bring back the fire to society. Others are here to create within the inner circle of society. Yet all of us can go to this edge in ourselves, pushing the limits of our awareness, expanding our consciousness into the darkened rooms of our lives.

Though we may continue to work within corporations and societal systems, the creative journey unfolds as an internal journey, which not only affects our way of being in the world but also produces a different quality of results in the systems we work within. Whatever role you play, the opportunities to do this work always exist.

Life in Station 7

Conception is an event that introduces the transformation of the energy released in Chaos into a new form. As we saw in the last chapter, there is a moment in Chaos when things become very clear. And now they go underground to grow.

Conception is the moment when the spark created in Exploration penetrates the Water of Incubation. It is the moment of bliss, when one sperm actually gets through, and the uterine lining welcomes it. The receptivity of the uterine lining where the tiny embryo embeds itself is the quality of my own nature—my receptivity, my moisture, my fertility.

What happens when fire penetrates water? The fire is extinguished, or the water boils and becomes steam. What is essential here is to have a container. Something magical happens here, when the spark of Life enters. Something is created here that did not exist before except as an idea, where Essence is distilled into pure and sacred Form.

Distillation: The Essential Toil

The process of making essential oils is a beautiful example of how we can work with the raw materials of our circumstances to create our lives as works of art. As a mechanical process, distillation involves placing plants in a closed container and applying steam (heat applied to water under pressure), which vaporizes the oil from the plants, releasing a mixture of steam and oil. Then, through the process of condensation, the oil is separated from the water.

There is perhaps no greater master of this art than Jack Chaitman, founder of Scents of Knowing in Hawaii. Inspired by his love of smell as an art form

and his respect for the souls of the plants he works with, Jack has spent two decades creating custom distillation apparatus and specialized methods to help plants release their essences. As different from the industrial methods of larger-scale production facilities as man is from machine, Jack's work is an expression of love, and his products are masterpieces.

We often speak of separation on a spiritual level as a bad thing, as if we should only be spirit and not human. But perhaps the process of being human is assisting us to refine and distill the essences of spirit in a way that can only take place in physical form.

The Experience of Conception: Wonder

The experience of Conception is wonder. From the annihilation of Chaos, if things do not end in failure, they become very clear. Wonder is the other side of annihilation; it occurs in surrender when you have stopped trying to control Life.

In order to experience wonder, you must first let go, which requires a choice. There is a great inhale of Life energy in Station 7, which must be openly welcomed, opened to and grounded in the body. This station is the funnel, where the enormous, wild and unbridled energy of Life released in Chaos gets transformed into the seed of the New Thing.

At this point of Conception, we are completely open to the Universe. We have experienced this dissolution to allow us to experience our oneness with it all: Earth, Air, Water, Fire and Space. Momentarily unplugged from Form, we become aware of essential energies flowing through our chakras, which become our experience of the material world. But it is all the same energy.

Here we experience an opening on every level. Floating in Air, our minds are loose and curious. Swept up in Fire, our spirits are connected and trusting. Swimming in Water, our hearts are tender and vulnerable. And grounded in Earth, our bodies are soft and relaxed.

The voice of Conception is: "Wade in the Water." Get in. Get wet. Let Life support you.

The Task of Conception: Be Receptive

The task of Station 7 is to be receptive. Conception is a resting place, though it is not a place for going to sleep. In Station 7, you are the funnel, bringing the grandeur of Life down into one tiny seed, from which it will grow again into Form. There are two aspects to this task.

Making the Space

Reduced to basic building blocks, the whole cosmos is nothing more than a cluster of atoms and molecules. It is pure energy surrounded by ether: the dark, empty portion of the cosmos, the same emptiness from which the original cosmos was born.

So first, Conception requires you to make space. Here you introduce the fifth element, Space, to go with Air, Fire, Water and eventually Earth. Here you create the space for the elements to commingle.

Receptivity is work, because we live our lives so guarded and controlled. The controls are blown apart in Chaos, so the work here is to go against all the years of habitual patterns to keep things open. You will not succeed immediately, but you will progress immeasurably over time.

This does not mean picking up a more enlightened version of being guarded. Outwardly, it means staying open even as you discover your limits, patterns and compulsions. It means taking care of yourself. Inwardly, it means listening to your inner voice before making commitments, acknowledging your inability to relax, allowing space for yourself to think (and feel and sense).

Being the Container

Second, Conception requires you to create a container for the distillation of Essence to occur. Like a child who looks over her shoulder to be sure Mom is still there just before taking the next step toward adventure, the tender fragile new seed within us must be kept safe from harm so it can grow with abandon.

Being a container means honoring your boundaries and taking responsibility for your choices. In order to truly say "Yes" to anything, you have to be able to say "No": "I choose this and not that." To conceive means letting go of blame, knowing that Life is reaching out to you all the time, in every encounter. We are not victims of our lives, only of our thoughts; and we are always choosing what we will create.

Like the active and receptive principles, both of these aspects are required. Making space without containment produces endless expansion without consequence. Containment without space produces unimaginative productivity. One without the other is not enough.

Shiva and Shakti

In Hinduism, Shakti is the personification of divine Feminine creative power, sometimes referred to as The Great Divine Mother. In Sanskrit, the word *shak* (to be able) refers to the sacred force or empowerment. It is the primordial cosmic energy and represents the dynamic forces that are thought to move through the universe. Not only is Shakti responsible for creation, it is also the agent of all change. Shakti is cosmic existence as well as liberation, its most significant form being the Kundalini Shakti, the deep psychospiritual force at the heart of mystical experience.

Shiva is the static, fixed or unchanging aspect of consciousness, the latent, formless principle from which the whole of the universe is manifested. Shakti is the active, fluid or changing aspect of consciousness, manifested outwardly. According to Swami Jnaneshvara, Shiva and Shakti are like ink and word. As the ink, Shiva is static, fixed and unchanging. The ink is always the same, whatever form it takes. As the word (or picture), Shakti is active, fluid and changing. Many forms are made with ink, but ink is always ink.

Shiva's influence on the mind creates separate, distinct forms. When these forms are abstract, we call them energy, which is the equivalent of Shakti. When the forms enter the material world, we call them matter. Energy is a neutral force, and when we are conscious and intentional we channel it first into abstract forms, ideas and then, using the four elements, into physical form.

This beautifully describes the relationship between Essence, Form and the human being as creator. The energy of the Universe moves freely and constantly beyond time and space. It finds containment, both temporal and spatial, in physical forms. As human beings we contain energy, too, and we move it from the infinite to the finite through the mental, spiritual, emotional and physical aspects of the creative process.

The Unifying Practices of Tantra

In Sanskrit, the word *Tantra*, associated with Indian yoga traditions, comes from two root words: *tanoti* (to stretch, extend, expand) and *trayati* (liberation). Reaching far beyond the West's trivialization of it as sexual practice, Tantra deals primarily with spiritual practices and ritual forms of worship that aim at liberation from ignorance and rebirth, and it sees the universe as the divine play of Shakti and Shiva.

In a broad sense, Tantra implies the continuity of spiritual and material, weaving our realization of spiritual truths, by means of personal experience, with energy and Life. In a nutshell, Tantra teaches that there is only one energy in the universe, and our task is to know that through direct experience.

Tantra teaches the way to use the divine power that flows through the universe (including through your body) to attain purposeful goals. These goals may be spiritual, material or both. The body is a sacred temple in which to travel the path of spiritual evolution. Sexual practice plays a powerful role, because it offers the dissolution of perceived boundaries at the door to oneness with everything.

Tantra also teaches that the currents of energy flow in two directions. What flows out through us is the way the world evolves; our work is to return the energy to its Source, and ourselves with it, liberating ourselves from our attachment to the Forms of our lives in the process. Two of Tantra's essential truths are, "One must rise by that by which one falls," and,

"The very poison that kills becomes the elixir of life when used by the wise."

In the first chapter, I talked about the art of textile weaving as a metaphor for our role on earth to weave the fabric of the universe by the way in which we live our lives. The vertical threads run between us and Source. The horizontal threads are the matter that makes up our world. Heaven and earth form the loom, and we are the shuttle, moving back and forth between them to weave the fabric with our thoughts, feelings, words and actions. This is the process of moving around The Wheel of Creativity, again and again in every area of our life experience.

Here in Conception, we step into this role wholeheartedly as we say "Yes" to Life and allow it to plant its seed in us. That is the first step.

What is required in Station 7 is a shift from doing to being. Being receptive requires letting go of the mechanics and techniques of control and allowing yourself to be used by the creative force that wants to come through you. When you allow yourself to let go and become one with the creative force, mechanics and techniques give way to spirit through the process of creation. The process itself replenishes the soil of your being, and what you create as your life is the byproduct of that.

The Reward of Conception: Fertility

The reward of Station 7, when you go through it with the conscious intention of being receptive, is fertility, the natural capability of giving life.

Like us, the earth is a living organism, so we can draw some conclusions about our own creativity by learning from it. Fertile soil is rich in the nutrients and minerals necessary for basic plant nutrition. It contains organic matter that improves soil structure and moisture. In general, it has a neutral pH level. A variety of microorganisms in it support plant growth. The quality of soil is determined by its capacity to sustain and produce the ecosystem that depends on it.

Good soil is typically the result of good soil conservation practices; that is, sustainable methods of growing food. However, industrialization has mechanized farming methods, coerced output, circumvented love and respect for the land, demanded product to the exclusion of process. When too much is demanded of a plot of land in these ways, the soil becomes depleted. When the soil is depleted, it will not support biodiversity, and the food it grows does not nourish.

Like the earth, we are naturally designed to give life. Our role as creators is to receive the seeds of Life and to nourish them within us until they sprout into independent living forms. When we try to make our lives too efficient, we deplete the soil of our own souls. Only when we live our lives with respect and care for ourselves as carriers of Life can we take our places in the cycle of creation.

What You Create Creates You

You are always creating. What you are creating is your life. In order to know your work as a creator, you have only to look at the canvas in front of you. What you create creates you.

Artists are constantly going up against the gap between their vision and what they see on the canvas. This is the process of life, if we can bear it. But you can make this process conscious, using desire and intentions to create different results than the default patterns of your past. You can use it to know yourself.

Conception is hard for us, with our need to feel in control. The idea of waiting, allowing, nurturing is unfamiliar and a little frightening. What could happen if we allow it? Waiting is never easy. There is the compulsion to be doing. By our society's standards, if we are not doing, we are losing ground. At the same time, we are longing for a more relaxed state, trusting, alert, receptive. That state is the divine Feminine.

Conception in Conclusion

There is something very active in this receptivity of the Feminine. It is moving, flowing, caressing and breathing. The process of Incubation is the process of filling up to overflowing. In Buddhism and Tantra, as well as Hinduism, the Kundalini Shakti describes the bowl (kunda) of universal Life energy we each possess, sitting at the base of our spine, flowing energy to us always unless we block it. If we do not block it, the bowl continues to fill and fill until there is no containing it, and it spills over in the creation of something new.

As Fire moves into Water, Kundalini moves into human form: you. Your work is to ground this fire in the soil of your body, letting it flow through all the chakras, not just keeping it up in the head. Your work in Conception is to receive the fire, to allow it to penetrate you, and surrender to it.

This way of life sees beauty in the simple ordinary things of life; every act takes on a sacred quality when performed with total involvement, with love and for its own sake. And, in fact, it is a much better way to achieve the results you seek than by striving to be brilliant or extraordinary. Eventually, when you accept this process, the extraordinary becomes the ordinary—commonplace, your usual way of being. There is no distinction between the phenomenal world and absolute Divine consciousness.

This leads us deeper into ourselves and the sacred awareness of Life present throughout our lives. When we experience ourselves not as the disempowered pawns in Life's game but as the channels of Life's love for its creations, we are ready to catch the train from Station 7 and move on toward Station 8, Gestation.

A Story of Conception

Alison Prideaux, Mindfulness Teacher
Current City: Nice Area, France

> "Today we were skiing through the woods, and had to be creative about how to get down the mountain and swishing about the trees. It's all creative."

Alison Prideaux is one of the fittest women and loveliest people you'll ever meet. A massage therapist turned mindfulness teacher, Alison is a shining embodiment of presence, poise and peace of mind. In the 10 years I have known her, I have watched her practice what she teaches through difficult times as well as good. And, as her life has evolved, she has learned to transform the dark times of her past into a personalized gift for the planet.

KATHERINE ROBERTSON-PILLING: How do you define creativity?
ALISON PRIDEAUX: There are a few words that come to mind, like an overflowing and an outpouring and a sort of welling up, and a natural process that comes right from deep inside and, for me, not from the intellect. That's how creativity feels to me. There's a newness—something that wasn't there before, even if it's just a moment, creating a fluid moment that's then gone. It's the stuff of life, the process of life.
KRP: How do you experience it? Where does it show up in your life?
AP: Everywhere. Doing a massage. Cooking a meal. Today we were skiing through the woods, and had to be creative about how to get down the mountain and swishing about the trees. It's all creative.
KRP: Tell me about your experience of skiing.
AP: It's actually a reflection of how I am. When I'm centered and confident, then I relate to the mountain in a masterful way, in a healthy relationship with the elements. And when I'm tired or filled with self-doubt or scared, then I'm not one with the elements, I'm in a challenging relationship with them. It's not one at that point; it's two.
KRP: How does creativity show up in your work?
AP: When I'm teaching mindfulness, creativity shows

up when I manage to make connections—between what somebody's experiencing, how that relates to my experience, and knowledge from other sources, like spiritual teachers or writers. Creativity comes when I can pull all those together in a way that makes sense and is helpful to the student.
KRP: I've heard jazz musicians talk about something coming through from somewhere else. Do you relate to that?
AP: I think that if I'm in touch with my true Self, then my true, inner Self is in touch with everything in the universe. So it's in touch with all the forces of Nature and all the accumulated knowledge. So it's natural that I would put two and two together and come up with something useful, because I'm connected. It is like poetry or a musical harmony. It's like a kind of "Aha!" And it's fun.
KRP: What has been the toughest time in your life to find creativity?
AP: When I'm depressed, I don't feel it at all; it's a desert. I have been depressed on and off since I was a teenager. There were times I was really debilitated with depression, lying in bed and not being able to move. In those very closed-down times, I felt no enthusiasm, no creativity, no spark of any kind.

Now, my depressions start but they don't develop because I apply the mindfulness techniques and they work. By studying the detail of the depression—the dead weight inside, the anxious thoughts, the kind of closing down on a physical level—by feeling and experiencing those signals, I allow all evidence of the depression to put me into a place of coping.

I also had a very black moment when I was diagnosed with cancer, and I used the mindfulness to get me through the dark moments, so I have a lot of confidence that it really works.

KRP: For me, the creative process has a lot to do with something ending or being lost. That launches us into a void, which needs to be filled. Sometimes we put ourselves into the void, and sometimes Life puts us there. Do you recognize a creative process in your physical healing?

AP: It was a time of transformation, inasmuch as I realized that I was really loved and supported, that I could be vulnerable, and that friends would be there, instead of being the strong one. And then through being afraid for my life I experienced a huge letting go and a release of all of the old resentments, things I'd been trying to let go of for a long time. I think that's the void that you're talking about. The illness got my attention and pushed aside the old resentments and doubts and made a space that had been filled up with them.

KRP: From what I know about your healing process, you did not use the traditional methods. You got very creative about that too.

AP: Well, yes. Fortunately I knew something about alternative treatment. But it was very stressful deciding what to do after the mastectomy. One particular oncologist said, "You can do that; it won't do you any harm, but it won't do you any good. You need to be on four months of high dose chemo." And I walked through the chemo department, and I thought I'm never coming back here. It was just too grim, and I knew I wouldn't heal. So then there was a big dilemma, what do I actually do?

And then there were a series of links, not really coincidences, but each avenue of inquiry led to another piece of information. And after several phone calls and an awful lot of research, I decided. And, once I decided, I felt a lot better emotionally.

I decided that my body was confused and that it needed some guidance, and that if my body had created it, then I could also uncreate it. I didn't feel like a victim. I didn't say, "Why me?" I just thought, "Okay, I've created this. I'm responsible, and I can love it better." Those poor cancer cells were all multiplying like mad because they'd gone a bit crazy, and they needed guidance and love and sorting out. So, I suppose you could say it was creative to put together an alternative treatment plan.

KRP: It's wonderful to hear you talk about how, if your body had created it, you could also create something else.

AP: I definitely did that. And the paradox is that, through all those depressions and many times not knowing whether life was worth living, suddenly when I had a life-threatening illness, I really wanted to live.

KRP: What strikes me is that there is a transformative period and then there's an integrative period.

AP: It's really interesting that you say that because I'm in what [road racing cyclist] Lance Armstrong calls survivorship. It's actually quite hard reinventing life with not as much physical strength. I've had another clear report, but I've gotten past the euphoria. It's taken away some of my oomph. So I have to come from a place of gentleness and femininity and that kind of creativity that comes with flow and enthusiasm rather than from a place of, "Okay, let's set some goals."

KRP: Would you say that the dark moments and the tough times in your life have given focus and direction to your skill set?

AP: I understand others who have also been in a dark place, and it's given me empathy. Ever since I was seven, I've wanted to heal the planet, and I didn't know how to do it. And in my 20s I just got this feeling: You have to sort yourself out before you can do anything for anybody else.

I've worked in South America, diving and sailing. I've worked as an environmental planner in Boston. I've worked in England and France. I've done all kinds of sports: canoeing, sailing, windsurfing and hiking. I've sailed twice across the Atlantic, traveled widely to India, Africa, Asia. I've studied with teachers and mentors. I've lived a very rich life, and am very grateful for having had all those opportunities.

I've always known my purpose; I haven't known how to do it. And now it's really clear. We're all connected. And the only way to raise consciousness is one individual at a time. Now I have something very concrete that I can do. I can see that it makes a difference in the individual lives of the people who study with me. And I can only hope that that kind of self-awareness makes a more aware society.

8

STATION 8 Gestation

Vulnerable we are, like an infant.
We need other's care
or we will suffer.
ST. CATHERINE OF SIENA

On the Platform in Station 8

Gestation is the second step in the Incubation Quarter. While the Exploration Quarter was a big, outward-pushing quarter, Incubation requires you to turn inward. The growth that occurs here is internal. There is a rest required, a quiet, calm, still place that more than ever requires us to return to our center. A lot of what happens in this station is not outwardly visible.

To Carry and to Move

The word Gestation comes from the Latin *gestare* (to carry or to bear). The range of its meanings is wide:

- The act of wearing (clothes or ornaments)
- The period of development of the young from conception until birth
- The act of carrying young in the womb from conception to delivery
- Being passively borne or carried, as on horseback or in a carriage
- The conception and development of an idea or plan

Gestare is also the root of the word *gesture*, meaning a motion of the body or limbs that expresses or emphasizes an idea, sentiment or attitude. So you could say that this station is a time of both carrying something within ourselves and expressing something that is important to us.

The Voice of Gestation: "Sittin' on the Dock of the Bay"

The Gestation Station is the point in the creative process where Water moves in Water. It is a time of mystery, where the work is to be watchful and waiting, trusting Nature to take its course and caring for the bearer of the new life as well as the life itself. Gestation is a time for taking care of yourself so you can nourish the new life and give it what it needs to grow.

This station is a crucial stop in the creative process, because time is required for new ideas to develop in the physical world. Not all times are meant to be productive in the external sense. We are the stewards of our ideas, and they need our patient protection while they develop.

Romancing the Seed

A seed cannot do what it is intended to do without gestation. It is the dark moisture of the soil that encourages the sprout to break through its shell and grow. A seed cannot be thrust into the world and expected to feed the world immediately. That's a ridiculous notion at a natural level, but that is often what we expect from our dreams and projects. This is not Nature's way. In The Wheel of Creativity, the seed is sown out of Chaos, carrying with it all the potential of a fully manifested idea. It must be taken in, buried safely in the moist soil of our hearts, and nourished while it develops into a physical presence.

Nature offers us this wisdom in countless species, in humans and other mammals, in plants, and in birds and sea creatures that gestate their young in eggs.

The egg has often been linked with creation myths throughout history. For ancient cultures from Egypt to India, the egg symbolized Life and the potential for life. Egyptian hieroglyphics show the egg as the seed of regeneration and the mystery of life. In many cultures, the universe was seen to have hatched out of a cosmic egg. The origin of the egg was a mystery to human beings, and thus it became a powerful symbol for the primordial chaos from which the universe emerged.

Water's Destructive/Creative Power

Eventually, whether egg or seed, there must be a metamorphosis in order for the New Thing to emerge. Water plays a key role in this process. In humans, the embryo is nourished and cushioned in the amniotic fluid, where it must develop into a fetus before it is ready to live in the world on its own. Similarly in plants, the seed's hard shell must be held in moisture in order to soften and open up into the embryonic seed, from which it becomes the seedling. The egg must open, the seed must die; they both must give up their identity in order for the New Thing to develop.

Throughout human history, water has been associated with the mysteries of gestation. It has evolved as a symbol for change, life and human emotion. Jung saw Water as a symbol for the unconscious and one of the four alchemical elements.

In alchemy, the symbol for Water is a downward-pointing triangle, suggesting downward flow. In mirroring the female genitalia, this symbol represents the Feminine across cultures. The symbol for Fire is an upward-pointing triangle, suggesting a rising force. It is hot and dry, and stands for the fiery emotions and spiritual aspiration. Together these two symbols represent the chalice and the blade, forming the basis of the alchemical interaction, which we talked about in the last chapter.

In arriving to Water from Fire (in Exploration), we experience an alchemical process of distillation, the refinement of our essential qualities and those of the New Thing.

In my experience, Station 8 usually goes on longer than I'd like. The unknown mystery inherent in something happening outside my conscious awareness makes me uncomfortable. But over the years, I've cycled through these subterranean growth spurts again and again, and I've learned the value of waiting:

- For direction when I had big decisions to make

- For work that was both profitable and meaningful

- For my husband to enter my life when I was 50 years old

It's much easier to trust the process now than it used to be.

In the Cosmos

The Incubation Quarter is closely linked to the receptive, feminine influences of the moon, which are strong here. One relationship between the moon and the earth is gravitational attraction. The earth tugs on the moon, which is why the moon is shaped like a football rather than a sphere. But the moon also tugs at the earth, deforming the water in the seas, causing the rising and falling of tides. It is a forceful antidote to inertia.

Gravitational attraction is strongest when the moon is closest to the earth. Its strength is related to distance and mass. The bigger the object, and the closer it is, the more powerful the attraction. Thus, when farmers plant their crops by lunar cycles, their crop yields are significantly affected, increasing by up to 50 percent depending on the days they choose to plant. Seeds actually absorb (attract) more water at the full moon, so they germinate faster.

In the Vision Quarter, we must move away from the status quo. We are influenced by the larger forces of Life in which we participate. The power required to overcome inertia must be built by drawing closer to what attracts us. It's there in the physical and it's there in the spiritual as well: The closer we move to what attracts us, the more powerful its influence on us, the more powerful our influence on it.

Now it is time to settle, and allow the influence of what attracts us to deepen and grow. It is a time for taking time, putting yourself first, honoring the sacred role you play in ushering in a new life to Creation.

To Everything There Is a Season

Nature clearly demonstrates a cycle of growth and rest within its seeds. These cycles exist for us as well, in our own creative cycles.

There are so many natural processes at work, not only in the physical world, and they are there to assist us in our journey as well. But we are either ignorant of them, or ignore them, or allow external influences to seduce us.

In seeds, there is a time of growth and a time of rest. And while growth is occurring but not yet exerting its influence on the world, it's a good time to rest and replenish. This is not the time to dig around and see what's going on in there. It's a good time to turn our attention to ourselves and the care we need as carriers of the New Thing.

It's a good time to look at our boundaries and our limitations. To admit to ourselves what we are committed to, whether we are willing to go the distance, and if we are willing to take on the job of raising this New Thing in the world. As it grows within us, it will pull us through our lives. And, as every mother has said at one point in her life, it becomes your greatest challenge and your greatest reward.

In Gestation, we are wooed to turn away from the external influences of our everyday lives, to return to our instinctual and emotional connection with the forces of Nature. We are called to go through our lives doing what we must, but to allow ourselves to be increasingly influenced by what is growing within us, what will soon appear in our world to change our lives forever.

The Skill to Get Still

Our work in this station is to open, and at the same time to be the container for the seed to shed its shell and grow and flower. But this is not so easy, especially in the world we all live in with its demands, deadlines and conflicting priorities. Technology is shifting our relationship with time, and many of us feel overwhelmed. Never has there been a more important task than to create the space for creativity to occur, the stillness where we can hear it speak.

Every few years, a new study comes out on multitasking. Some say it makes you feel good, some say unhappy, but one thing they agree on is that it does not make you productive. At the same time, people who develop the practice of mindfulness and meditation discover the paradox that when they make the space, time expands. They actually get more done in fewer hours by learning to focus on the here and now.

In response to that reality, we must develop the skill to get still and go within in an instant; to pull in no matter what we have to do 30 seconds later. I call it "resting in motion." If I'm present, I can do whatever I need to do and still be at peace within myself. But this is one of the greatest challenges of life.

The Moon Lodge

In Native American tradition, women were recognized as carriers of Life's creative energy. As such, they were respected for the enormous contribution they made to the entire tribe. A woman's time of menstruation was called her Moon Time, when she was deeply connected and empowered with the Life Force of the Universe. It was seen as a gift to the entire tribe.

During Moon Time, the entire tribe took up the responsibilities of its menstruating women, giving them the opportunity to separate themselves for their own replenishment. As the men participated in Sweat Lodge ceremonies for their physical and spiritual purification, women had a lodge of their own—the Moon Lodge—in which they could reconnect with their roles as the carriers of Life.

The Sacred Gift of the Feminine

Native Americans are not the only society to hold this belief as sacred. In the early 20th century, Japanese labor unions demanded that Japanese women be able to take time off when they were menstruating. In 1947, the Japanese Labor Standards Act guaranteed Japanese women menstrual leave. Similar laws have been passed in other Asian countries—including Indonesia and Korea—and Australia. In 2007, sports apparel and equipment manufacturer Nike included menstrual leave in its Code of Conduct, applicable to all the countries in which the company operates. But many women do not take the leave, for fear of not being competitive with their Western counterparts.

My personal experience of menstruating, during the first day or two when the pain was strong, was a feeling of being wounded—in a way of beauty, in a way of something good and fruitful. And on those days there was a softness in my experience of life that touched me so much, when I could make the space for it. But most of us see, and the world around us tells us, that we have to be strong and get the job done, operating in a Masculine way in the world. And this Masculine way, by itself, will not fulfill us.

Not for Women Only

If you are a man reading this, I want to reemphasize that you are not excluded. The creative process demands that every one of us develops the receptive as well as the active aspects of our human natures. Beyond male and female, the Masculine and Feminine forces are present in all of life. Just as both bicep and tricep are required to use an arm, both active and receptive forces are required to create a life.

As carriers of the Life energy for the entire community, then, the entire tribe's well-being requires that we all nurture our connection with Source. Matriarchal societies have long recognized this. But in our contemporary society, all of us are required to plow through the natural rhythms of life in our bodies. We have become so externally oriented that we do not stop to listen to these rhythms, much less honor what they offer the world. There are times for plowing through, to be sure; and there are times to stop, look and listen.

Creating Optimal Conditions

It's a well-documented fact that industrial farming requires such high levels of production from fields that the soil becomes depleted and the food grown in it is not properly nourished. It is not just the level of productivity demanded that causes this, but also the absence of a resting period. If soil cannot replenish itself, it will not have the nutrients needed by those things that grow in it. Is this why the tomatoes we find in our supermarkets have no taste? It's like painting a copy rather than creating an original, because we have no spirit to put in it.

The conditions encountered by the seed are crucial to the healthy development of that seed. The better those conditions, the better life the seed will have. So the work in Station 8 is to tend the soil and nurture the ground in which the New Thing is growing. It's about creating optimal conditions to support that seed to germinate and grow.

What does this mean for us? We are here in the center of Quarter 3—in the deepest part of the element Water. Our work now is to sink ourselves deeper into Water's Feminine energy in order to nourish and protect what is being created through us. Again, we are ourselves watered and nourished in the process.

Life in Station 8
The Experience of Gestation: Urgency

The experience in Station 8 is urgency. There are many varieties of this, but in general it's some version of: "There's nothing happening. When is this going to happen? I need it to happen now." The New Thing is developing what it needs to survive when it comes out. It has its own process, and I am not in control of that process.

While in physical gestation each species has its normal gestation period, this is not the case in the creative process. If you know what normal gestation is ("Okay, nine months; I can relax.") then it is easier to manage your expectations. Everything arrives in its season. But with the creative process, this is a mystery and an unknown, which makes it more difficult to wait and trust.

Many great artists throughout time have indicated that their gestation periods were short, often in contrast to very lengthy periods of execution and production. In the creative process, it takes what it takes for the seed of the New Thing to sprout. Each has its own gestation period, and some are definitely longer than others. A song will likely take longer than an airport, for example. Trying to speed things along too fast can result in a premature birth and a lower survival rate. At the same time, prolonging the gestation period can result in stillbirth, damage to the baby or the mother in childbirth. This is where your relationship with the New Thing is paramount; relaxed awareness and "response-ability," your ability to respond to it.

To Serve and Protect

What does it mean to be the carrier of this seed? To be the soil in which it chooses to take root and grow?

For me, Gestation is a recognition of the sacred unfolding of Life and my participation in it. It is about letting go consciously and deliberately, recognizing that I am not the New Thing, though I, too, am transformed by the process. The New Thing is the natural product of the union of the material and the spiritual, the offspring of the sacred marriage of the Masculine and Feminine, the synthesis of active and receptive.

Real Physical Changes in Your Hands

This sense of urgency, the result of doubting yourself and the process, produces tension. Tension, which is perceived by your body as stress, produces a number of automatic responses in your body:

- The flow of oxygen is shut down in your extremities to make it available to your brain, heart, lungs and liver.

- Endorphin production jumps to reduce pain, increasing your blood pressure, heartbeat and pulse.

- Adrenaline is released, to fuel your muscles for a quick getaway if needed.

- Your reproductive system shuts down, as energy is redirected elsewhere.

- Cortisol release makes you hungry.

- Your immune system is weakened as energy is diverted to respond to stress.

What to do?

The Task of Gestation: Relax

The task of Station 8 is to relax in order to stay open and receive the seed, and in order for that to germinate inside and grow. First, we need to strengthen the container. We do this in a number of ways:

1. Making choices and having boundaries between our inner selves and the world. This involves discriminating between those with whom it is safe to share what is gestating within us. It means saying "No" to certain things, so that we can say "Yes" to others.

2. Nourishing the soil within us with the things that nourish us, which brings us back to the work we did in the first quarter, moving through Anorexia to be able to choose love, to choose what we love. This is what makes the soil of our hearts fertile.

3. Aligning with natural cycles of Life. For example, when we're tired, we rest. It's about choosing not to continue demanding industrial strength mechanical performance from the wondrous human beings that we are.

4. Creating systems to get the support we need from outside—the guidance, the wisdom, the experience of those who have been through the process. In the Native American Moon Lodge, a lot of information is passed on and guidance given about what it means to be the carrier of Life for the tribe. We in Western culture are sorely lacking in these models today. Isolated and individualistic, we have lost the nourishing wisdom passed on by elders from generation to generation.

From Doubt to Trust

All these things support you in moving from the doubt that produces the tension to trusting the process. As you learn to trust the process—that seed is becoming a seedling and the seedling a plant—you also develop deeper trust in yourself.

What is required of you here occurs in three stages:

1. Breakdown. This is a time of doubt, the feeling that this is out of your control,

nothing's happening, or it's not happening by your timing.

2. Expansion. This is a time to get bigger, take a breath, recognize and dare to trust the rhythm of Nature, and merge with Nature.

3. Contraction. This is a time to turn inward, a time when in action and nonaction you stop trying to control and instead surrender to the process in its own time.

Bonding with the Seed

A bonding occurs in this station as you create the relationship with the seed wanting to be born. Whenever you fall in love, the hormone oxytocin is produced, making you crave the person you love. Its properties were first described in relation to its physical healing and emotional bonding effects during and after childbirth. It is a bonding hormone, especially for women. As we make space for the dream, as we let ourselves love what we love and what wants to grow inside us, we put ourselves in deeper relationship with the Life energy, which is creativity, which is love, which wants to flow through us.

As time goes by, you begin to see more and more evidence that something really is happening. By the end of this station, what has been hidden begins to be revealed. Through your process of staying with it, the urgency based in doubt is transformed into faith. There's excitement, too, about the new life developing within you, and about being of service to something greater than yourself.

The Reward of Gestation: Faith

The reward of this process is faith. Here you work with the tendency, when developing something new, to focus only on its external evidence in the world. What will it look like? What will be the result? Is anything happening? Much like the reward of meditation, this station teaches you to detach from the distraction and the spinning of the world out there and return to the breath of Life within you. The inevitable change that occurs in you changes everything you do.

When you're willing to deepen and change yourself, then the work you put out into the world is imbued with spirit. It is original. Without that spirit, it is the equivalent of a knockoff. When rose bushes are forced to produce more stems or faster, the roses have no fragrance. The fragrance is the spirit.

Method and Wisdom

The Dalai Lama speaks of the Sanskrit Buddhist chant "Om Mani Padme Hum" as the way of transforming the negative things that come through us into positive things.

The principle in Buddhism is that everyone can be a Buddha, and everyone is in the process of becoming a Buddha. The Buddha was not only one particular person who became enlightened under a tree; we are all Buddhas in the making. We are all in the process of personal transformation. In this alchemy of transformation, method and wisdom are inseparable. It is through one that the other is attained.

Tibetan Buddhists use a prayer wheel in chanting their prayers. The prayer wheel is a cylinder on a stick, which is turned back and forth between the hands. "Om Mani Padme Hum" is written on the outside of the wheel and on paper wound inside it. The prayer wheel is understood as a vehicle for setting prayer into motion.

From Breakdown to Breakthrough

Gestation is union with the silence, the emptiness, the waiting to be filled, the waiting for the seed to crack open and germinate. We do not have the privilege of watching this happen but must sit by in our stillness and allow it to begin its own life. It is how we do this that can either expedite the process or cause it to stall.

And the Wheel, by its turning, moves us from active to receptive to active, unifying those energies within us so that whichever aspect we are stronger in, we are also moved to use its opposite, balancing our natures as it turns.

Gestation gives motion to what we find important. This is where we begin a relationship with something else, the soul of the idea that has come to us. And a relationship with anything other than us requires that we honor its process as well as ours.

Then, when what is growing inside you is ripe, it will signal to you that it is ready to be born, ready to break through. It's time to push it out of its anonymity and into the world. This is the point you move into the next station, Breakthrough.

A STORY OF GESTATION

Susan Cherian, Film Producer
Current city: Mumbai, India

"Even before I open my eyes in the morning, I acknowledge myself before God and say, 'Look, today is going to be a great day. I'd like you to guide me, and whatever I need to accomplish, help me accomplish.'"

I first met Susan Cherian in graduate school in Chicago in 1980. We lost touch, and 25 years passed before she found me on the Internet. We finally met up again in 2010 in Los Angeles. At the time of this phone interview, Susan was in Mumbai, India, working on a film project about the 105-carat Kohinoor Diamond, which the British took from India under Queen Victoria. Susan's story illustrates the necessity of Incubation and the reward of waiting with the process.

KATHERINE ROBERTSON-PILLING: Tell me about this film.

SUSAN CHERIAN: It's called *Kohinoor*, which is the name of a gem that was part of the Peacock Throne in India for a long, long time. When the British invaded India under Queen Victoria, they took it. Today it is part of the Queen's crown jewels, and India would like to have it back.

KRP: How's it going?

SC: Talk about creative process! We have been working on what we're doing now for two years. Last April we got the attention of an A-list actor in Hollywood. He loves the script and spent a week with us to suggest some really good changes. Then it had to go through the rewrite, but our writer was writing the sequel to *Salt*. And finally, that is done. He will send us the rewrite, and we will send it to the actor and wait for him to say, "I like it and here's my schedule." Then it becomes a very focused endeavor.

Development—the creative process of getting any project from idea to incubation and waiting—is the longest part of the process. It takes the patience of a saint and a lot of faith and trust that things will work out in the end.

KRP: How does being in India affect your work and getting things done?

SC: Where do I start? First of all, you've got to wake up with the attitude that today is a great day, and things are going to work out. Even before I open my eyes in the morning, I acknowledge myself before God and say, "Look, today is going to be a great day. I'd like you to guide me, and whatever I need to accomplish, help me accomplish."

Whatever I need to accomplish I'm going to accomplish, and I'm just going to go with the flow. That is the only way to work here. I would assume that's the way to work anywhere, but things are a little [easier to accomplish] in the West.

Some days are difficult because the way people communicate is different. There's a lot more corruption here, so you have to have your guard up. So, it's a little more difficult. But life is short. You have to drive your life, otherwise you fall into traps of whatever is in front of you. That's the way you go in India.

KRP: Has this process revealed the difference in the values and priorities of the two cultures?

SC: There is a huge difference in the values and the culture. Indian families are very tight-knit. They will stick together and do anything for the family. But transparency and integrity are subject to interpretation. I am of the mold that everything is above board. What we consider integrity, openness, straightforward, aboveboard, all of that, it's highly negotiable here.

You have to know how to work the system, and

you just have to go with the flow. You cannot be uptight. And you have to be very open to what is happening now. It's a very different thing than how I lived in America. I'm going back there, but it has been very good for me to learn how to be present.

KRP: How is creativity viewed in Indian culture? Is there a view of life as a creative process in which we participate?

SC: A lot of creative things happen in India. An amazing number of films are made. Lots of music is done. Painters, poets, authors, artists are all celebrated in this country. It's not done in the corner. It's in the news. People are very sensitive to these things.

Bollywood is very different. It's high entertainment and star based. The artistic creation of anything that happens in Bollywood is centered around four or five big stars who sell product, though now there are a lot of indies coming.

Then there is also the struggle for survival in India. Seventy-five percent of the population lives in villages. There is a growing middle class and a big push to move the real poor to the middle class. But there is still a lot of fight for survival.

Most people are religious. They have a very strong connection to the Supreme—Hindu, Muslim, Christian, whatever. And they worship: They go to the temple, the mosque, church most days, and before they have a big exam or project.

There are so many people, and everywhere is paradox. So there is this unsaid connection to the mystery of life. TV and the Internet have come, and people are very engaged in social networks. Most have a phone, whether poor or not. It's all part of the survival and the connection.

In the States and Europe, it feels different. There is a disconnect. Everybody does their own thing, and then they go back to their house. But people here are very engaged in life, and there is a connection to depth. That connection is there.

KRP: Do you see your own life as a creative process?

SC: Absolutely. I feel that everything that is created inside, it's manifested outside. I love projects, and I've got nine projects that I'm juggling. But for me, to focus on the creative process within is more

important than the projects. Pay attention to what is happening inside, and then things fall in place. If you look at it from a Christian perspective it's, "Seek ye first the kingdom of God, and all these things will be added unto you." That happens inside.

KRP: Do you recognize a trajectory in your life? You talked about driving your life, but what's the connection between you and the greater force in your life?

SC: I'm an American citizen, and my base is in the US. I was supposed to be here only a few months, and then it got longer, and I got deeper into the project. And it became very difficult for me to leave.

This period in my life is an incredible experience of how to work with two diametrically opposite cultures, in every sense of the word. If you can make this happen and succeed without being damaged or damaging others, I think you have growth. And that is my whole purpose, that I grow in the process and help others to grow in the process.

Second, I've been able to reconnect with my family and, when there's been a gap, I've helped them with other things. I would have never been able to do that, and I wouldn't have planned it. At the end of my life I'm sure I'll look back and say, "Oh my God, I'm so glad I was able to do that." I see that. I just need to keep my overall purpose in life and be very aware of what's happening.

So I've learned to pay a lot of attention. If I hadn't gone through this process here, I wouldn't have. I'm just a goal person. I know exactly what I'm doing next, and I go on and do it and get it down and then move on. So this has been personally a very creative time, and it gives me so much peace. As a human being I should be going nuts. "Oh, how long is it going to go on? What is next?" But no. What I create inside every day is what's going to manifest outside. I know that.

This is not something I knew before or planned. I read Deepak Chopra and people like that a lot. I knew it in my head, but finally you become aware that this is exactly what's happening in your life, and the more you engage with that, the outer life just falls in place. But you have to pay attention.

KRP: It's a shift of attention from the outside to the inside.

SC: Mind you, I get up in the morning, and I have things to do, people to call. All that is there. But there was a series of obstacles, and a waiting period; and I had to pause and be still. All that is an opportunity to engage with yourself and what is happening around you. I didn't even know this idea existed before.

And faith plays a big part in all this—faith in yourself and faith in something greater. And to let things incubate. And I knew all this, you know, timing is everything. But experiencing that in life is a different thing.

KRP: What is your definition of your faith and something greater than yourself?

SC: My faith right now is very little talk. It's a connection. It's a relationship and conscious awareness of that relationship. And I'm happy with that. Then I'm connected, and the more I'm connected, the more peace I have. That's it.

I used to think, "Oh my God, I'm hanging by a thread. I'm just going out on a limb. I don't know what I'm doing. I have taken all the chances, sacrificed everything. I've taken the biggest risk." This used to be my conversation. There are times I get panicky, and you have to pull yourself back. But I've seen that I'm connected. Things will happen, and things will be okay.

KRP: How do you define the creative process?

SC: For me, creative process is just living, and living is connection with God—the power above—and connection with people. All the things that we do— whether films or events or art—are just a celebration of that.

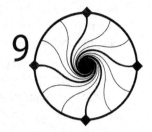

9

STATION 9 Breakthrough

You are not accidental. Existence needs you.
Without you something will be missing in existence
and nobody can replace it.
That's what gives you dignity,
that the whole existence will miss you.
OSHO

On the Platform in Station 9

Station 9 is the third and final station in the Incubation Quarter. In Breakthrough, we are coming out of Water and moving into Earth, where Water permeates the soil of Earth. Power, danger, energy and will are involved in this station. As the one who gives birth, you must release the New Thing, allowing it to separate from you.

This is the final station before we go through the Gate of Return, which changes direction back toward Home. Through Return, you are coming out of the internal, feminine, receptive, hidden (esoteric) time and moving back out into the world, into a more masculine, active, external quarter with something new. A young, fragile, tender thing it may be, but it is something physical.

At the Moment of Faith, Everything Is Possible

Breakthrough is defined generally as:

- A sudden, dramatic, and important discovery or development, especially in

science, such as a major breakthrough in DNA research

- A significant and dramatic overcoming of a perceived obstacle, allowing the completion of a process, such as a breakthrough in performance

In The Wheel of Creativity, I define it as a sudden change in which what has been developing inside you completes its gestation, detaches from you and pushes out into the world. There is an experience of one becoming two. At the outset of this station, the New Thing still has no face and no name and isn't there yet. The completion of this station is the birth of the New Thing; the Breakthrough. But it is still uncertain where it is all taking you.

Breakthrough is part of the process of focusing the New Thing. In Conception, the seed embeds itself in another to receive nourishment while it becomes ready to face the external world. What-could-be becomes more specific and complex. In Gestation, the simple seed matures into an organism directly connected with Life. Incubation is the part of the process through which it does this. We are the container. Breakthrough is the final stage of Incubation, in which this New Thing moves out of gestation into external form.

While we know the gestation periods of animals and plants, our creative seedlings are unique to us. We can't be completely sure what is developing inside us. And it is not always possible to know its gestation period.

In my own experience, Breakthrough is a difficult process. I do not decide when it is time, but it is up to me to be present and facilitate the process. We cannot push the process; premature birth is dangerous to the unborn. But equally, delayed birth can be dangerous for both newborn and mother.

On top of that, our process may not look familiar to anyone around us. So we must be particularly sensitive to the signals and make time for the birthing process, as it is unique to us. It is the moment when the mystery is revealed.

The Moment of Birth

Humans. For the human baby, Breakthrough occurs at the moment of birth. Birth is a moment when the fetus faces the world for the first time. In humans, birth normally occurs at a gestational age of 37 to 42 weeks. Childbirth before 37 weeks of gestation is considered preterm, but viable after 25 weeks. Premature birth reduces the survival rate. Equally, delayed birth is dangerous for baby and mother.

Plants. For a plant, there are several definitions of Breakthrough. The plant begins its life cycle when the seed cracks open and germinates. But for our purposes, Breakthrough is the time when the seedling makes its first appearance above the earth's surface—when it becomes visible.

Stars. One of the basic principles of physics is that energy is never destroyed, nor is it created. It simply changes form. All matter comes and goes out of existence as a result of these changes. When something is destroyed, energy is released; when it is created, energy takes form.

Stars, for example, begin in what astronomers call stellar nurseries: gaseous clouds called giant molecular clouds (GMCs), massive clouds of gas molecules in space. GMCs average 50 to 300 light-years across and are 100,000 to 10 million times the mass of our sun. Inside a GMC, the density of molecules is several million times greater than in the rest of space.

What causes the birth of a star is actually a gravitational collapse of a GMC. There can be a number of external triggers for this collapse, including collision with another GMC, passing through another dense area in space, or supernova explosions nearby. As the GMC collapses, it is compressed and fragments, breaking into smaller and smaller pieces. Potential energy is released, and the fragments of gas condense into rotating spheres of superhot gas known as protostars; and the spheres grow larger. Not all protostars grow large enough to become stars, but for the ones that do, their core temperature increases radically. The heat generated by the release of massive amounts of energy eventually leads to nuclear fusion. The internal generation of energy is so massive that it stops the collapse, and equilibrium is reached. Thus the star becomes stable relatively quickly.

The process unfolds as a balance of expansion and contraction. The gravitational force acts to collapse the cloud, and the internal pressures act outward to prevent the collapse.

In creativity, this conflict of pressures—the external pressures to "keep it in" and the internal pressures to "get it out there"—must be acknowledged and their energies integrated. Otherwise the New Thing is made vulnerable in our attempt to relieve the pressure of our own discomfort.

Life as a Hero's Journey

Even before there was a Wheel of Creativity, I was intrigued with the idea of life as the archetypal Hero's Journey. No matter what our external role in life might be, we are all engaged in a journey through life to overcome internal weaknesses and external blocks in order to win the prize and bring it home. This is why the stories that touch us most reflect this theme.

Across cultures around the world, the classical Hero's Journey has common features. The hero:

- Departs from the family or "the fold" to set off on a quest
- Must enter an unfamiliar and challenging world
- Must pass through and respond to a test
- Returns to the ordinary, but now expanded world

In early attempts to decipher the mysteries of the human psyche at the start of the 20th century, psychoanalyst Otto Rank and his contemporaries, such as Sigmund Freud, sought in numerous ways to demystify the workings of the human psyche. Rank studied many cultural hero myths, including Moses, Oedipus, Perseus, Tristan, Romulus, Hercules and Jesus. In his book *The Myth of the Birth of the Hero*, Rank interpreted the myths and revealed the progression of the hero's life, which I summarize here:

- The hero is born to distinguished parents, often a king.
- His birth is preceded by difficulties or obstacles.
- There are often warnings against or threats to the birth.
- When he is born, he is placed in a container in the water.
- He is saved and nurtured by simple folk or creatures of the earth.
- He grows up and discovers his parents by chance.
- He returns home for revenge and ends up being acknowledged.

Even in his birth, the hero makes a journey into the world. His character is formed out of loss, leaving, finding and return. It is a challenging journey, but it leads to purpose and the fulfillment of destiny in the end. In Station 9, it leads the New Thing into the physical world.

Life in Station 9

We arrive in Station 9 from Gestation, where urgency builds as time passes without much, if any, visible progress. As we learn to relax and have faith in what is coming, Station 9 arrives with a bang. After all this time, something is finally happening. It is a relief to finally be able to see something, to relate to it out there in front of you, as separate from you.

The Experience of Breakthrough: Appreciation

When the New Thing appears, there is an experience of appreciation. You are coming into relationship with something other than you. You are falling in love with this new expression of Life, the fragile beauty of it, and its preciousness to you.

It is something of a loss, too, as you move from the dream to reality. What is born is not necessarily what you want. The New Thing may not be exactly what you want or what you said you wanted when you launched. You conceived, you gestated and now you have a New Thing. But you get what you get, and you don't have much control over what it turns out to be.

What you have is evidence of where you are in your relationship with your original desire expressed in Vision, your journey toward it in Exploration, and what has actually shown up through Incubation. Now, heading into Cultivation, you are engaged not only with your own creative process but also the creative process of the New Thing as it begins its journey around the Wheel. There is still much work to do, to grow this New Thing, to nurture and prune and harvest it in Quarter 4.

The Voice of Breakthrough: "Free at Last!"

This station is an important part of the process, because even as the New Thing is revealed, it changes you. It is a paradigm shift, from having a dream to the reality before you. From something mysterious growing inside you to something real in front of you with real demands, here you are required to get involved. In the presence of this thing outside you, your world is transformed.

This moment is perhaps most clearly seen in the plant, where the seedling sticks its shoot above the soil and you can see it. It is fragile still. It needs protection.

I first identified the importance of this station in the early 1990s. I was living in Chicago in an apartment where I had a small room for an office. In that room I had a keyboard and a guitar. I had written a song and gone to bed, leaving the sheet music on the keyboard. But I was too excited to sleep! I had fallen in love. So I kept getting up and going into my office and looking at the music and playing it on the keyboard. And I thought at one point, "I am like a new mother getting up and going to look at the baby in the crib." These verses from the song express what I felt:

> Where could I go to hide from feeling
> Where could I go to stop the pain
> I saw the graves of all my dreaming
> And knelt beside them in the rain
>
> There on my knees I found my children
> A hundred souls across the years
> The seeds of Life I had abandoned
> I saw them clearly through my tears

It was the first time that I realized that this is what we do: We give birth to creative children. They are our children in the world. But no sooner do they appear than we proceed to judge them. We hide them, we go into shame, and we have all these reactions: "Nope. Don't like that one." "Oh, that one over there sounds better." "This will never be good enough."

If it were a baby, we would never do that. Okay, maybe if it were missing a finger we'd be a little disappointed. But we would love and work with it, and we would do all we could to help it grow and

develop and mature to be able to take care of itself in the world. And it would change us.

I have a dear friend in Florida who has a beautiful eight-year-old daughter. Early in her life, her daughter was diagnosed as autistic. My friend is very bright and positive, and committed to ensuring that her daughter has all the support she needs. Reaching beyond preconceived limits previously ascribed to autistic children, she is determined that her daughter not only survives in the world, but thrives and takes risks and enjoys her life.

My friend tells me that parenting an autistic child—or perhaps any child with a disability—is a very different experience than parenting a "normal" child. Instead of planning for her daughter to grow up and move away and become independent from her parents, they are planning for her to be taken care of after they are gone. Financially, emotionally, professionally, socially—in every way, their lives have been changed forever.

But my friend has stepped into her role with the fierceness of a mother lion. Not only does she live this at home but also in the political and educational systems around her, even as her daughter tests and discovers her own inner resources within those systems.

The Task of Breakthrough: Be Present

At this station, the New Thing takes a form of its own. And when it does, it's surprising not only to see it out there, but also to love it so much. And now suddenly everything—all that has come before in your creative process around the Wheel (which was not even visibly related before)—now makes sense.

So the task of Station 9 is to be present. You must be present with what is. And here, too, you must make a commitment to it. You have to engage yourself and say, "Yes, I'm willing to take this one on and to see it through." And the New Thing will bring you face-to-face with yourself when you don't do that.

The first manifestation of the New Thing in the world is incomplete, and could be construed as a failure. But now you have a form. Now you have something to work with, to take it to the next stages of its development. There is still a lot of work to do.

For a parent, this is a newborn baby. For an author, it is a first draft. For a sculptor, it is a lump of clay. For a hostess, it might be a party theme and a menu. For someone in advertising, it might be a storyboard. For a manufacturer, it is a prototype. This is the place where possibilities are put on the table, given space, explored and appreciated. It is not the time for testing or perfecting. Not yet.

In business, this is a tough call to make. Companies whose cultures do not make time and money available for failure do not have room for innovation. And it may be a tough sell to shareholders.

On a personal level, it could be having a transitional relationship after a painful divorce. You go back in the game and try it, even if it doesn't work out. Remembering that this is the "seedling" is crucial. It is not a failure. It is something to work with.

Not every project we give birth to, nor every New Thing, is meant to go the distance and go on to completion. You might decide, when you get the business to profitability, to take it public and sell it. You might decide that a simple recording of voice and guitar is enough. But you must decide. If you do not decide, if you give up because you can't face another revision, you will end up carrying around the incompletion forever. In this station, the moment is all there is.

How we do this makes all the difference, affecting who we are and all those around us. It's balancing receptivity with focus, presence with intentionality. And when it comes to giving birth, there is no giving up midstream.

Nature's Way

Lamaze is a technique that prepares a woman to give birth naturally. Developed in the 1940s by French obstetrician Dr. Fernand Lamaze, the technique was for the West a natural alternative to the predominant methods of childbirth of its day, which all required medical intervention.

I love the principles espoused in Lamaze, which offer natural wisdom for creators as well. Lamaze proposes that:

- Giving birth is a normal, natural and healthy part of life.

- The experience of birth profoundly affects us and our families. How we go about giving birth to what's inside us profoundly affects who we are and all those around us.

- Our inner wisdom guides us through the process.

- Our confidence and ability to give birth is either enhanced or diminished by the people we look to for support in the process.

Essentially, the Lamaze method teaches us to:

Wait. Let labor begin on its own, when you are both ready, as opposed to trying to push and force. Deadlines will come. When the time is there, you have to engage. But still you must stay present with the process, or the product will suffer.

While I was writing this book, I was also facilitating a three-month creative-process group. Each week, the lesson, exercises, meditations and sharing focused on one station in the Wheel. Between sessions, I wrote the chapter on that station and shared it with the students. It was a challenging schedule, and I began to feel a difference in myself and in the group. I was coming to realize that it was not working when one of the students, Petra, said "The last two chapters have been really theoretical; they are not concrete. You're not in them."

I had to step back and look at myself. I knew she was right. And the rest of the group confirmed it. When I looked at what was going on in my life, I had slipped out of my own center. I stepped out of my own creative process and into production mode: Get the job done, make the deadline, and check the boxes.

By the time I got to this station, I realized that each

of these chapters were in gestation. And I was taking forceps and pulling them out. And the weeks that followed occurred really differently for me.

This is exactly the awareness that the Wheel offers. And it was offering it to me. How can I be in it, how can it be anything but theory if I'm not present? The work of the Wheel is to step back from the Form when needed, to be present with reality, to breathe spirit in and return to the Essence at the center.

Move. Move through the birth-giving process, which facilitates the baby's coming into position and being born. This means staying active in your life through the process. Don't disengage from everything else in your life.

Keep doing the things that nourish and support you. Otherwise, you lose your connection with the Life Force. I can find myself doing this when I feel the pressure of time: not going to the beach, not seeing friends. And I think that's what happens to artists. They start to go a little over the edge when they stop engaging with the people in their lives that ground them in day-to-day life.

Partner. Have a partner or buddy you trust for continuous support through the process. A clear witness through the process is crucial.

Another member of the group put it this way: "It's that little pause that I take to check in with myself and say, 'Well done!'" A partner also fulfils the need for a mirror. She continued: "I need to tell someone. I need to share with someone, who reflects it back, because I feel like I'm in a vacuum. I'll get depressed because I feel like I'm doing something, and yet it doesn't really count. I want someone to tell: 'Look at this little thing I've done today. Somebody, tell me it's a start at least.'"

Allow. Avoid unnecessary interventions to force, rush or direct the process. That is, have what you need to support the process and to handle risks if they occur. But don't try to direct it too much or to do the work of Nature. It knows better than you do what needs to happen.

Another member of the same group made a trip to Bali to introduce her son to his father. It had

been a 10-year process for her. From the moment she knew she was pregnant (at 42), she made the choice to have her baby and bring him up entirely by herself. Even so, she stayed in contact with the father, knowing one day she would make this trip.

Even as she boarded the flight, knowing that she wanted her son to meet his father, she did not go expecting it to happen. And yet, by following her intuition and allowing the process to unfold, the trip was an amazing success: "I couldn't have imagined it or dreamt it any better."

Stand. Let your body guide you and stay upright. And this gets back to the task of Station 9, being present. If you trust the process and remain awake and aware, you take your place at the center of your own life. By becoming aware of your connection with Life in all circumstances and engaging with it consciously, everything you bring into the world comes with greater ease.

Delphine came to the group struggling to find her place in her own life. "I am a very high achiever," she says. "It's easy for me to achieve many things, so I dismiss my achievements. As a result, I don't get pride out of them. I hide my achievements and a huge part of myself with them. That's what I'm fighting: the lack of confidence, lack of me taking my place, having my voice, showing myself."

Stay. Stay with the New Thing. Give it time. Let yourself appreciate it. Feel the sacredness of the moment. Often we achieve something and never celebrate it, never acknowledge it. We just move on. That is dishonoring to ourselves and to what we've achieved. But even small jobs offer the opportunity to create something different.

Diane described a perfect example: "Last Saturday, I took on a project I had been wanting to do for months. I touched up all the spots on the walls and ceiling in the kitchen. I started at 9:30, and it took until 3:00. Then I stopped and appreciated it. 'I'm so proud of myself,' I thought. I was really proud that I had finally, after I don't know how long, just done it. Later in the afternoon, my son came to me, saying, 'I'm so proud' of something he had done, which clearly overshadowed my achievement. But the appreciation of what we do, even if it's the slightest thing, feels so good. And who else says it? No one."

What Is Required to Be Present?

It is a big piece of the work in this station to bring yourself, with whatever exists in front of you, to a place of appreciation. You must deal with:

Expectations. I love the saying, "Expectations are premeditated disappointments." And I have certainly found it to be true in my life. Presence means acknowledging what you actually have in front of you as opposed to what you wanted, or what you think it should be, or what it's going to be. It's easy to see this with a baby, because you love it. But with your own work, you want it to be perfect immediately, because it reflects on you. The New Thing is going to have its own course of development; you are its guardian, but you are not in control of that process. Being present means managing your expectations to make space for what is.

Comparisons. Worrying about what other people are doing is one of the most destructive distractions I have engaged in. Nothing will pull you out of your center faster. The presence of a supportive partner or community reminds you who you are and what you're about. It's like having a midwife present at the birth. She gives you confidence and guides you; and her experience gives context to yours in a way that keeps you safe and helps you do your job. Someone to share yourself with intimately helps you stay present through the ups and downs of Breakthrough.

Impatience. I also love the saying, "When you ask God for patience, he puts you in line." Presence means not demanding that the New Thing pay for itself immediately. Presence is not jumping ahead to the reviews, not imagining the market share, not predicting the Nobel Prize. Those of us in creative professions do this all the time: We don't get the pen on the paper before we're hearing the critics praising us or tearing us to shreds. In these moments, we're in fantasy, and the truth about ourselves lies just out of reach. Being present means being neither in the past nor the future, but in this moment.

When you can't stay with the timing, when it's not your timing, you tend to get bossy (that is, controlling) around the process. At these uncomfortable times, it's easy to turn to artificial interventions to manage the discomfort and numb the pain. Chemicals and technology are two of today's most extensive epidemics. From taking the edge off with antidepressants to avoiding all moments of down time with hand-held entertainment, we can use just about anything as a distraction. Lamaze encouraged using the breath to work with pain and move through the process naturally, rather than numbing the pain. And I think that's really relevant to the creative process as well.

As the New Thing breaks through, a new challenge arrives with it. If your expectations are instant perfection, it's painful to look at this unformed, undeveloped creative work. Whether it's a business, product, lifestyle change, relationship or new way of being, there is risk. And that is uncomfortable.

But remember, the third quarter is all about the prototype. Quarter 1 was the idea. Quarter 2 was the research. Quarter 3 is the prototype. It gives you something to work with, and you go about making continual improvements until it is ready to go to market. It's meant to be worked with and improved. That is its function.

The Reward of Breakthrough: Confidence

Life is a process, expressed physically from birth to death. During the course of a lifetime, we move through many different forms: egg, embryo, fetus, baby, child, young adult, mature adult, aged adult. Each of these forms has its own developmental stage, and each has to give way for the next one to appear.

But the Form is not the equivalent of Life. Life moves through the physical forms, but it extends infinitely beyond them on either side, before and after their existence. To own the Form that is here now is power, and with that comes the confidence to live this part of the process fully, without shame and without judgment.

It takes courage to give birth and make visible a work in progress, unfinished and undeveloped. But in reality, that is all there is. It is all we are: works in progress, transforming energy into form after form.

Completing this station prepares you to move on through the Gate of Return and forward into Cultivation. As the New Thing comes out into the world, its world expands; but your world contracts, as you are required to choose it and commit: "Not all those other possibilities out there, not all those other dreams. This is the one." And that requires commitment. It's the commitment to nurture and tend the New Thing so it can grow to the point where it can fulfill its purpose.

As I've grown in my understanding of this process over more than 30 years, I've observed that ideas do not come to just one of us at a time; rather, they are sown like seeds, and wherever the ground is fertile they grow. This is where I began to sense that ideas have souls, and when they come to us, they have chosen us. When Life has sown the seed and you receive and gestate it, a relationship forms. We meet an idea that comes to us, and we choose each other; and in our collaboration with it, we step into the flow of Life through the creative process.

We left Home with a longing, and set out on a journey, believing the answer to our longing was out there somewhere. As the obstacles on the path bring us back to our center, we return to Source, to Life, and realize it was there all the time coming through us. But now our longing is linked with a new life, which we care for and bring into the world. It leads us then not only to the fulfillment of our own longing but also to a New Thing that nourishes the world as well.

Why Bother?

If it all leads back to where we started, you might ask, "Why bother making the trip at all?" In reply, I would ask, "Why do we travel?" Do we travel in order to move to another place? Sometimes. But usually we travel knowing that we will return home again, because the overall experience gives us pleasure. It may not be easy; the experiences may trouble us. But whatever the experience of the journey, we return home richer and more deeply alive because we made it.

Breakthrough brings you to one of the most beautiful moments in the creative process. Pleasure becomes bliss. Our greatest challenge here is to actually experience that moment, by being present with what is and what comes up in us to remove us from it.

If we do not do this work, we will move on into the production aspect of creation without the confidence achieved here. Then the inevitable discomfort of giving birth will throw us into our reactions: Either we will feel compelled to get the New Thing out there as fast as possible, putting it at risk of failure from its very first breath, or we will avoid giving birth at all, holding onto the New Thing and wasting away as it drains the creative Life energy from us.

Externalizing the Internal

My song acknowledged all the children I had abandoned through my life, all the projects I brought to this point and then stopped. Countless times in my life, I came up against that shame of "Oh my God, it's terrible," and the fear of ever looking it in the face again.

The process I became aware of in that song pushed me to deal with the patterns that had me abandon and abandon and abandon. I could look back and see project after project through my whole life where I had repeated these patterns. And the projects were always the important ones, the ones that meant the most to me.

That process led me to get more training, to develop my skill, to enable me to produce what I envision. An artist friend of mine took four years to perfect the material and the technique she uses for her current work. Her process involved a lot of research, drawing on the experience of other artists and experts in raw materials. She tried things and they failed. She encountered resistance from her neighbors to her use of toxic materials. And finally, after four years of perseverance and hard work, she got there.

This process led me to a lifelong pursuit of personal development as a creator. Somehow we have come to believe that it should be easy, that if it doesn't just plop right out, perfect the first time, then, "I'm a failure, and it's not meant to be."

This station asks you to choose, to see it through— or not. Not until you let go of the judgment of the New Thing does the choice become visible. It is, once again, the opportunity for a paradigm shift and personal transformation. As staying with the process in Gestation rewards you with faith, staying present with the process of the New Thing taking shape in the world rewards you with the confidence to go forward and create. And that leads us into Quarter 4.

A STORY OF BREAKTHROUGH

Suzy Girard-Ruttenberg, Business Coach, and David Ruttenberg, Music Producer
Current City: Boca Raton, Florida

"How do you raise a perfect child in an imperfect world? How do you take a kid that has all that creativity and not drain it out of them, so that they fit into a world that needs the very thing that makes them so distinctive to begin with?"

I met Suzy Girard in Chicago, in the late 1980s. It was crystal clear that the young woman serving my table at D.B. Kaplan's Deli was seriously underemployed. We instantly became fast friends, and though our paths have taken us far apart geographically, she is a soul sister of the highest order. With an equally fabulous husband, David, at her side, Suzy has surmounted the suicides of both her parents, transformed the lives and businesses of her coaching clients, and taken on the public institutions failing young people like their daughter, Phoebe.

KATHERINE ROBERTSON-PILLING: How would you describe yourself and your life?

DAVID RUTTENBERG: I am a music producer, engineer, composer, arranger publisher, husband, father, son, soul mate. And part of the reason that I'm all that is because I have two great parents, and a fabulous wife, and an equally gifted and fabulous daughter. I wouldn't be doing what I'm doing if it wasn't for them all.

SUZY GIRARD-RUTTENBERG: I would say my life is an adventurous wonder filled with blessings. I feel surrounded by unconditional love and support and acceptance, regardless of what each day brings. And I'm very, very lucky.

I operate the same way in my professional life as I operate in my personal life, which is that I'm committed to helping people design the lives they would dream for themselves if there were no obstacles or limitations. I want that for my daughter. I want that for my husband. I want that for myself. And I certainly want that for all my clients, and for anybody in the world.

KRP: How do you work with obstacles?
DR: I'm a typical male. So instead of trying to find meaning in them at first, I just try to find a solution. Then I go back and find the meaning. Suzy can focus on the duality between why this is happening and how do I navigate through the process at the same time.
SGR: I think that obstacles are really just unidentified or uncommitted raw material. For most of us, when things happen, we know where they belong. And I think we identify them as obstacles because we haven't planned for them, or we're not sure we can overcome them, or they require us to be more than what we feel we're capable of. Really they're no different than anything else in our lives. They reintroduce us to our potential.
KRP: How do you define creativity?
DR: The first thing that comes to my mind is something from nothing, or being able to identify the opportunity to synthesize something from nothing.

As a composer, even before there's a feeling, or the thought of a feeling, of a musical line, or of a drum groove, there is nothing. And at some point there is a spark that initiates that process you call creativity. The rest of it is almost like making a sandwich; it's not profound. It's like, "Okay, now I got that spark, now I got the idea, here are the things I need to lay out." And I think we're all like that.
SGR: For me it's just the reverse: 80 percent mulling around in my mind and 20 percent execution. Sometimes I intentionally wait until the last minute, but I've been working on it all along. That's the way I do things. When I coach my clients, I tell them, "Don't go earn your money. Make it on paper first,

and then producing it will be a lot easier." It's all on the front end for me.

My definition of creativity would be the sandbox of "What If?" Even though this was never done before, what if we tried this? It's just playing around in that.

KRP: Tell me a little about Phoebe.

DR: The first question you ask is what's the deal with Phoebe? So, she was diagnosed early on as high functioning on the autism spectrum.

SGR: Her diagnosis was PDD, which is pervasive developmental disorder, which means there are two or more coexisting delays, such as speech, processing or fine-motor skills. Under the umbrella of PDD, you can have "not otherwise specified," which means we don't know exactly what's going on. Asperger's [syndrome] is the diagnosis *du jour* that gets the most media attention, and—if there is one—the preferred version of autism. Someone with Asperger's is usually somebody who's not particularly social but is unusually highly intelligent. Autism contains a very wide spectrum that includes everything from kids who seem trapped in their own world to children who are extremely high functioning. Then there's the Einstein syndrome: very, very bright kids who are very focused on one or two areas of interest but are late in developing socially.

Phoebe doesn't squarely fit into any one category.

KRP: What are you learning from Phoebe about creativity?

SGR: The biggest thing I've learned from her is that there is a dance between preserving what makes her unique and helping her adjust to the world she lives in. She has just an enormous imagination, and she is powerfully connected to and appreciative of her creativity. And I fear that these are the first things compromised when she is taught to act like an adult. In our society, to some degree, people exchange individuality and creativity for acceptance. They make tradeoffs, limiting their self-expression in order to fit into the mainstream.

How do you raise a perfect child in an imperfect world? How do you take a kid that has all that creativity and not drain it out of her, so that she fits into a world that needs the very thing that makes her so distinctive to begin with?

DR: From my vantage point, having taught several hundred kids and adults for almost two decades, I've seen some pretty amazing people and some fairly typical people, too. I've seen lots of creative spokes on the wheel.

Phoebe is great at so many different things, whether storytelling, language, violin, karate, animals, or now sports, she's pretty remarkable. She's one of the quickest studies I know at mastering stuff.

Some of the people who use the dojo where she studies karate—people with black belts—were like, "How did she do that?" because she had progressed much faster than they had. As I'm working with her on violin, what typically takes my students about 12 weeks to learn, she grasps in about 5 to 10 minutes. But while she really started to master the instrument, I've had to backtrack with her, because she still needs to improve her ability to understand the language and read music in more detail. That combination is pretty emblematic of her creative process.

SGR: For example, we had to do some standardized testing to zero in on a couple of major gaps she has in comprehension. So they informed us that she has the vocabulary of a 16½ year old. In science, she's on an eighth-grade level. In math, she's doing sixth-grade work. And she's in third. All moms think their kids are geniuses, but she's in the 99th percentile for her age group on both of those subjects. And yet her social and processing delays are significant.

KRP: So how do you support her?

DR: Our goal is to expose her to as many types of experiences as possible.

SGR: It's very daunting and depressing for parents to hear this, but only about 10 percent of the autistic population are employed or employable. My feeling is that that's not necessarily an accurate depiction of their potential. Parents need to, as soon as possible, identify what these children are creatively drawn to. And you have to have almost a Svengali-like approach because it takes a much more focused approach, much more time, and a lot more support, to have that child be independent. But I think it's completely doable.

DR: The way we employ this creativity toward Phoebe is a natural extension of what we've done in our own lives. Launching our Internet company and then closing it to follow our passions took a leap of faith and courage and creativity and new ideas. It also prepared us to think out of the box, because every day we need to think out of the box for Phoebe.

SGR: Parents are not being educated about how to steward their children's creative process. These kids are ultracreative, and they have highly honed sensitivities to their area of interest. And you can capitalize on that.

We live in a world of generalists. Look at people who are supersuccessful in whatever arena, who don't have special needs. At some point somebody took them by the hand, and they became singularly obsessed with something. Whether it was pulling themselves out of poverty, beating the odds, achieving something somebody told them wasn't possible, whatever it was, there's a lot to be said for that singular obsession. It's looked at as an oddity, but it

can be a huge asset; it just has to be channeled in the right direction.

KRP: Is this part of why you're trying to not use the label with her?

SGR: David put it the best when he said, "Everybody else feels the need to have her understand that she has this label, when Phoebe doesn't have the need. Phoebe's fine with who she is. It's everybody else who's not fine with it."

DR: The diagnosis is so broad in my opinion that there are many people walking around with it who don't do anything about it. Even her pediatrician says there's nothing wrong with her. The last thing I'd want to do is say, "This is what you're tagged with," and then have her crawl back into the shell that she's blossomed out of.

SGR: The child will let you know what they need and when they need it. We think that for the dignity of the child, you have to be willing to give up control and let them lead the way. You also have to realize that the outside conversation doesn't necessarily reflect what's going on with the kid.

I feel that autism is a set of components she will need to contend with, but in no way should it tell her who she is. It is part of what she manages as a challenge, but she is so much bigger than that. And I'm at peace with that.

10

STATION 10
Nurturing

Some say the creative life is in ideas, some say it is in doing.
It seems in most instances to be in a simple being.
It is not virtuosity, although that is very fine in itself.
It is the love of something, having so much love for something
—whether a person, a word, an image, an idea, the land, or humanity—
that all that can be done with the overflow is to create.
CLARISSA PINKOLA ESTÉS, PH.D.

On the Platform in Station 10

Station 10 is the time of the newborn, right after birth. Here we begin to work with the prototype we incubated in the third quarter. What was at one point a powerful longing was then clarified, crystallized and embedded in us. It developed in its embryonic state and finally separated from us to take its own place in the world. Now we must learn to create a loving connection with it, and with ourselves, in order to support its growth beyond us.

Nurturing is the first of two stations that work hand in hand. Nurturing and Pruning provide the mothering and fathering that the New Thing needs to survive the inevitable tests ahead.

In terms of creating something tangible in the world, these two stations are the most important in the Wheel. They are to be worked and balanced together. Nurturing welcomes, embraces, gives space and protects, bringing the new life to a certain point of maturity. Pruning disciplines the New Thing, cut-

ting away what is not necessary and giving shape to what is. But not yet.

The Voice of Nurturing: "Someone to Watch Over You."

The word *nurture* originated from the Latin word *nūtrīre*, to suckle. It is defined alternately as:

- To nourish and tend (a growing child, animal or plant)

- To take care of a young thing: to give tender care and protection to a young child, animal, or plant, helping it to grow and develop

- To encourage development of (a project, idea or feeling, etc.) to encourage somebody or something to grow, develop, thrive, and be successful; to flourish

- To educate; train; helping someone grow up to be an accepted member of the community

Nature's natural intuitive response to a newborn is to nurture it. There is something outside you now. It has a powerful developmental process of its own, but it is unable to survive on its own and is still totally dependent on you for its very life. At this early stage, the New Thing depends on you for unconditional acceptance, protection and support. This is your job. Now you are required to keep the commitment you first made in Conception.

The Third Gate: Return

In the Wheel, Nurturing is the first station in the Cultivation Quarter. We come from Breakthrough, where the fruit of our longing is first made visible in the world. This passage requires a decision, the decision to make love visible. It is a turning back toward Home.

Changing Quarters

While Incubation was the quarter of Water—the heart, feeling and receptive—Cultivation is the quarter of Earth—the body, sensing and active again. So we need a shift of energy from the internal to the external again, and this is the first part of that shift. Quarter 3 was the process of falling in love; Quarter 4 is the response with what is needed to see that love mature. Here in Station 10, you are required to keep the commitment you made in Breakthrough. There is something outside you, with a process of its own; and it is dependent on you for its development.

This station is Earth receiving Water, being nourished in order to grow the New Thing. We pass through the Gate of Return, and the energy shifts again, this time from internal to external.

To bring Water into Earth is to imbue the physical world with the depth you have plumbed in the third quarter. Your emotion, personal discovery, unconditional love, understanding, your truth, your tenderness, your dreams, your magic, your feelings—these are all the things held in the element of Water.

Now you are returning home to the community

you left, bringing the New Thing home, where it can make its contribution to the world. Although you are returning home, you are clearly not the same person who left. The process itself, even before it is complete, has transformed you.

Life in Station 10
The Experience of Nurturing: Tenderness

The experience of Station 10 is tenderness. This is the first point in the Wheel where you can actually see something out in front of you, separate from you, which needs your time, resources and attention to grow.

Having a new life in front of us calls up from within us the unconditional love and acceptance it needs (we need) to grow. Even when we are unable to nurture ourselves, we can receive Nurturing as it flows through us to this New Thing that demands it from us.

At the level of Form, on the outside of the Wheel, this station moves us into the duality of life. What was once our private longing now exists outside us, in front of us, in its elemental form. No longer is our creative process alone in its work; the New Thing has a process of its own. We are separate and in relationship with it.

What is required here is delivering on the commitment you made back in Conception. You chose to take the seed and plant it, to make space for it in your life, to say "Yes" to Life's longing for itself through you. Now there is no going back. The baby has been born. It is all or nothing. You must deepen your previous commitment: "I am here to do whatever it takes to see you come into fulfillment."

In the space of duality, there is also a synthesis. As you look at the New Thing, you see yourself. As you love it, you love yourself. Though not always easy, the process is self-nurturing and self-caring. And as you move through the challenges of this process into Essence, your commitment to its unfolding deepens. By making the commitment, you become more than you were before. Having this baby and never having been a mother in quite this way before, you have no experience to rely on. But you learn. And you become more than you were.

Becoming a nurturer occurs on two levels:

1. The moment the New Thing breathes its own air, you are a nurturer.

2. As you learn how to nurture, you become a nurturer, changed by the effects of your own actions.

As in every station, you have the opportunity to use what Life requires of you as a process to transform yourself. As you take your place and create a relationship with what Life has given you to nurture, you nurture your own destiny.

Nature Versus Nurture

There is a long-standing debate in the social sciences about how much of whom we are is inherited genetically and how much comes through environmental influences. It is called nature versus nurture. Nature signifies an organism's genetic inheritance, what it shows up with; nurture is the influence its environment has on what it becomes. Nurture is our response to Nature; what we nurture grows and flourishes, for better or worse. And Nature rewards that which strengthens the organism and helps it survive negative influences.

In Station 7, Conception, we talked about how the seed has to grow through the conditions in which it is sown. The better those conditions are, the better its development will be. This is the external version of that. Now that the New Thing is a life unto itself, it is time to work with the environment in which it must grow.

Why Is This Station Important?

Everything and everyone needs nurturing in order to develop, and in our early days we need to have a connection with someone or something greater than us from which we receive it. The myth

of the overnight success reveals the degree of training required of artists before they are suddenly "discovered." Personal relationships certainly need time and attention just to get to the point where you can see where they're headed. And anyone who has started a business knows just how much energy and resources must be invested before receiving a cent of profit.

In so-called civilized society, across cultures and throughout time, one archetypal figure has been historically associated with nurturing: Mother. While the classic image is the Madonna and Child—selfless, perfect, unconditional love for a perfect baby—this is an ideal. Those of us with imperfect childhoods and unmet needs we're still trying to have met (in other words, most of us) are wounded in this area.

Our ability to nurture is limited, especially our ability to nurture ourselves and things that come from us. We censor ourselves by default. We become perfectionists or underachievers, judging ourselves and our work first so that we don't have to bear the judgments of others. In this way, we also limit our ability to receive nurturing when it is offered.

Nurturing is a skill. We develop this skill as we nurture others, but also as we become aware of our own need for it. Our willingness to work on ourselves to clear away the scar tissue of our old wounds enables us to nurture our own creative work in the world and ourselves in the process.

Monkeys' Mothers Matter

Harry Harlow (1905–1981) was an American psychologist best known for his research on the effects of maternal deprivation on rhesus monkeys. His controversial social-isolation experiments on the monkeys demonstrated the importance of caregiving and companionship in the early stages of their development.

Harlow set up two groups of baby monkeys that were given the same amounts of food and water, and exposed to the same environmental conditions except for one factor: The monkeys in one group lived with their natural mothers, while those in the other group were given surrogates—mechanical mothers made of terrycloth-covered wire. All the baby monkeys clung to their mothers. The first group thrived, but the second group withered and become severely disturbed.

Harlow's findings proved that baby rhesus monkeys deprived of early nurturing contact end up severely disturbed and unable to participate in society. The only difference was the presence of a nurturing, natural mother.

The Soul of Creativity

Mozart said, "The soul of creativity is love, love, love." When we come back to the understanding that ideas have souls and that we are in relationship with them, we recognize that Life has called us, through the process of nurturing this New Thing, to transform ourselves. So there is a real creative blossoming that occurs with us as we take on this task.

What we create thrives on our love more than anything else. The foundations for the eventual contribution of that New Thing to society are laid here. In the Nurturing Station, we learn to care for the newborn and protect it from the harshness of Nature in its early, vulnerable days. This protection can be soft or forceful when required, but through our vigilance, we empower the fragile new life to eventually flourish on its own.

What Nurturing Looks Like

Nurturing is one of the most far-reaching foundations of human culture. To a greater or lesser degree, it is something every life form needs to thrive.

On the Kabbalah's Tree of Life, it is Binah—the Feminine, the Mother—understanding or contemplation. Binah is the ultimate Object, the receptive principle behind the cosmos. It is often compared to Shakti in Hindu mysticism. It channels the flow of energy, giving birth to all of Creation. It is something like mothering, but not exactly that.

In 1950, psychologist Erik Erikson pioneered work on the developmental stages all children go through in order to live in and contribute successfully to the world. His psychosocial stages trace how a person's development progresses through life, from birth to death. The foundation of all future development—positive or negative—occurs in the first year, when the child is most dependent and learns to trust or mistrust its environment in response to how it is treated.

As the child develops, the mother must gradually let go, with greater distance but still with tenderness and care. In order to do this well, she must work with her own needs so that the child is free and supported to move out into the world safely and autonomously.

Nurturing in Nature

In the animal kingdom, I have watched the seagulls near where I live—babies and mothers—go through this process together. It is incremental, from the parents' total (and aggressive) protection of the nest, to the baby's emerging fuzzy and fragile, growing, stretching its wings, discovering lift, skipping a few roof tiles and then, one day, setting out over open air. I watch them, distinguished from their adult mentors by their adolescent cries and their dark coloring, learning to soar and glide, still under the watchful eye of their parents. It is a process that blends the energies of Mother and Father, Nurturing and Pruning.

In the plant world, nurturing is the gardener's attention to her plants. It is the watering and feeding. In early days, weeks, years, they need to be protected from the elements. While food and water are enough for survival, tenderness and affection are required for blossoming. Each plant needs careful and individual attention, with environmental conditions monitored for optimal health.

While previous experiments have shown the impact of music on plant growth, in 2009 the Royal Horticultural Society in England studied the effect of the human voice on plants. In the month-long study, a group of tomato plants "listened" to different readings by different voices via MP3 players and headphones attached to their pots. Certain plants grew almost two-thirds of an inch more than the plants in the control group, which heard no voices. Women's voices seemed to be more popular than men's.

Nurturing and Pruning need to be informed by each other. Nurturing comes first in tenderness with a voice to say, "Now you have 'someone to watch over you.'" It accepts this newborn thing as it is. It provides for its survival needs: care and feeding, holding, and protection. Pruning comes in the next station.

Most of us censor everything that comes out of us. We compare it to others, measure it in the marketplace, and judge it as better or worse, not good enough or unacceptable, long before it has had a chance to develop. How many far-reaching solutions would we have patented today if they had been given room to develop and mature?

Nurturing is an evolving process, responding to the evolving needs of the New Thing as it develops. It is acceptance, abstaining from judgment and censorship in its early days. When we judge an idea prematurely, we shut down the flow of Life to us and through us. Thus, an important aspect of Nurturing is keeping it to yourself—not exposing it to outside judgment, not expecting it to perform until it is (and you are) strong enough to be seen and judged by others.

This is not always feasible. There are times when you must reveal something to the world before it is fully developed. But keep the effects in mind when you make the choice.

The Task of Nurturing: Protect

The task of Section 10 is to protect the New Thing. This station is about respect for and responsiveness to the fragility of new life. It is about listening as well as guiding. "I have no idea how I'm going to get from here to there, but this is what's on the table in front of me, asking for my attention."

This station also requires you to do your work so that you don't force your own agenda on the New Thing. If we don't look within ourselves and acknowledge the repetitive patterns, then we will continue to fail to nurture what is most important to us. And we will not develop beyond where we are. But this thing, so important to us, motivates us to look and to grow beyond where we would otherwise give up, or where we have always given up before.

To Serve and Protect

Protecting the New Thing comes in many different forms, depending on what that thing is, what our circumstances are and what our particular approach to life is. In general, we need to protect it from:

- Premature expectations. Think of a field of corn. Each corn plant needs 60 to 90 days from planting before it is ready to harvest and eat. We would never expect young corn plants to feed us when the shoots break through the soil. But our expectations for the New Thing are often not so realistic.

- Outside influences. I have a friend who is a painter, who avoids seeing other people's creative work when she is creating something new. She doesn't want her work to be influenced by someone else's.

- Other people's visions for your work. Everyone has an opinion, and very often if you talk about your vision, someone will say, "Oh, you should do this." That can be a discouraging distraction from your own creative voice, unless your work is collaborative at the start. This will be addressed in Harvest.

- Naysayers. Often family or people who have known you for a long time will tend to limit you: "Oh, you always . . . ," or, "You never. . . ." They have their own ideas of who you are from their experience of you, and your process of transformation will not fit their pictures.

- The inner critic. Most of us have an inner perfectionist who would never permit the release of the New Thing because there is still too much work to be done. This voice must be moderated or it will become toxic to creativity.

- Comparison. Someone will always be better, and someone will always be worse. Someone will do it faster, and someone will fall behind. When we compare our process to others, we are pulled out of our center and find ourselves being spun around the outside of the Wheel. We all have our own unique life processes; it is our work to trust them.

- Other people's jealousy. Likewise, as we compare ourselves to others, others compare themselves to us. When we begin to move through our lives deliberately, on purpose, drawing closer to nourishing ourselves by our own hand, other people notice. And they are not always happy for us, especially when they do not yet trust their own ability to do the same.

My Experience of Station 10

We all have our own story with regard to nurturing. This is mine.

In general, I was nurtured as a child. I was certainly loved, and my physical needs were always met. But there was an unhealthy dynamic in my relationship with my mother that left me wounded in my ability to nurture myself.

My mother was deeply deprived of nurturing in her childhood. Her family was poor and times were tough. Her mother became ill and was taken away at a very important age for her. In order to survive the loss, she learned to get her needs met by giving to others, to be nurtured by nurturing. There are many people like her, and the results for others are not altogether bad. But this form of self-nurturing does not fill the void within.

I was her primary focus in this pattern. As she gave to me in order to meet her own needs, there were strings attached. Her need for me to fulfill her unmet needs left me struggling to know my own, struggling to nurture myself. Everything that emanated from me was not good enough for me, as I settled into a pattern of perfectionism, thinking that the solution was always somehow out there still.

Never Alone

Ideally, we would all receive this nurturing in the early days of our lives. Sometimes people come along later, in school or business, who believe in us when we do not believe in ourselves. They help us flourish, for our own sake, without a hidden need for us to be a certain way for them. Perhaps this is why historically so many artists have thrived with patrons and sponsors.

Of course, we need this nurturing from ourselves, but given our own childhood wounds, it's often too much to ask. The wounds we form in childhood limit our ability to nurture what is important to us. We have to be conscious of that and work with it. We overcome our own emptiness in order to nurture the New Thing, and we must nurture ourselves in order to do that.

We also sometimes expect ourselves to do this all independently, be lone rangers, able to nurture ourselves and not need anything. We can get along to a point, but eventually we need someone who will say, "You've got something here! Believe in yourself! Take your place in the world. Don't doubt. Don't second-guess. Stop apologizing for yourself."

I know I experienced this at earlier times in my career, and I still do today. When I am doing something I have never done before, when I am testing my wings, I need someone standing behind me, watching me as I step off the rooftop, someone who knows what I am capable of when I am in doubt.

This is the value of healthy feedback systems: coaches and mentors, patrons, peer support groups, advisory boards and friends. These are not investors or shareholders; these people need to have no direct financial stake in the success of our work. Their aim is only to support us in our own fulfillment and manifesting what we are made to be and do.

This is our role for the New Thing in Station 10. As we give it, we develop our capacity to give it. And we nurture ourselves.

A Return to Wholeness

Nurturing is the re-enactment of the experience of wholeness we felt in the womb. In reality, wholeness comes only when we draw on the inexhaustible supply of the cosmos. We are eternal beings in finite forms here on earth. Thus we must tap into the eternal in order to be whole. Until we do, we end up always seeking something spiritual in the material world, something that is not material at all. What is needed is quite simple really: Stop, get still and touch that which gives us life.

More than the support of any human being, we need to feel our connection with the cosmos. We need to experience that the Universe's attitude toward us is benevolent; that it believes in us, supports us and encourages us. That's what tells me I'm on the right track—even if people around me are questioning and doubting me. When we tune in to our deepest, most authentic desires and feel that support from the Universe, nothing can shake us.

When I first moved to Los Angeles, it was because I had received an intuitive calling. I had no job, no home and one friend. During my seven-day drive from Chicago to LA, the house-sitting job my friend had arranged for us fell through. We found ourselves sharing a tiny studio apartment that was offered to us. Within a week of my arrival, my car was broken into and everything in it was stolen. When the thief tried the doorknob of our apartment, we were both too scared to utter a sound. I knew I had to find a better place. And that's when I once again realized the mysterious ways Life delivers what I need when I acknowledge my dependency on it.

It was not always easy, but my old friends in Chicago and a new community of like-minded friends in LA helped me remember the truth of who I was. And because I knew and trusted what was calling

me, I was not caught on the edge of the Wheel. I was able to return to the center, to my Essence. There I could experience Life as nurturing, no matter what was going on around me.

There have been many stories along the way of Life's nurturing hand on mine. Things show up in my environment that I need to survive, to feel safe, to earn a living. I ask a question and get the answer the next day. I meet a stranger in the square who tells me to believe in myself. I learn that an idea I shared empowered someone I didn't know to change his life.

Serendipitous experiences and chance encounters make me feel connected with and affirmed by the cosmos. These things touch me deeply and affirm that what I'm doing is connected to truth in some way, and I should keep going with it. They remind me that I am on the right track, doing the right thing. I need that from time to time. We all do. This is Life nurturing me.

Our connection to the Source makes us whole on a moment-by-moment basis; no matter how disconnected we may feel, it is always available. Living life conscious of its creative process connects us to this Source. For me, the creative process is a powerful mechanism to open this channel; and, unlike the exclusivity of religions, it is inclusive and available to all.

Commit to Something Big

This station of the Wheel can be tough to enter, because nurturing does not always come easy. Sometimes it's easier to nurture plants or pets or political projects than ourselves and the ones (people and ideas) we love. Sometimes we are so uncomfortable with our needs that we don't allow others to nurture us.

The commitment we fulfill in this station requires a leap of faith. If we wait to *feel* nurturing before we nurture, we may continue to wait, while the New Thing starves. When we are willing to commit to something out of our reach, without knowing how it will develop, we initiate the flow of Life to us, through us and beyond. What the New Thing needs to thrive is what we need as well.

This New Thing you have chosen to give birth to and cultivate in your life in the world is bigger than you. For one person, it is a longing for passion in work that launches him; for another it is the longing for serenity; and for another, it is her longing for home. But at this station, each of us renews our commitment to the feeding of our own hunger.

Taking on the commitment to nurture something we have created out of our own longing confronts us with all the closed places in ourselves. In taking on the challenge to feed your own hunger, not as a dream but as a commitment, you will be transformed. And never forget your place in the Field of Wheels. The value you bring forth is not for you alone, but for everyone whose lives you touch.

As that energy flows through us, and we experience ourselves as creating what we long for, we make choices that nurture that process, to be happier and more fulfilled. Nurturing is not just something we do, it is essentially who we are, and we evolve positively from there. Everyone in our lives will benefit. It's part of the movement of Life energy.

What It Takes

In the Nurturing station, we learn to care for the newborn and protect it from the harshness of Nature in its early, vulnerable days. This protection can be soft or forceful when required, but through our vigilance, we empower the fragile new life to eventually flourish on its own.

The essential ingredients of good nurturing are:

- Commitment. You must commit to being there and to keep being there until the New Thing is weaned and ready for shaping. The commitment is to honor the desire, will and intention of the soul of the New Thing and to assist it in taking its place in life.

- Presence. Harry Harlow showed in his research that just the presence of a natural mother was enough to nurture a baby to thrive. Attention, intimacy, listening and clear response, love and acceptance are all components of presence.

- Mirroring. Mirroring is the opposite of the premature expectation (which sees the child or the New Thing as a possession). It is being a clear witness for what the New Thing is and wants to be rather than what or who you need it to be. When the ego takes control, the result is narcissism, and it will always be reflected in the developmental process of the New Thing.

- Self-care. To truly, freely nurture the other, you must be fulfilled yourself.

The Reward of Nurturing: Maturity

The Reward of Station 10 is maturity, of the New Thing and of yourself. It is bringing the New Thing to fruition, seeing it become more and more real in the forms of your life. In order for this New Thing to become real, you must step into a new gap from which you emerge changed into someone you have never been before. Thus, as you change to give the New Thing what it needs to thrive, the reward signifies your own maturity as well.

So this station calls us to take on something bigger than ourselves. We do it not out of duty or obligation, but out of love. As Clarissa Pinkola Estés says so eloquently in *Women Who Run With the Wolves*, "It is not a matter of wanting to, not a singular act of will; one solely must." (Clarissa Pinkola Estés, *Women Who Run With the Wolves: Myths and Stories of the Wild Woman Archetype*, USA: Ballantine, 1992, 1996) This station puts us in relationship with something outside ourselves and requires something from us. Thus, something we once felt a victim to becomes the very thing that empowers us.

The boy who grew up in horrid conditions and manages to get out knows he must go back to offer a hand to those still trapped. He does not do it out of obligation, but because by doing it, he cleanses himself of the past and creates a future not only for others but also for himself.

As we nurture that, we are nurtured. As we take responsibility for something larger than ourselves, then we begin to free ourselves from our insecurities. It's like taking on a project we are not quite sure we can do. We get bigger; we expand. We have to find strength we don't know we had, which was there all along, waiting for us to use it.

I love the phrase, "Love is coming through." When we love, when we say to the New Thing, "I love you, I want you, I'm committed to you," love passes through us to it, and we are nourished by it in the process.

The Ability to Deal With Uncertainty

Someone told me years ago that maturity is the ability to deal with uncertainty. Humans crave security. We need to know how things are going to turn out. We want to know that this New Thing is going to lead us to a successful place. But we don't know for sure.

We arrive in Station 10 sometimes after many days, weeks, and years with no nurturing at all. It is the oasis in the desert, the cool, clear stream on a hot summer day. And its loving-kindness flows through us, rather than to us.

We might have had all kinds of ideas about what this New Thing would look like, or how it would sound, or what it would become. But the baby in front of us now is what needs to be nurtured. The others will come in their own time, but they are not the ones here now.

When we allow ourselves to commit to and engage with something, not knowing how it's going to turn out, the process of living is so much richer and more creative. When we have to know, we shrink the possibilities for it and for our lives. We don't know where our longings are taking us. But if we stay open, they can really take us into great adventures. Enjoy this station because you're about to get on the train again, and it will take you to a new neighborhood and a new task to achieve there.

A STORY OF NURTURING

Amy Blake, Opera Singer
Current City: Nice, France

> "Only because I'm being 'selfish' in the old definition can I be of service. I have to come back to always taking care of myself, being obstinate for my own talent, for my own space, in order to have this connection to Source, which enables me then to be of service and to be creative."

Amy Blake came into my life a couple of years ago in France, though we both hail from the Lone Star State of Texas. A red-haired beauty with a radiant countenance and a spirit to match, she made a leap of faith in love and life, which led her to the life of her dreams in the south of France. Her story, so much like mine, reveals the secret mysteries of a journey from someone else's life to one's own, and the value of tender vulnerability along the way.

KATHERINE ROBERTSON-PILLING: How do you define creativity?

AMY BLAKE: Creativity is that Source of energy for which I am the vessel. So, if I have prepared, if I'm calm, if I'm connected to my higher self, then creativity flows through me like a river. I'm not invested in the reaction of what's happening; I'm just the channel.

I consider my training as a way to access what, as you say, everybody has—this connection to the Source, the energy of Life. Our training as artists and our disciplines enable us to experience these moments of transcendence more often. So I've discovered that I have to be disciplined; it's the work that enables me to have this connection to the Source.

Creativity is about owning my responsibility for my own happiness. And what makes me happy is I have to sing. Every day. I have to look at music. So about a year ago I decided to consecrate three hours a day to song, to making sound with my throat. When I would do this on a daily basis, I was extremely happy. I realized I had to protect the space around this daily time when I prepared and I worked.

KRP: When do you feel most creative?

AB: As a performing artist, or for anybody that does anything temporal like music, we are creative in our preparation. Every day I have to take care of my preparation for the next thing. Sing my scales for a good hour in order to have that juice, or those moments of transcendence.

KRP: And what if there's not a performance?

AB: Great question. I had to deal with that when I moved here. I had nothing on the horizon, and I kept waiting for people to give me opportunities to sing. It took a good year to realize that I missed singing for the pleasure of singing, and that's when I realized I had to get my butt in gear and do the discipline. Even if I didn't have anything coming up, I needed to sing, breathe deeply, open that throat and make sound.

There are a million lyric sopranos in this world, and they all want to sing Violetta in *La Traviata*. Why should I think that I can add something? Then I realized I don't give a damn. I have to do this because I love it. But I had to refind that passion and take my own pleasure and protect the time around it in order to have more and more of that. I just followed my curiosity, learning music that I loved.

KRP: One of the tasks in The Wheel of Creativity is to choose love, to choose what you love. Does that ring true?

AB: I had to learn to love myself. From there, I can love others freely. I thought that if you loved others you sacrificed yourself. That did not work for me; I had to search for another belief system that would help me live and not feel like an evil person. At the end of my life, it's only going to be me, not my next of kin, my mother, my father, my brother, my next-door neighbor. Can I serve others by first taking care of myself?

And I said to myself, "Forget Jesus. Save yourself." It was so important to take responsibility for my own salvation. Everything shifted after this revelation.

KRP: Tell me about that change.

AB: I was in New York working full time as a secretary and trying to pursue a classical singing career as well. And everything began to unravel. My marriage broke up. I had two huge professional opportunities. A wonderful conductor chose me to sing for a reputable festival telling me, "You are one of the most wonderful voices of your generation." And I did not prepare well enough. I was also chosen to sing an audition in Chicago for their young artist's program. And I was a complete mess.

I felt so much shame, and I realized that I wasn't being of service to anyone because I was so bound up. Just then, a friend gave me a way to calm myself down—a kind of meditation—to connect the energy of the sky and the earth, the energy of Source and love. And I had this incredible moment when I actually felt all the ropes that bound me—all the exterior influences—and I just decided to take them off. And then I saw this golden light, and I knew that was me, my higher self.

The change was gradual. I made the *Four Agreements* [by Don Miguel Ruiz] my bible. I slept a lot. I worked. I went to yoga. I felt like I had to learn to take care of myself. I realized that if I really wanted to sing professionally, I needed to leave my job and try. I wanted to make a big change.

KRP: And how did your life respond?

AB: The following summer I had the opportunity to come back to France to sing for a small festival. And there I met my current partner, and we fell in love. And this man made me an incredible proposition: "If you're coming to Europe, why don't we try to live together as well? And you can try to sing." And I said yes. Immediately.

Coming here four years ago and finding a new culture, a new language, has been very, very healing for me personally because I'm able to leave that old perception of self behind. Here I can be this light, this radiant creature that I feel I am, which we all are.

A year ago, even after all these wonderful liberations, I was still dealing with feelings that my ship had passed me by, that I was never going to have the opportunity to do what I want to do. And I felt terribly guilty and sad. And I just thought, this is not very interesting, for me or my partner.

So I just decided to change my thoughts. That's the past. What if I say, "Now I am in the perfect place at the perfect time doing the perfect thing for myself." And that changed everything. I started to believe all the past had been necessary. I started to cut myself some slack and to see myself doing what I wanted to be doing.

And it's so amazing, because ever since that change I have had something on my calendar every two weeks, if not more. I have such a feeling of abundance. I live in the south of France. I have a vegetable garden in Italy. And I live with the love of my life. And I'm not just a singer. I always loved plants, and I have found a passion for the environment, for taking care of the world. It's such a pleasure to make things grow, to follow a lunar calendar, to make less trash, consume less energy, to look at the birds in the trees, to hear water running, and to just be well. I've allowed these other passions more space than before. They nourish the singing and nourish me.

Only because I'm being "selfish" in the old definition can I be of service. I have to come back to always taking care of myself, being obstinate for my own talent, for my own space, in order to have this connection to Source, which enables me then to be of service and to be creative.

11

STATION 11 Pruning

The enemy of art is the absence of limitations.
ORSON WELLES

On the Platform in Station 11

Pruning is the 11th station of The Wheel of Creativity. It sits at the midpoint of the Cultivation Quarter—the body, sensation and the physical world. Cultivation is active and Masculine, as opposed to receptive and Feminine. We are in the middle of the element of Earth, as we move gradually back toward Home with the New Thing we've given birth to.

In terms of creating something tangible in the world, the first two stations of Cultivation are the most important in the Wheel. Nurturing makes space for the New Thing to develop, protecting it from the destructive powers of the outside world, accepting it and encouraging it to grow strong. Now we've moved out of Nurturing, and Pruning gives the New Thing shape, setting limits and removing the nonessential with loving discipline.

But there's a lot of work still to do, externally and internally. Not only do we shape the New Thing, we must shape ourselves in order to do so. Stations 10 and 11 work hand in hand, informing each other, and both are required to create. Each alone is less than half the job done.

The Voice of Pruning: "Time to Say Goodbye."

Pruning is traditionally defined in two key ways:

- To cut off or cut back parts of for better shape or more fruitful growth; e.g., prune the branches of a plant

- To reduce, especially by eliminating superfluous matter; e.g., prune the text, prune the budget

At this point in the Wheel, in this quarter, you are required to keep your commitment. There is something outside you with a process of its own. But it still depends on you for its development. In Station 10, you began to cultivate the New Thing. Here you begin to shape it into a useful, concrete form.

This is a very different point in the process than where you began. The longing you felt in Hunger—the vague sense of restlessness—has evolved into a clear commitment. You stand between heaven and earth as the energetic link between what-could-be and what-will-be. Think back to where you began, and feel the difference in your energy.

153

You enter this quarter having made a commitment to raise this New Thing in the world. The strength of your commitment positions you like a lightning rod that draws energy to it and aligns it for a purpose. At this stage, what you say you want is meaningless. The only thing that matters now is what you're committed to. What are you willing to bring to the table to raise this New Thing?

Here you bring the energy of Nurturing from Station 10 into the next developmental stage of your New Thing, and you make it active. The task of Nurturing was to protect; the task of Pruning is discipline. Both are required to make a new life stand on its own.

Pruning gives form and focus to your whole human experience—mind, spirit, heart and body—as it does to the New Thing. Without this focus you float, you are lost. New Things need focus and limits and discipline to refine them, just as you do.

Since 1992, the Institute of HeartMath in the United States has been conducting research into heart-brain interactions and their impact on the human body's largest electromagnetic field, which is produced by the heart. According to research director Dr. Rollin McCraty in a videotaped interview, the impact is clear, not just for us individually but for those we touch:

> What we've found is that if we look at the spectrum analysis of the electromagnetic field radiated by the heart, the emotional information is actually encoded and modulating into those fields. So by learning to shift our emotions, that's changing the information we're encoding into the magnetic fields radiated by the heart, and that can impact those around us. We are fundamentally and deeply interconnected with each other and the planet itself. And what we do individually really does count. It matters.

So you work with your thoughts, energy, emotions, sensations and the real stuff of the world in order to produce a particular outcome. You are not in control of the process, and you can't always see where you're headed. You don't know what it's going to become. You can set limits, but you can't make it turn out a certain way. And the process itself transforms you.

The creative process is a challenging dragon to ride. And this transformation does not happen overnight; it can take days, weeks, months or years, because everything is continually in evolution. We prune and discipline ourselves while working with what's out here. The process itself changes us. In order to produce a different outcome than we have produced before, we ourselves have to change.

Building the Future, a Stage at a Time

Erik Erikson was a Danish-German-American psychoanalyst whose life spanned most of the 20th century. Erikson's groundbreaking work described the human experience of life as a series of developmental stages, from birth to death. Each stage has a task that must be achieved in order to move through life successfully:

1. The infant must learn to trust or he or s/he will learn to mistrust.

2. The toddler must learn autonomy or s/he will develop shame and doubt.

3. The preschooler must develop initiative or s/he will feel guilty.

4. The school child must achieve industry or s/he will feel inferior.

5. The adolescent must develop identity or s/he will end up in role confusion.

6. The young adult must learn intimacy or s/he will become isolated.

7. The adult must learn generativity or s/he will stagnate.

8. The mature adult must develop integrity or s/he will end up in despair.

If each stage were a stone in the pyramid of a successful life, the stability of that life would rest in the stability of each stone. Failure to achieve the task at any stage creates a faulty foundation for every stone above it. At each stage, if the developing person does not achieve the task, she carries that failure throughout her life until she does. The Wheel of Creativity offers her a framework to use her present circumstances to confront those failures and reinforce the cracks in the stones of the past.

Life in Station 11

While the reward of Station 10 is maturity, the reward of Station 11 is mastery. What begins as a baby grows to a child; the child becomes a youth; the adolescent becomes an adult. At every stage, new skills must be learned and mastery achieved in order to move on with a stable foundation on which to build a contribution to the world.

As you master what is outside, as you develop the skills to produce the results you say you are committed to produce, you also master yourself.

My Garden, Myself

Pruning is most often associated with plants. Gardening is a wonderful, creative activity. Nowhere do I feel more intimate with Life than in my garden. Watching how my plants respond to my care, or the lack of it, puts me in closer touch with the flow and fragility of Life in me and around me.

Plants are the only life forms that make their own food. We have talked about metabolism in humans and animals, the process by which our bodies break down living matter and use the energy released to build new tissue. Plants, through the process of photosynthesis, convert the inorganic energy of light into the organic elements of life directly.

Plants are the only life forms that feed themselves directly from light energy. And they make enough food for themselves and every other life form in the world that consumes food to live. The rest of us live off of what they produce naturally.

A Good Cut Heals

Gardening expert Lee Reich, Ph.D., opened an article he wrote for the Associated Press with the words, "Pruning can't help but wound a plant." So why would you do it?

We prune a plant to stimulate and promote its growth, health and well-being, and to increase its fruitfulness in the world. How does a wound stimulate growth? According to Reich, the wound we make marshals energy to the area around it. Once the cut is made, all the cells around it burst into activity; they work to prevent the spread of infection and seal off the wound. Instantly the plant enters a period of rapid respiration (hyperventilating) and rapid cell division. It's a natural process in which "antimicrobial chemicals are released and new cells grown to seal off the wound."

Plants have an uncanny ability to deal with wounds, whether caused by wind or storms or the gardener. But the way the cut is made is crucial. The same cut, if not done properly, can stunt the growth or even kill the plant, can cut off or limit the Life Force flowing to and through it.

Pruning is a skill. We learn the skill through the circumstances of our lives, and we practice it to develop ourselves as well as our work in the world. As we put ourselves through this process, we learn new methods of pruning that actually promote our health rather than stunt our growth.

A Steady Hand

Good pruning requires precision. A good cut is made with love, attention and expertise. Think about a surgical cut, as opposed to a tearing, ripping or breaking. It's much easier to recover from a hip replacement than a broken hip because the first is deliberate and controlled, while the second is random, uncontrolled and accidental.

Whether you pinch a bud, snip a stem, lop off a branch or saw off a major branch, pruning requires precision. It's much easier for a plant to recover from smaller cuts than bigger ones. A pinch is better than a snip; lopping is better than sawing. Cuts need to be clean.

Good pruning requires balance. Leaves are the food-producing tissue of the plant. One must cut off enough leaves to stimulate growth, create a pleasing shape and eliminate dead and diseased tissue, but not so many that the plant can't feed itself. It is a matter of wisely assisting the New Thing to develop, rather than forcing your will on it and keeping it under control.

In childhood we are all growth. We are insatiable in our desire to learn, and so impressionable. The discipline we received as children was not always loving, precise and clean. So, we sealed off our wounds to protect them. Scar tissue forms around those wounds, which causes us suffering still and blinds us to our choices. When you cut, when you prune, you must be present and aware. You must set boundaries for yourself, internal and external, to make the cut without cutting yourself off.

The Task of Pruning: Discipline

The task of Station 11 is discipline. *Discipline* has many definitions, but these are the most relevant to us:

- A branch of knowledge; a field of study or learning; an art form, such as dance, music or writing

- Training by instruction and practice that produces moral or mental development in a particular direction

- Systematic instruction of disciples as students in a craft or trade, or a code of conduct or "order," the enforcement of which is often regulated through punishment.

The word *discipline* may seem harsh at first, but discipline gives direction to our energy; it focuses it. *Discipline* basically refers to teaching, and to be disciplined means to be teachable.

If you think of discipline in terms of children, it's giving them the tools they need to learn to stand on their own. It's helping younger children develop the self-control they need to respond to the world, direct their decisions and live in society. As they get older, they integrate what they learn as self-discipline, enabling them to choose to practice techniques and methods in order to perfect them.

A disciple is a follower or learner of a mentor or other wise figure. People become disciples because they want to learn and master something new. And discipline serves the disciple in two ways:

1. Imparting knowledge (information, techniques, methods, etc.)

2. Directing away from what doesn't work.

To educate—to teach—is to lead out (from the Latin word *educare,* to lead forth) into the world. From what began as a seemingly unattainable longing, we have brought our dream this far, inches away from existence. We can either do this consciously, where we are simultaneously developing ourselves, or unconsciously, where we continue to work only with external forms. We have the choice: doing as an expression of our being, or just doing for its own sake. We can almost see now how it's going to happen, but not quite.

The Case for Trial and Error

Around the Wheel we've come, quarter by quarter, developing our relationship with the New Thing until we are almost ready to bring it Home:

- In Vision, we clarified and specified what we wanted.

- In Exploration, we gathered energy by overcoming obstacles.

- In Incubation, we agreed to incubate the seed of the New Thing.

- In Cultivation, we are making it real.

A big part of the creative process is trial and error, and Station 11 is where the product of the trials begins to take shape. So it's important to have a system by which to maximize resources (energy, time and money) by focusing on specific directions and responding to outcomes. How many times did Thomas Edison fail with his light bulb before he found the one that worked?

We have to make mistakes. We have to make choices. We have to set limits. We have to give boundaries to the New Thing and to ourselves in relation to it. We have to continually train ourselves to set our priorities by focusing on what works and letting go of what doesn't. This stimulates growth and increases energy. Otherwise, we end up wasting resources and exhausting ourselves, continuing to recycle what we've done before.

Here we begin to make the New Thing real. We're beginning to put this vision, which we have captured out of Chaos and nurtured from the seed, into space and time. You can imagine it will not necessarily be an easy fit. You're taking something formless, enormous and immense, your vision, your dream, and cramming it down into space and time. And it may be uncomfortable for a while.

As part of the process of Cultivation, discipline is: "No." "This way, not that." "Do it like this." "Follow me." It is compassion in action. Discipline is the Masculine energy of the Father, which separates the child from the nurturing Mother so it can survive in the world and contribute to society. This is the way of Nature.

What Discipline Looks Like

On the Kabbalah's Tree of Life, Discipline is Chokmah—the Masculine, the Father—wisdom. Chokmah is the ultimate Subject, the active principle behind the cosmos. It is similar to Shiva in Hindu mysticism. It is the primary (beginning) force in the creative process, driving the cosmos forward. It is something like fathering, but not exactly that.

Time's Up

About five years ago, when I was first developing the concepts of Nurturing and Pruning, I was having a coffee in a square in Villefranche-sur-Mer. I overheard a conversation between two men about 50 feet away. They were speaking loudly, one of the men in particular. His accent gave him away as an American, and I immediately thought, "Of course."

But this extremely audible man told the most amazing story. As a boy in the American Midwest, he was part of a family that raised homing pigeons. He talked about how the mother and father guard the nest. One parent stays with the babies while the other goes out to get food. They take turns. The babies grow to the point where they begin to fly. The parents go out with them. The mother always welcomes the young birds when they return to the nest. Then the man described a moment when there is a big shift. One day, the father takes Mom's place in the nest. When the young birds try to return, he bats them with his wing to say, "No. Time's up. Now it's time for you to go get your own family and make your own way in the world."

I love the idea that the mother and father share the nest. Nurturing and Pruning work hand in hand (or, in this case, wing in wing). We need to give ourselves space for where we are in the process, and we also need limits. Here in this Cultivation Quarter, we have to learn to balance the Feminine and receptive with the Masculine and active energies in a new way.

Why Is This Station Important?

Filmmaker Orson Welles was quoted as saying, "The enemy of art is the absence of limitations." And this is exactly where we are. What we want to grow in our lives will not mature if we do not make space for it and set limits to direct its growth. Life lived without guidelines is confusing and troubling. Limits are the framework of refinement.

The I Ching, a classic Chinese wisdom text, tells us, "Voluntarily chosen limits empower your growth." This means taking responsibility for what you have chosen so that you have a clear idea of where your energies are to be aimed. How we set those limits makes all the difference. The I Ching offers us guidelines:

- Determine your own limits rather than take them from others.

- Be gentle in the process rather than harsh.

- Be patient and allow yourself to progress gradually.

- Balance discipline with moderation and pleasure.

Discipline Without Judgment

Just as Nurturing needs to be informed by the Masculine, so Pruning needs to be informed by the Feminine, done with compassion and balance.

Gurumayi, whose ashram in India is described in Elizabeth Gilbert's memoir, *Eat, Pray, Love*, notes that, "Discipline and punishment have become interchangeable for many people. … When people have this fear [of punishment], instead of wanting to improve, they want to rebel. … Instead of seeing hope in the path of discipline, they see pain and torment."

Most of us have this resistance to discipline embedded in us because of our pasts. Either we are harsh with ourselves, working ruthlessly to overcome our own self-judgment, or we blame and rebel against others. In either case, we lose the value of the teaching.

But when our relationship with Life is not harsh and punishing, we recognize that Life disciplines us in love, and we respond by making loving choices. Wherever our weaknesses are—whether we are too sensitive, get discouraged and lose faith in ourselves, or are overconfident—we must push into that. We have to work with our weaknesses and make different choices in order to get the job done.

My experience of this station is that there is pushing, there is cutting, there is setting new limits in order for the New Thing to be more, do more and be clearer than in the past. I have to do things differently. Sometimes it's painful. Sometimes I cry tears. But on the other side of the tears is an opening, a clarity, an awareness I didn't have before.

What Is Required of You?

We must integrate what we need in order to be able to have what we want. Our habits, the ways we've always done things, got us the results we have today. And that may be fine; they may be excellent results overall. But Life is always evolving, like water, flowing and seeking the next place to flow. Living life is the process of refinement; what brought us to this place in the Wheel, and what will take us around it again, is the desire for something more.

In order to keep growing you must cut away dead and diseased parts: the unhealthy beliefs, thoughts, actions and attitudes, the ways of doing things that don't support you in what you're committed to. You must eliminate:

- What doesn't nurture you

- What is not aligned with your vision

- Things that waste your time

- What no longer fits (externally and internally): relationships, jobs, ideologies, activities

- Opportunities that pull you off track

- Destructive and/or energy-draining habits

Fulfillment does not come through the senses alone. Without the connection to Essence, the senses leave us always with a feeling of wanting more. What nourishes us is the experience of uniting heaven and earth.

Sometimes Pruning Means Training

Pruning may require you to learn techniques and methods, practice new skills, seek and listen to guidance and wise counsel, and make mistakes, the absence of which reveals a lack of reach.

When I was in my late 20s in Chicago, I was very involved in music. I was studying singing, guitar and theory, and had just begun performing at open-mic venues around town. My greatest deterrent was stage fright, which rose up from a deep well of self-judgment. When the lights were in my face and I was on stage in front of people I did not know, I sometimes forgot entire phrases of my own songs.

But through consistent training with good instructors, I learned tricks and, more importantly, methods to see me through. The most important of these was practice. If I practiced playing each song until my fingers went through the motions without my brain, then nerves were not a problem. My body knew what to do, even when my mind forgot completely.

You can see those who have discipline and those who don't. You can see it in the way they move, the intentionality of their actions. It is not rigidity necessarily, but something that reveals their training, their fluidity and familiarity with the task. The skill is embedded in the muscles and cells.

A Pot for All Seasons

Sometimes Pruning means choosing a new pot. Without self-examination, changing situations that don't fit can make things worse. But sometimes change is required to make space for your own roots. It's only when your roots reach deep into the Earth of your life that you will really receive the nourishment you're longing for.

The Experience of Pruning: Fatigue

Pruning—not only your project but also yourself—is hard. It wouldn't be hard if you continued to create the same old thing. But this is new; you must become new. It hurts to cut as well as to be cut. And it's tiring.

The Wound That Heals

Poet Robert Bly was one of America's leaders in the men's movement. He did a great deal of work around the concept of wounding and how it affects men in particular. But the truth is, it affects us all. Bly has said, "Where a man's wound is, that is where his genius will be." It is out of our wounds that our gifts to the world come.

I've seen this again and again in my life. The places where I am wounded, the places I feel vulnerable are the places where I have the most to give because I've been opened to Life there. If I can back

off my self-defensiveness around that long enough, Life will flow through me there, not only to me but also to the world around me. What I write from that depth—whether music, articles or blogs—touches people at that depth as well. What has transformed me has the greatest power to transform others.

I like to say, "Where your treasure is, there will your wound be also." If you think about it, our capacity to be wounded occurs in places where something means a lot to us. If you think about relationships, it is the people we love who can hurt us most, and by contrast these are the people we tend to hurt the most as well, because we are most vulnerable there. These are the places where we stand to lose the most.

Discipline is a gift to the child, the New Thing or the immature within us. We all may certainly resist, just as Daniel in *The Karate Kid* resents having to go through the motions of his training. Like his training program, it is the way of practice: doing what is required of you when you don't see how it will give you what you want and you don't want to do it. Then, one day, after obeying for days and days and weeks and months, something happens, and boom! Suddenly you realize you've got it. The skill is there when you need it—the skill you didn't know you were learning.

If you look at your work, growth, a greater facility with skills, always comes when you stretch into something you didn't want to do, didn't think you could do. And this is where support is so important. We want to isolate ourselves at those times, but we need someone to believe in us when we don't believe in ourselves, someone to remind us who we really are.

When it comes to this principle, I always remember my business partner in my early 20s. Marvin Mews was a television producer/director, I was a writer/producer, and so we partnered for a time to offer our services to companies in Chicago. Marvin had contracted with a client to produce a business meeting, and we were supposed to be there together. Something came up at the last minute and he was not able to make it. So he sent me on my own. He was confident I could do it, but I was not.

There I was at the hotel, and when problems came up, I became scared. I can remember calling him in tears from the hotel room, and he simply said, "I would not have sent you if I didn't think you could do it." His belief in me saw me through. He didn't let me back down in the way I would have on my own. He believed even when I didn't. So I did it. I managed it. And I grew.

We all need people in our lives who remind us of who we truly are. By pushing us beyond our comfort zones, they dispel our broken, faulty opinions of ourselves. They are our teachers. That is the role we play in each other's lives.

But even more than people, perhaps, we need this view of Life. We need to come to trust the process of being alive so much that we know it would not have brought us here if we were not capable of handling it. Even when we don't believe it or feel it and certainly can't prove it, we are changed by the process.

The Alchemy of Creativity

Alchemy is an ancient path of spiritual purification and transformation. Evolving within mystical traditions of both the East and West, alchemy presents a system for connecting with the Divine through esoteric symbols embedded in everyday life.

In the West, alchemy can be traced to Ancient Egypt. During medieval and Renaissance times, it spread through the Western world and, as noted earlier, functioned on the levels of the mundane and the spiritual. In the 1920s, Carl Jung explained alchemical literature in psychological terms, as manifestations of a "collective unconscious."

I think of creativity as an alchemy of its own, the art of working with what's out there in order to transform ourselves. The raw material of our lives—our circumstances, our experience in any form of creation—is the base metal we transform into gold. The Wheel of Creativity is based on the idea that we can use whatever is happening in our lives symbolically to understand life at a deeper level, and we can learn to use the process to connect directly with Source.

Through the process of not liking what's out there, wanting it to be different or better, we require ourselves to do things differently. And that transforms us and clarifies who we are through the process. We are taken down a path that leads us to produce the results in our lives authentically. We produce them as a natural expression of who we are rather than as something we have to force.

At its essence, the creative process is not an outer process at all. These living arts in which we engage, like alchemy, are the external game we play through which we do our real work: creating ourselves. Like martial artists, we sculpt our bodies and our minds, not with a chisel and blade but with discipline and practice.

Supporting Your Mind, Body, Spirit and Heart

So how do you take care of yourself here, when you are going through the process of wounding? How do you cope when you need to wound your dream to make it real?

Everything we do is an opportunity to detach from the outer circumstances and return to our center, to transform what's out there by returning to ourselves. The practice of consciously working with that focuses the energy you channel, and that is how you create what is next. Whether you're sitting, walking, dancing, eating or riding the bus, you can engage in a simple practice of moving your awareness between the outside Forms of your life and the Essence of it at the center. So, everything is an opportunity for meditation.

The Reward of Pruning: Mastery

We have a habit of seeing life as something to get through. If I can just get through this, then everything will settle down and I'll be able to enjoy my life again. But did you ever notice that life doesn't work this way? We can get along okay on will power and force for a while. But the results come from a different place.

What does discipline look like? It is getting up day after day and wrestling with the problem, writing the words, practicing the moves, reworking the numbers, until finally it all comes into view.

According to Gurumayi, enduring happiness is born of restraint: "[T]he practice of discipline is the mainstay of purification. As long as the mind is not channeled in a positive direction, it compulsively paints one dreadful picture after another—of your past, your future, your character, and the world you live in."

There's no getting around it—discipline is ultimately self-control.

The moment of truth occurs when we reach our limits. That's when change becomes possible. Then it is time to re-Source ourselves with our own Life Force and life process. The key to this process is to learn to master the moments of growth, when things are tough, learn to find your center, spread out your roots and draw your nourishment from Earth, from your own connection with Life.

Discipline is rehabituation. It is developing new habits and new ways of responding. And it may also involve shifting things around in your world if you can. But that's not always possible to the degree that you would like. So you have to learn to prune your thoughts, feelings and reactions to promote your own growth.

A New Way of Life

Only when the young seagull finally steps off the rooftop does he put himself in the way of mastery, does it become possible for him to perfect what he's made for. It's a new way of life. No longer is he limited by his feet, or by gravity; a whole new world is available.

Pruning brings greater blossoming, greater fruitfulness and greater fullness. Plants really fill out when you cut them back to the base. Each plant needs to be cut a different way that is unique to it. Pruning also brings more space, which is something we all need now.

Mastery comes not only for the New Thing but for you as well. Not only do you get the book written, or the patent approved, but also whatever inside you wants to give up along the way is confronted, expressed and moved through. You're creating the New Thing, and it's creating you.

This process of creation is the path to personal transformation. By the very fact that we take it on to create a new way of life uniquely ours, we put ourselves in position to change, because we put ourselves in position to have to change. Then we not only discover what we're here for but find ourselves living what our nature is asking of us. So the fulfillment of what we long for requires some faith, and some choices.

When we're young and developing, we're open to mentors and guides, but as we get older, we have to learn by practicing ourselves. When we reach adulthood, nothing can come to us except by our own choice. And Pruning is the process by which we develop those skills. We have to choose. We have to choose the support; we have to choose to show up.

So many young people today are growing up without limits, without the strong guidance of the Masculine in their lives. As has been stated for centuries, from ancient texts such as the *I Ching* to contemporary scientific research, without limits, New Things grow up wild.

Structuring a Purposeful Life

As a teenager, my husband trained dogs. He and his black Labrador, Helga of Thornber (affectionately known as Pod), were a team. They trained five or six times a day, heading off into the woods to explore or hunt (an activity my husband long ago gave up). He has always said that a trained dog is a happy dog.

"I think dogs like to please; they enjoy showing off, being trained to do things. It gives them a role and a sense of purpose. A dog enjoys a relationship with his master in which he feels useful, is in control of himself, and is successful. You can see it.

"Pod had really basic instincts. One night when we were out shooting, we were waiting for the ducks to come over. The ground was frozen hard, and she dug a patch to make the ground soft, she patted it around and then curled up in it to get warm. That was all done by instinct.

"On the other hand, dogs instinctively do not put their heads under water; but Pod learned how to do so through training. In order to train her, I put straw inside a long gray sock and threw it out into the field. She went out to fetch it, and I trained her to pick it up, bring it back, walk behind me and give it to me before she sat down. When it went into the stream, she would actually go into the stream to get it.

"Training dogs helps them focus, and it makes them happy. Untrained dogs have no function in life; they are just trying their best to survive. I don't think they understand that there is purpose, reward and love. Discipline gives structure and boundaries to life. Without those, things in life tend to be meaningless."

Projects, like animals and people, can grow wild, get out of hand and exhaust us by their constant pulling if they are not given limits to grow within.

What Life Is Asking of You

What are you committed to? What are you willing to bring to the table to change the results you're producing? How far are you willing to take it?

The creative journey doesn't just have to be about your own life. It could be that Life is calling you to create something more in the world, in your country, for your family, for society. In fact, it probably is.

By the age of eight, Emmanuel Jal was a child soldier in southern Sudan. At five, he saw his village burned, his aunt and sisters raped and his mother killed in the war that ripped his country apart. Unable to read and write, he was sent to "school" where he was trained to fight. And he was a soldier for the next five years.

When Jal was 13, a young British aid worker named Emma McCune found him, rescued him and gave him a second life. That's not the happy ending we'd like for our story, however. McCune was killed soon after in a car accident, leaving Jal to find his own way on the streets of Nairobi, Kenya. From there, Jal took one step after another, following the journey of his extraordinary life to become the hip-hop star he is today, described by singer, musician and songwriter Peter Gabriel as having "the potential of a young Bob Marley."

Jal went on to found Gua Africa, a UK-based charity whose mission is to help individuals, families and communities overcome the effects of war and poverty. He is raising money to build a school in southern Sudan that he calls Emma Academy.

With music as his "weapon of choice," Emmanuel Jal is doing the real work of the artist in society, transforming his suffering into light. But this work is not for the artist alone. It is for us all. For we all suffer. And the world is in need of light.

Mastery is the reward of this station. And Mastery occurs because you've done the work. Once the work is done, it's time to get back on the train and move to the next and final station of the Wheel, Harvest. From Harvest you will take the New Thing Home, finished, ready to serve the community, and feed the world, born of the very Hunger that launched you on your journey.

A Story of Pruning

Mike Birch, Jazz Trumpeter
Current City: Petersfield, England

"It's a hard taskmaster, jazz. It really is. But I love it dearly."

I met Mike Birch in 2011 near our home in England. He runs a weekly jazz workshop at the local arts center for the love of it. It's a place where musicians like me can go to play, experiment, make mistakes and grow. And that's just the kind of guy Mike is. His story illustrates the power of Discipline to release the true spirit of creativity in whatever you do.

KATHERINE ROBERTSON-PILLING: Of all the directions to take in life, how did you choose jazz trumpet?

MIKE BIRCH: Whenever I listened to bands, my ears always swiveled toward the trumpet player. When I was about 20, I went to see the great trumpet player Ray Nance, who supported Duke Ellington, at a little gig in Hampshire one Sunday lunchtime. It had never occurred to me to be a musician. But suddenly, hearing this guy playing the trumpet, I thought, "That's fantastic. I've gotta be that guy standing on stage, making that sound with his horn."

A couple of years later, in 1967, I left Portsmouth and took myself to London. I worked as a technical officer for London University, sort of a scientific odd-job man, building different types of equipment: electronic, electrical and mechanical bits of hardware.

And I decided to have a go with the trumpet and see what would happen. I bought a beat-up old horn and took solo lessons from people who were pretty good. There were no jazz courses in England back in those days, so I went to the UK's first summer jazz course at Clapham Common, run by some British greats. The tutors were fantastic. It was an eye-opener of a week, not only to how bad I was, but how dedicated they were, and the fact that you only get better with a lot of hard work; it won't

just happen. It made me practice more and properly, and to work to pass my classical exams.

I got a better horn and found a very fine trumpet teacher, a black American guy called Gerald Abbé, who taught classical trumpet and was quite a jazzer. It was the best of both worlds for me. I've been playing for 45 years now.

I got early retirement 10 years ago, and I've really done nothing but music since: writing, arranging it, running classes and workshops, and I've got two bands that I play in.

The thing that really excites me about playing and listening to jazz is the improvisation element, because it's the only art form—unless you count standup comedy—where you actually observe the creative process. A jazz soloist is creating it in his mind as he's playing it in front of you. And that is an absolutely fascinating, riveting, wonderful thing to be able to do.

You can be well warmed up, and the trumpet's feeling good, and the band's swinging, and everything feels great—and it's just okay. And at other times, you've got a hangover and a cold coming on—and you play great. When I know I'm playing my best is when all of a sudden it seems to be doing it by itself. It happens to me about twice a year. All the work, that day, that moment, the form, the music, your practice and the listening, it all comes together and it's all clicked in place. And then you put the horn on your face, and suddenly it's there. It is very odd, that it suddenly comes from somewhere else. The really great guys, they're like that all the time.

The other big demand in jazz is the self-discipline to never repeat yourself, which is practically impossible. "I played that in the last tune; I mustn't do that again." But you do, because it falls under the fingers. But that discipline of never repeating, being fresh and original all the time, is terrifying; I don't know how else to say it. It's a hard taskmaster, jazz. It really is. But I love it dearly.

KRP: Why do you love it?

MB: I like the immediacy, the excitement, the fact that, when the guys are really firing, it really taps into their total being somehow. You can hear that. They are just being themselves, and presenting you with their life, transmuted through musical notes. That sounds a bit airy-fairy, but that's the thing to aim at all the time.

KRP: You're talking about telling the truth, and not hiding behind a façade, which is what we do in our normal lives.

MB: It's like nakedness, really, which should be nothing to hide behind. It should just be you coming out through the music and hopefully touching other people at an emotional level. And that is powerful stuff.

KRP: What fascinates me most about the creative process is how a human being can take the forms in the world—we could say, notes—can take them in and send them out again in a completely different way. And in that process, they transform and are transformed too. Have you experienced a way that music has saved you or seen you through difficult times?

MB: Without a doubt. When I was married the first time, we didn't like each other. I didn't quite like my job, and I hated the people I worked for. I had a terrible commute, with [subways] not working much of the time. I was living in a grotty flat. Everything was cracked! And the only thing I could hang onto, and what to some extent saved my sanity, was the fact that I was beginning to get deeply involved in jazz. It gave me a sense of purpose: Just get better at this. It was very good for me. I don't know what I would've done without it.

KRP: Absolutely. I think that's what art is, the transformation of the muck of life into beauty.

MB: Yeah. That's a good phrase. I've seen it in other guys I've met. Being a musician or being involved in music, it's just having this other sort of self-discipline, to practice every day no matter what. I've met quite a few guys who said that it saved their bacon, intellectually or mentally, many times. It's not uncommon, though it's a difficult thing to talk about in a funny sort of way.

I believe in the power of jazz particularly to uplift people. To be involved in some crappy little pub gig in southwest London, where obviously nothing really comes out of it, but somebody comes up to you and says, "That's really great. I really enjoyed that." And I think, "God, I've actually done somebody some good." It's powerfully uplifting for me.

KRP: I hear you use the word discipline a lot.

MB: Yeah. It concentrates the mind. In the really early days playing the trumpet, I'd practice when I wanted to and not when I didn't. And that is just rubbish. This morning I woke up a bit late, felt a bit dozey, and didn't really want to practice. But now, every time I think like that, I make myself do some trumpet practice. When you want to do it, it's easy. When you don't want to do it, you do it anyway. It's gotta be done, and you've got to do it virtually every day.

KRP: You admired Thelonius Monk.

MB: Yeah. He had absolutely no clichés. I saw him play every time he came to the UK. There would be great stuff coming out of the piano; it was still his solo, and then he just stopped. If the creative process stopped, he would stop, with his hands on his knees, just sort of nodding slightly, waiting for the process to kick in again. He wouldn't just fill in with some nice little runs. And that requires gigantic discipline and bravery. The space was always as important as his musical notes, and the tension in that is fantastic.

12

STATION 12 Harvest

Often have I heard you say, as if speaking in sleep,
"he who works in marble, and finds the shape of his own soul in the stone,
is nobler than he who ploughs the soil.
And he who seizes the rainbow to lay it on a cloth in the likeness of man, is more than he who makes
the sandals for our feet."
But I say, not in sleep but in the over-wakefulness of noontide,
that the wind speaks not more sweetly to the giant oaks
than to the least of all the blades of grass;
And he alone is great who turns the voice of the wind into a song
made sweeter by his own loving.
Work is love made visible.

KAHLIL GIBRAN

On the Platform in Station 12

Station 12 is Harvest, the final station in the Wheel. Whatever you've been given, whatever you began this journey with, here is where you bring it Home. Here you harvest the crop you've grown. The name of this station honors the full-ness of the journey of your life and your creative response to it:

- The longing that you felt in your heart, the acknowledgement of that longing

- The willingness to go along with Life where it took you

- The return Home with something you didn't have before

Harvest is a compound word, derived from the Old English *haer* and *fest*. *Haer* has an Indo-European root in the world *kerp*, which means to gather, pluck or harvest. It is comparable to the Latin word *carpere*, made famous in the phrase *Carpe diem* (Seize the day). And *fest* means feast or celebration. So the word *harvest* originally described the celebration of the gathering of mature crops from the field.

The word *harvest* has long been linked to autumn and to the full moon nearest to the autumn equi-nox, which is known as the harvest moon. Until the 16th century, *harvest* referred to the entire autumn season. Later, as farmers left their agricultural roots to live in towns, its meaning became more closely linked to the reaping of crops, and the season took on the names autumn or fall.

Today *harvest* is both a verb and a noun, describing an activity and a product. To harvest is to gather or reap anything, from grain and fruit to fish and timber.

In The Wheel of Creativity, Harvest occurs in Station 12, and it completes the Cultivation Quarter. The Harvest of Station 12 is internal as well as external. It is the harvest of yourself and the New Thing you have created. It is the fulfillment of your creative act of transformation, giving form to a mysterious longing that did not have form before.

Station 12 is a place of gratitude—for the harvest, for the journey, for the way of ignorance through which you have passed in the discovery of something new, for the abundance you have met on the road, which has shown you your own grandeur.

Station 12 is the threshold that leads you back Home, where life again is stable and familiar. Passage through this station opens you up again to your world, with something more to share. The community you left needs your contribution. Once back there, you experience how you have changed and how it has changed in your absence.

In Station 12 you complete the entire creative cycle by sharing the fruit you have grown with the world and by celebrating the harvest.

Mirroring the origins of the word, Harvest has two parts, which are connected but experienced distinctly. Part one is a definitive cut, and part two is the celebration of that cut. Both are required to complete this station.

Harvest in Greek Mythology

Of all the deities in ancient Greece, Demeter, the goddess of the harvest, was considered the most generous and empathetic to the human experience. Demeter (called Ceres by the Romans) made the land fertile, taught humanity to cultivate the land and harvest its produce, and rewarded human efforts with harvest-time abundance. While the other gods and goddesses kept their distance from humanity, Demeter was involved with it daily.

Demeter is said to be responsible for the seasons. When her daughter, Persephone, was abducted and held in the underworld by Hades, Demeter searched the world for her, refusing to nourish the earth. Without her attention, the earth (which had been continually fertile up until then) stopped supporting life, so animals did not multiply, vegetation withered and human beings began to die. Even when Persephone was ultimately reunited with Demeter for eight months a year, she refused to nourish the earth for the other four months, and these remained infertile. This was the beginning of what we know as winter.

Demeter nourishes the earth and teaches humanity how to work with it in order to nourish ourselves. Ancient Greeks defined in her their awareness of human dependency on the earth to live. For millennia, traditional cultures around the world tended the earth with respect and appreciation of this relationship.

Man Versus Machine

Today we live in a highly mechanical society. Harvesting is done with huge machines, and the people sitting in them are hardly connected to the earth. Things have been made so efficient that we have lost touch with the earth and our place on it. But efficiency and effectiveness are not the same thing. Either we act as agents of advancement, or we fight Nature and destroy that which keeps us alive.

Honoring Our Connection With the Earth

What can we learn from traditional knowledge that can affect our lives today? Let's look at Native American culture.

Until recently, many non-Native Americans viewed all Native American populations as supporting themselves solely through hunting, fishing and gathering, and living on land that was natural and wild. But in its final report to Congress in 1996, the Sierra Nevada Ecosystem Project revealed that Native Americans commonly used a variety of sophisticated horticultural techniques to manage and enhance the fertility of the land. In fact, the techniques they used are still considered highly successful for effective land management, some 100 centuries later.

While today we tend to assume that human impact on the land is always negative, this was not always the case. For more than 10,000 years, native people in the Sierra Nevada managed biotic resources intensively as part of their overall sustainability plan, and their influence on ecology and the environment was significant.

They were strategic about their harvesting methods in a way that promoted diversity, variety and crop yields, because they worked directly with the life in the earth. They respected it, they honored it, they saw themselves in relation to it, as stewards of it, rather than dominating and industrializing it as modern people have done.

It is estimated that in late prehistoric times, about 100,000 humans lived in the Sierra Nevada, so their impact on the land was enormous. And the report by the Sierra Nevada Ecosystem Project shows that their departure from the land there and the loss of their influence has left a vacuum:

"There is currently an ecological . . . disequilibrium . . . in the Sierra resulting from the departure of Native American influences. The recent decline in biotic diversity, species extirpation and endangerment, human encroachment into fire-type plant communities (e.g., chaparral), and greatly increased risk of catastrophic fires are but symptoms of this disequilibrium."

The report strongly recommended that Native American traditional knowledge be incorporated into ecosystem management policies and programs.

Man Is Not a Machine

Why all this talk of crops and harvests when the vast majority of us do not grow and harvest our own food? We are part of the ecosystem. Our influence is a given. Whether our impact—positive or negative—is conscious or unconscious is up to us.

The methods used by the Native Americans in the Sierra Nevada replenished the earth. They made the crops stronger and more resistant to external forces like weather and pests. But we have so lost touch with our relationship with the earth. They knew their place in the process of Life.

The creative process is inherent in our lives, and Nature gives continual evidence that even the smallest contribution has a huge impact. A worker bee will spend its entire life making half a teaspoon of honey. To fill a jar with a little over one pound of honey would require an entire hive to fly almost 56,000 miles and visit two million flowers. But bees do more for us than sweeten our food and drink. They pollinate 70 out of the 100 crops that provide 90 percent of the world's food.

The work of The Wheel of Creativity seeks to make the process of creation conscious. And that returns us to our awareness of our role in that process. So it's not about whether what I have to offer is good enough. It's that I take my place in the circle of Life. And if even one of us is not there, we're missed. And if my gift is not presented with all the others, the abundance of the harvest is less. Take your place. Follow your true nature. Live the adventure.

The Web of Life

For Native Americans, the traditional agricultural methods practiced by many early aboriginal people were grounded in a unified ethic that transcended cultural and political boundaries.

Native Americans saw humans as part of the natural system, rather than above it, and they taught that because we are related to all life forms, we are to coexist and interact with them respectfully. This ethic was a founding principle of native society, expressed and reinforced through every custom.

Each person in the society was recognized as having an important role to play in the health of the community. And tending to the land was an important aspect of that.

Taking Your Place in the Web

Echoing the principles so beautifully embodied in native culture, The Wheel of Creativity turns on the idea that your place in the world, as a human being, is as an agent of change. You are here to transform. It is your nature.

Our task as evolving humans is to ensure, wherever possible, that our intervention in the natural system produces a harmonious result. To do this we must curb our greed and gluttony for immediate gratification and measure our results instead in terms of the world we will leave to our children and theirs.

We are part of the ecosystem. Our influence is a given. Whether our impact—positive or negative—is conscious or unconscious is up to us.

Harvest is the final step in the process by which we assist the evolution of our species, and it is required. Without Harvest, the entire creative process stalls. It is not enough to play with creative energies and enjoy the process, though there is value in that as well. But the creative product is the ultimate purpose of the process. Until your book or CD or widget or theory is in the hands of people who can use it, it does the world little good.

The process itself has merit, and there are times in the cycle to detach from the product and just be in the flow. But the process alone is not complete. The harvest is not in. We are not here just to play with our gifts; we are here to use them to contribute to the world.

Don't Quit Before the Miracle

In *Sacred Path Cards*, author Jamie Sams writes that the Iroquois teaching called the Field of Plenty describes a vast cornucopia covering the earth through which Great Mystery provides the world with what it needs. All new things—solutions to problems, medical cures and educational advances, everything that would exist throughout time—first came into being as thought-forms or ideas. The idea gives way to its development in physical form. When there is any need on earth, the solution already exists here. Human beings have only to tap into this eternal resource to bring them into physical form.

This same principle of creation applies to us all:

teachers, doctors, artists, dancers, musicians, homemakers, entrepreneurs, architects, cooks, therapists, inventors, scientists, poets, journalists, waiters, computer geeks, priests and salespeople.

Every one of us is an inventor, an agent of evolutionary change. Life is continuously knocking on our doors with new ideas. The knock comes in the Hunger that pulls us from the comforts of Home and calls us to a journey to something better. Following that call makes us collaborators in the creative evolution of Life.

The New Thing that we produce in that process is unique to us. And at the end of the game, what it is or how much it costs is really unimportant. What is vital for our personal well-being and that of the planet is that we answer the call that comes to us. For then, we sow that which nourishes—first ourselves and then our communities. Our willingness in this station to finally make the cut and let it go to these very communities gives purpose and meaning to our entire life experience.

Life in Station 12

As the final station in the final quarter, Station 12 completes your journey around The Wheel of Creativity with regard to this one New Thing. You have moved through four elements: Air, Fire, Water and Earth. Weaving your way between form and formlessness as you circumnavigate the Wheel, you have integrated their energies within yourself and formed something with them in your world. Now you are in a place of bringing it home to the tribe.

Station 12 concludes your sojourn in the Cultivation Quarter, where the nuts and bolts are put in place. Nurturing and Pruning—the mothering and fathering energies—are worked together here. The prototype is accepted, uncensored. The manuscript is saved and then edited. The solar theory is tested and refined. Processes are mastered, results are achieved, and in Station 12, the product is interpreted into the language of the marketplace.

The Task of Harvest: Release

Harvest is an opportunity to share, but timing of the Harvest is very important. If the fruit is picked too early, it will be small and bitter. If it's picked too late, it's likely to be tasteless and dry. To be effective in its purpose in the world, the fruit must be cut at the peak of its juiciness and flavor.

This is true for us as well. When we guard and keep close that which is so precious to us because we don't want it to be hurt or damaged out there, our contribution passes its prime.

We all have feelings about releasing our precious New Thing to the world. You might feel pride. Or regret. Or reluctance. You might prefer to give something less than your all, holding something back. But in this station, you release the New Thing into the world so that you both can take your places there. "Okay, here it is now. What works? What doesn't work?" And that is challenging. Letting go and turning it over to someone else is challenging. You are releasing control.

The How of the Harvest

One Native American practice was the aboriginal idea of selective harvesting. When natives picked wild plants, they took from every seventh plant, leaving plenty for those who followed them. In farming, they would harvest certain rows and allow others to grow. This practice encourages certain features of the plants, which leads to evolutionary advancement of the species. It actually makes the plant grow fuller and richer and be more productive.

It is not just *that* you harvest, but *how* you harvest that produces your results. The sustainable harvest is:

- Conscious versus unconscious

- Consistent versus sporadic

- Responsive versus controlling

- Intentional versus inadvertent

- Collaborative versus dominating

- Sustainable versus sweeping

The Definitive Cut

Cutting is the first step. For the final session of one of my 12-week creative process groups, I cut a lemon from my tree. I had had two lemons on my tree for months, and I had not wanted to cut them. I had an idea of what I was going to do with those lemons, and it had to be perfect, just right. One year I made limoncello because it would make the lemons last. But this particular year, I just left them on the tree way past the time they should have been harvested. I wanted to save them for a special occasion.

And that final night of group seemed just the occasion I was looking for. There is something final about that cut. Once made, the fruit cannot be reconnected. It is not done lightly. In the end, my lemon was still juicy and delicious. But in cultivated crops it must be done, or the crop will pass its peak and rot in the field.

This has been a struggle for me with The Wheel of Creativity as well. Coming to the place where I had the courage to commit to the idea and put it out there has taken time. As in Gestation, Harvest has a season. It can't be rushed, but it must be observed and acted on.

Harvest is the end of the season of labor in the fields. It is the gathering of mature crops from their growing places. It marks the end of the growing cycle. Here you reap what you have sown, cutting it from its connection with the earth. It is required, not only so that you may eat, but also so that the crop, the fruit, does not die in its place. It is the act of cutting the New Thing at its peak, at the height of its ability to nourish.

What is required of you in the Harvest station is a definitive cut. When orchard growers harvest their fruit, they do not pull the fruit from the tree. It is too hard on the plant. The healthier method is to cut the fruit, as close to the fruit as possible. The cut is clean and quick and gentle. This takes the fruit and leaves the plant without trauma.

In this Harvest, we are the plants. So we need to hold lightly what we're growing for the world, not get too attached to it or take it too seriously. And when the time comes, we need to let it go, making space for the next fruit to take its place on the tree.

In the throes of creation, we may find ourselves acting as if this is the only thing we're ever going to bring into the world. We all fear the horrible fate of the "one-hit wonder." But no matter how much space is left on the branch when that fruit is cut, there will be another branch, another fruit to follow. Only when we block the flow of Life through us does the next fruit not appear.

The Experience of Harvest: Satisfaction

Harvest is the process of loving and letting go, and the experience of satisfaction comes at the end of the station. Each of us passes through this station many, many times in a lifetime. Each time you recognize a need in the world, hear the longing of your own heart and respond, you step into your place in the world as a creator. And the process itself manifests your longing, making it concrete in your own life. It is a journey of discovery and invention:

- For an entrepreneur, this is the product launch.
- For a scientist, it is solving a mystery.
- For a young couple, it might be moving into their own home.
- For a single woman (or man), it could be marrying their soul mate.
- For an architect, it is the day the doors of the building open.

But the Harvest need not just be a change in external circumstances. It can also be a change in your relationship with those circumstances:

- For someone struggling with depression, it could be the shift to a new experience of appreciating the moment.

- For someone battling compulsive eating, it could be the willingness to make a different choice.
- For a dejected retiree, it could be discovering a long-suppressed passion he never had time for.
- For someone who can't find a job, it could be the courage to start her own business.

Station 12 is as much about harvesting a new way of being as it is about harvesting something outside yourself. It is passed through with awareness, gratitude and humility.

Celebration!

When the journey is complete, then comes the celebration! This is part two of the Harvest. Typically, the harvest is the most labor-intensive activity of farming. When it is done, everyone is ready to blow the whistle, shut down the production lines and throw a party. So it's not surprising that festivals often accompany the harvest in cultures all around the world.

The Harvest Festival

The harvest festival has been a part of cultures around the world for as long as human beings have grown crops. It occurs when the labor in the fields is complete and the harvest is in the barn. The celebrations bring families and communities together, each culture celebrating in its own unique ways. But across cultures, harvest festivals have certain things in common. There is much feasting on foods freshly gathered from the fields. There is time off to rest and replenish. There are games, contests, music and dance, romance and togetherness. It is a time for thanks, appreciation and celebration.

- The Chinese Mid-Autumn Festival, or Moon Festival, occurs in September or October. It is celebrated as a public holiday in China, Vietnam and Taiwan, typically with moon cakes, incense, paper lanterns and romance.

- In the Iranian calendar, the September equinox marks the first day of *Mehr*, or Libra. The festival called *Jashne Mehragan* is celebrated on the 10th day of the month *Mehr* and usually corresponds to the day when farmers gather their crops. It is a festival of sharing, love and gratitude to God for food through the winter.

- In Ghana, West Africa, the Ga people "hoot at hunger" in their *Homowo* festival. With processions, dance and feasting, they celebrate their survival through long periods of famine by helping each other.

- Throughout the year in India, the harvest is celebrated in festivals bearing different names in different regions. A few are *Makara Sankranti, Thai Pongal, Uttarayana, Lohri* and *Magh Bihu* or *Bhogali Bihu* in January; *Holi* in February to March; and *Onam* in August to September. People set aside days for feasting, games, music and dance, decorating cattle and a ritual of throwing colored powders on each other.

And of course in America, the Plymouth colonists' first harvest, in 1621, is still celebrated each year on Thanksgiving Day. On the final Thursday of November, families come together to give thanks and feast in their homes. Originally called Harvest Home by the colonists, this festival actually sprang from the Wampanoag Indian harvest festival, which combined feasting, dancing and ceremonial games. Often included in these festivals was a "giveaway" in which families gave personal possessions to others in the community who were in need.

In fact, the first American harvest itself was a kind of giveaway, as the native peoples assisted the new arrivals with corn for planting, as well as knowledge, tools and experience in a climate and land they did not know.

One of my personal favorites among harvest festivals is the Jewish Festival of Ingathering, called *Sukkot*, which occurs each year at harvest time. American business coach Suzy Girard has celebrated *Sukkot* many times through the years:

"My experience of the holiday is grounded by three words: abundance, nature, gratitude. Judaism is very focused on the interplay between human and nature. *Sukkot* is very focused on the concept of harvesting and giving thanks for what we reap and how it nurtures our family. Around the world, families come together either at their local synagogue or in their own backyards in order to build a shelter from branches or palm fronds and to pray and eat under the shelter. My interpretation of this ritual is that it is to remind us that we are Mother Nature's tenants and the beneficiaries of her bounty."

What I especially love about *Sukkot* is the reminder that the harvest is a time for feeding ourselves. We gather together and we take for ourselves. We must take time to nourish ourselves in order to nourish others.

Many of us are conditioned to skip over the celebrations of our achievements, to check them off our lists and move on. We harvest the New Thing and send it out into the world without taking from it to feed ourselves. This is a disservice to ourselves and the creative Life Force, which gave us both Hunger and Harvest. Only when we take for ourselves is the creative process sustainable.

The Reward of Harvest: Purpose

The reward of Station 12 is purpose. Harvest gives purpose to what we've created because the creative cycle is not complete until the New Thing is offered to nourish others. The need you recognized with your own Hunger has led you on a creative journey, but the purpose of the journey was greater than you. In the Native American concept of the Field of Plenty, you received the thought-form from the Source of all things in order that the world's need might be fulfilled. Now, in bringing it home, you complete that purpose. Life sends out the call, and we are invited to collaborate in the solution. The one who responds gets the joy of creation, the love of Life, the glory of contribution and (in product development) the trademark.

Harvest also gives purpose to everything you've experienced to get here. All the breakdowns along the way and all the tough places on the journey where you lost faith, here they all have meaning. Every one of them has gone into feeding the soil that you are and nourishing the plant you are growing in the world. The very nature of the Life Force is that it takes the energy released in the destruction of other things, other experiences, even other parts of yourself, and transforms them into beauty that nourishes the world.

That's why I call this the Sacred Harvest, because it makes sacred our lives. The sacrifices we have made along the way, the things we've had to leave behind, have made space for the new. This awareness puts us in touch with a sense of honor and reverence for the purpose of all things. What each and every one of us is creating is necessary and honorable.

Native Americans really felt that the thing that we give or create embodies the spirit of the elements it's made of and our spirit as the giver. So nothing should be wasted. Nothing should be thrown away that is still useful. Not one of us, no matter how poor the quality of our lives might seem, is not useful.

On January 8, 2012, as I was writing this chapter, Stephen Hawking celebrated his 70th birthday. At age 21, Professor Hawking was diagnosed with amyotrophic lateral sclerosis and given only two years to live. His health has declined steadily throughout his 49 years of grace, and today he is confined to a wheelchair and able to communicate only with a computer and speech synthesizer he controls with his hand. Yet he has made some of the most remarkable contributions of all time to our understanding of the universe. He also has a wife and three children. What if his gift for theoretical physics had not been recognized? How would we have failed to evolve?

This process of Harvest puts you in connection with the Life Force in everything, not just what you create but everything created by everyone else. Everything has value because it carries the spirit of its creator and the spirits of the Earth, Air, Fire and Water it is made of. It is a completion of a cycle and a celebration. It leads us back to Home, back to the place where we are part of a community, where we can rest and replenish ourselves before we begin again.

The Voice of Station 12

The voice of Station 12 is "Homeward bound." What does it mean to go Home again? What is Home now?

When I left the United States in 2001, I didn't know where I was going. I knew I needed to leave where I was. I knew something was missing for me there, but I didn't know where I needed to go. In my mind's eye, I could see my back, see myself going, but not coming back. My intention was to do a six-week walkabout and come back and be clear: "This is where I'm going to live now." But it didn't happen like that.

The journey I really took was a journey of learning to recognize Life meeting me in all the different ways it did, and learning to trust that. It was a journey in which the circumstances in my life shifted into something much bigger than I could have imagined. I met my husband. I learned a new language. Opportunities for work took me in a new, more meaningful direction. I discovered a different way of life. I discovered The Wheel of Creativity.

In one Harvest after another, I have seen the culmination of so many seemingly disconnected and broken pieces of my life, now polished and rounded and made into symbols that can be meaningful to other people. My life has meaning for other people because of my willingness to meet it and engage with it consciously. And it's exactly the same process for each of you.

So when we go Home, we have to let go of our expectations—what it used to be and who we used to be—in order to discover where Home is now, what it means, and what it has become for us.

We set out on our journey. We don't know where it's taking us. We have to leave our comforts. Even though they may not fit anymore, we cling. It takes courage to leave, but we know we must in order to be true to ourselves. And letting go gives us a new vision. It's a symbol. It represents where we come from—the community and tribe that held us, which we have outgrown.

A woman in one of my groups, with her own journey like mine, put it so eloquently:

"It's what we call Home, but not necessarily the good home. Maybe the going away and coming back is what gives us the knowledge of what the good home needs to be in our life. And it's only the going away that makes you understand the true concept. Only then can you know that the place you held as home wasn't."

When you're a blue dot in a blue room, you cannot see yourself. You stay in the place you know, until one day the red room across the hall catches your eye. And in moving your blue self to the red room, suddenly or gradually you see your shape, your form, your outline and your texture, and you learn who you are. It is by leaving the familiar that we are transformed.

Weighing In

After the Harvest, Home again. When we re-enter the community we left for our journey, it is a time for celebration. It is also a time for evaluation.

Detached from the frontline demands in the field, once again you can relax in the comfort and safety of Home. Here you can take time to listen to the community about what is actually needed, and your next step is a response to that.

It is time now to evaluate your results:

- What is the yield of your efforts?
- What kind of crop have you produced?
- How many did it feed?
- How well were they nourished?

- What changes need to be made to improve results?

The yield of the Harvest gives evidence of all that came before. It is too late now to improve the results; you have to make those improvements next time.

In the mid-1980s, when I started my first business as a freelance writer and producer, one of my best clients was Motorola at its corporate headquarters in Schaumburg, Illinois. It was a time when global competitiveness was becoming tougher, and electronic imports were surpassing exports in the United States. One of the business strategies Motorola developed during my work with it was Six Sigma, which has since been widely adopted across business enterprises around the world.

The goal of Six Sigma was the continuous improvement of manufacturing processes, and Motorola put the people and systems in place to virtually eliminate manufacturing defects and variations. I would not seek to apply this level of precision to daily life, but the company's commitment to continuous improvement certainly changed its position in the marketplace and changed the entire electronics industry in the United States.

Continuous improvement is a core principle of The Wheel of Creativity and not to be forgotten in the creative process. After Harvest comes a period of rest within the community of Home. But the Wheel will continue to turn as the next feeling of restlessness initiates the next journey through it.

Living Well in the World: The Seven Principles of Kwanzaa

The African celebration of Kwanzaa takes its origins from the ancient First-Fruit Harvest celebrations and the modern black freedom movement. It teaches principles and practices dedicated to co-creation and sharing. The seven days of Kwanzaa focus on seven principles for living well in the world. I think they are applicable here as we evaluate our place in the stream of Life:

1. *Umoja* is unity, recognizing the interconnectedness of us all.

2. *Kujichagulia* is self-determination, and teaches us to define ourselves by our actions in the world.

3. *Ujima* is collective work and responsibility, and speaks to our role in making the world better than it was when we got it.

4. *Ujamaa* is cooperative economics, teaching us to satisfy our needs without harming others.

5. *Nia* is purpose, and invites us to develop ourselves in our own interests and those of the world.

6. *Kuumba* is creativity, encouraging us to constantly repair, renew and rebuild for a better and more beautiful world than it was before us.

7. *Imani* is faith, the faith to believe in the capacity of all and support all in bringing good into the world.

And for The Wheel of Creativity, I would say:

1. We are part of the cycle of Life and Nature.

2. It is not just what we think, or have or are that defines us, but what we do.

3. The joy in life comes from making the world a better place, one action at a time.

4. Let your footprint on the world be light and, as far as possible, harmless.

5. Follow your longing and your hunger, and create something from them.

6. Whatever you have now is the raw material for something new, more, better.

7. There is something more than this; whatever it is that keeps you alive, let it be for good.

How Does Your Garden Grow?

One of my English clients has a garden. When, during our business coaching calls, I asked him what he was passionate about, he described his garden. And when he spoke of it, his energy changed. So I decided to go see this garden for myself, and what I saw amazed me. It was a huge terraced garden cascading down a hillside with dozens of varieties of flowers and fruit trees and vegetables. It was an enormous living canvas, requiring a great many hours a day during the growing season.

He had spoken to me of how much he loved working in his garden, and told me he had begun the process of making notes. At the end of the season, he made notes about the methods he had used to tend each species, how much water and sun and food and pruning, and the result his methods had produced. He did this so that he knew what he needed and wanted to do the next year. What had worked and what had not. In this way, each year was an evolution of the year before. In this way, he advanced the quality of life in his little corner of the world.

This is what we all do, in our little corners of the world. The creative process, this journey away from Home and back again, can be a physical journey, like mine, or not. It can be political, ideological, spiritual, emotional or social. It can be horticultural, architectural, medical, scientific, artistic or romantic. It will always be unique to you. It is the journey of making all of life's moments sacred, as you recognize that it is Life itself that leads us through them all.

What have you achieved in your journey? When you look back to Station 1, where you first felt the Hunger you have now fed, what do you see now that you couldn't see then? Where has your Hunger taken you? And what have you created along the way?

- In your journey through Vision, what awareness, direction and torque did you achieve?

- In your Exploration of the unknown world, what freedom did you win, discovery did you make and prize did you capture?

- In your Incubation of the new, how did you find your fertility, your faith and your confidence?

- And in your Cultivation of the New Thing, how did you achieve maturity, mastery and purpose?

Whatever creative journey ends for you here, a new one is beginning. After a book is published, a book tour begins. After a product is completed, it is placed on store shelves. After a song is written, musicians begin to rehearse it. After a meal is prepared, it is eaten.

And so the Wheel continues turning, with yet another opportunity for creation, evolution, contribution and personal transformation.

This is all there is: you in your place in this grand and glorious adventure we call life.

What are you hungry for now?

A STORY OF HARVEST

Heather Larrabee, R&B Singer
Current City: Denver, Colorado

> "In the midst of it all, my creativity—pursuing my music, writing and pushing myself to really dive into that—gave me sustenance and gave me something to anchor myself with."

I've known Heather Larrabee since she was 20 years old. She continues to be one of the brightest, most beautiful and inspiring young women I've met anywhere. I have watched her reach for and succeed at her dearest passion, singing, while at the same time evolving a meaningful professional life as well. This interview describes Heather's experience of going to Los Angeles to sing, and then returning home to Denver, Colorado. Heather's story illustrates how the journey brings us Home with a Harvest, even when things don't turn out as we had planned.

Heather's story illustrates the value of having made the journey anyway, and how you can never know where that road will lead.

KATHERINE ROBERTSON-PILLING: Heather, are you aware of something shifting for you in going to LA and coming back?

HEATHER LARRABEE: I would say that it was really good for me to leave, and to extricate myself from the community that I'd grown enmeshed with. I was living vicariously and making choices through relationships and activities that were very external in focus and kept me always busy, always running. I didn't take time to regenerate, to feed my own creative interests.

And so, stepping into a new landscape, where I had very few friends, I had a lot of time on my hands. And I had an essential choice: "What am I going to do at this time?" So I used it to go really internal, go really deep inside of myself and spend intimate time with myself. A lot of things were falling away, a lot of things were breaking down, like a relationship and feelings. In that process, my expectations of what the move would produce in my life totally shattered, and

then I was just left with, "What am I going to do with this? Am I going to continue on, and let this make me stronger? Or am I going to give up?"

And I chose to use that energy to try to grow, which I did. And, in the midst of it all, my creativity—pursuing my music, writing and pushing myself to really dive into that—gave me sustenance and gave me something to anchor myself with. It was only about me. It wasn't about anybody else.

And, at the end of all that, I came out knowing just how strong I was, just how capable I was. And I wouldn't have known it unless I'd had that level of testing. Then after that was done, I kind of felt like, "Well, I'm 32 years old, and I have a rich community in Denver that I love deeply." Staying in LA would've been a pride and ego thing around not wanting to seem like I had failed. Instead, I felt like I wanted to be in a place where there were people that I loved and cared about, in a community that felt like the right place for me, on a soul level; where people were unself-conscious, and they were generous, and they were involved, and they were kind. And they were supportive as a community.

KRP: As opposed to the competitiveness of Los Angeles?

HL: Yeah. I didn't even really feel the competition so much as I just felt a hyperfocus on wealth, and a hyperfocus on work, and a lot of agendas. Like people would go out in order to meet people, or in order to advance some career prospect, instead of just going out to enjoy things. And I just didn't really resonate with that after a while.

KRP: And how is your experience of Denver different than it was before you left?

HL: I've realized that it's okay that I like this place. You know, before I used to think that I was settling, because it's not the glitzy, glamorous world of LA or New York where "real artists" live. Instead I found that for me, there's a lot more vibrant, creative things happening in Denver, and people really pushing more. It's from the heart, you know, taking risk and supporting each other. So I just learned that it's okay that I like it here and that this is where I fit.

KRP: There's less pressure to make money or be the top in Colorado. So in a way, there's more room for the plant to blossom into what it actually is, as opposed to having to fit into somebody else's agenda for it.

HL: Right. And I don't know if this is going to bear out, but I do have this intuitive feeling that in places like Denver—and I think Austin's also a good example of this—audiences want authentic art still. And so, you know, I think it's better for artists to come out of the place they're from. Like the Flaming Lips; they're based in Oklahoma. That's who they are; that's their fabric, and they're resonating with that. And it's true and it's honest. But transplanting, unless it really is a part of your soul's journey, becomes about something else, and that shows up in the art. I feel like people who make strategic moves to these cities can spend so much time just trying to make something happen, as opposed to letting it come organically from where they're really rooted, that a lot of the art gets twisted or watered down. It's not flowing out at that point, it's being created with an audience and a critic in mind. It's too crafty at that point.

KRP: How did this process change your music and your relationship with music?

HL: It taught me a lot about what I want from a band. In LA, I got really good at the business side of things. So again, it was something that strengthened me and made me feel more confident about my abilities. And I also lost a lot of my creative feeling there, because the musicians I was working with were in LA only for financial gain. There wasn't that spirit of abundance or of giving or of nurturing. I felt like I was racing against the clock in rehearsals, on gigs, and asking for their time. So when I came back here, I was more interested in, and made sure that I aligned with, people who would play with me, whether it was for free or for pay, because it was about self-esteem and worth. I'm worth it. You know, what I bring is worth supporting.

KRP: It certainly is. Would you make the move again?

HL: Absolutely!

KRP: And why?

HL: It showed me so much what I never would have been able to see about myself in any other way. And the strength that I generated from that experience, even though it was very, very painful, was amazing. And I would never give it up.

KRP: And what has happened in the three years since you've been back?

HL: It's funny. Literally within two weeks of returning, I had 12 shows booked that paid really well and with a group of musicians that I adored and respected and who were excited to work with me on the bandstand. Within two months, I landed what was, by all accounts, a dream job for me with a really conscious company that does great work in the world. I [had] a very isolated, lonely day job in LA where I learned that, although I'm an introvert, I really need heart-to-heart connection with people on a daily basis and to feel connection and movement. And so I went from a tiny office environment where I had almost no human interaction for a year to a work environment where I had meaningful daily interactions with over a hundred soulful, conscious people every day and got to do great work in the community to give back.

I've described it to people as feeling like my life just cracked wide open and everything good came rushing in. And I really believe that when you're in the right place, things just flow. There is a natural, strong, forward-moving surge that brings everything into alignment over and over again, and it just keeps building. It's exhilarating and it feels like that sense of "right place."

And each month longer I stay, those connections keep deepening, and the pool keeps expanding, and I find more and more people overlap here—all doing good work. All trying to live their dreams and shine their light. And so many days I think to myself how grateful I am to be in my right place and really know it down to my bones. That's my hope for everyone— that we could all feel this way.

Part Three

Coming Home to the Adventure of Life

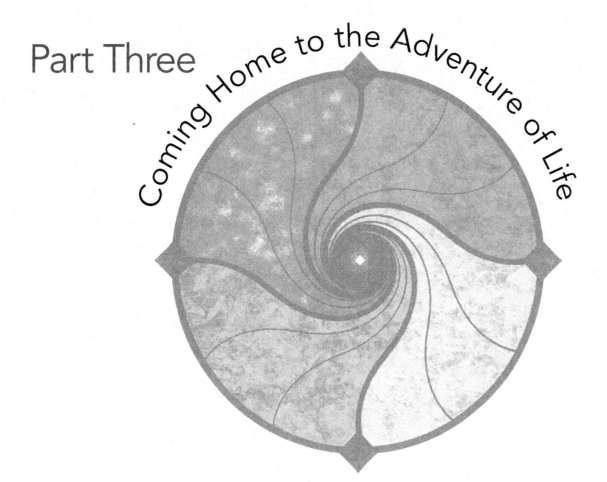

There is a vitality, a life force, an energy, a quickening
that is translated through you into action,
and because there is only one of you in all time,
this expression is unique.
And if you block it,
it will never exist through any other medium
and will be lost.

MARTHA GRAHAM

Taking Your Place in the Adventure of Life

A dream doesn't become reality through magic; it takes sweat, determination and hard work.
COLIN POWELL

Finding the Magic Wherever You Are

You have a place on this earth. Wherever your feet are, that is your place. But taking it and owning it and making something with it is up to you. And that determines whether the quality of your experience of your brief stay on this planet is heaven or hell.

When my husband and I visited Sri Lanka in 2010, we were guided through the countryside by a pair of angels whose names were Kamal and Victor. Kamal was a 40-something father of three daughters, and Victor was an 80-something wise man. Sri Lanka is the oldest continuously Buddhist country in the world, and Victor has been a practicing Buddhist all his life. He imparted his wisdom in between archaeological side notes, and the advice that resonates in me still is simply, "Keep your mind where your body is."

Whatever the circumstances of your life, and whatever your thoughts or feelings or judgments about them, that simple wisdom will be your way back to your place. You must let go of everything that is not here in order to be here. And that is where we begin this chapter.

How Do I Use This to Get Where I Want to Go?

Everything in your life is the product of a creative process. Conscious or unconscious, deliberate or by default, personal, cultural, solitary or in collaboration. Everything that exists began its life as energy, then was collected in someone's mind as an idea, quickened and captured in the spirit, nourished and grown in the heart, and produced in the physical world. Each of us is here as a lightning rod for capturing and focusing the energy of the Universe to create our worlds. And when we become fully present, we can begin to realize that we're here to enjoy the process.

So far you have been given a bird's-eye view of The Wheel of Creativity, and you have read the descriptions of its 12 stations. You have read the stories of people in all walks of life, in their own words, about their experience of the creative process, which will hopefully inspire you. Now you are asking, "What do I do with all this information?"

While the previous twelve chapters focused on the experiences, tasks and rewards in each station **181** of the Wheel, this chapter shows you how to understand and use the Wheel in your creative projects and daily life. For each station, this chapter helps you deal with the experience, personalize it and achieve the task. I've developed a creative toolbox of meditations, writings, intentional actions, exercises, games and rituals to stimulate and channel the different energies required to move through the entire creative process. For example, running may be more appropriate to reinforce the work of the Exploration Quarter, while yoga might be a better choice for the work of Gestation.

A Map, a Compass and a Set of Points

I have friends in Colorado who regularly engaged in the sport of orienteering. As a family, they set out on foot once every month or so into the foothills of the Rocky Mountains with a map, a compass and a series of points to find. The clock was ticking, and their objective was to navigate their way from point to point, validate their presence there and complete the circuit. I never went with them, but it always sounded like fun to me—like a scavenger hunt in the wild on the hiking trails.

   The Wheel of Creativity is something like that. It is the map, the compass and the points in the creative process. The terrain includes the circumstances of your life. The 12 stations are the stops you make on the journey to get your bearings, develop your skills and build your muscles. The entire journey takes you where you need to go to find your lost pieces and reintegrate them to make yourself whole again. It is Life's perfect creative design.

The Experiences of Creativity

Each station of the Wheel has an experience. The quickest way to find out where you are in the Wheel may be to simply identify what you are experiencing now. It is the entry point to each station, where you do the work required to win the prize and move on toward your goal.

Station 1. Restlessness	Station 7. Wonder
Station 2. Desire	Station 8. Urgency
Station 3. Paralysis	Station 9. Appreciation
Station 4. Enthusiasm	Station 10. Tenderness
Station 5. Despair	Station 11. Fatigue
Station 6. Panic	Station 12. Satisfaction

The Tasks of Creativity

Each station has a task. No matter where you are in the Wheel, no matter how hopeless or impatient you may be feeling, there is a path from here back to your authentic Self, your true nature, your connection with Source. Each task, when achieved, brings you through that station and out the other side. No matter where you are, the Wheel keeps turning. Get on the train again, because you're always on your way to a new station and a new task.

Station 1. Tell the truth	Station 7. Be receptive
Station 2. Pay attention	Station 8. Relax
Station 3. Choose love	Station 9. Be present
Station 4. Leave home	Station 10. Protect
Station 5. Stay vigilant	Station 11. Discipline
Station 6. Focus	Station 12. Release

The Rewards of Creativity

Each station has a reward. That reward, reached through the experience and task of that station, sits in the center of the Wheel, in the place of stillness, resting in timeless perfection. It is pure Essence, where you and your Source are one.

Station 1. Awareness	Station 7. Fertility
Station 2. Direction	Station 8. Faith
Station 3. Torque	Station 9. Confidence
Station 4. Freedom	Station 10. Maturity
Station 5. Discovery	Station 11. Mastery
Station 6. Capture	Station 12. Purpose

Celebrate each small step. Enjoy the reward. Be grateful for what you've learned there, no matter how it felt at the time. And allow it to take you to the next stop on your journey. Completion of that part of the process moves you naturally into the next place, and closer to the fulfillment of your desire.

How Do I Know Where I Am in the Wheel?

The most important part of using a map is first to establish where you are on it. You can begin by choosing words from the previous lists. Then use these questions to help you find the "You Are Here" label on your map. Where do you begin your journey?

- What does the status quo look like in your life today?
- Where do you see creativity already at work?
- How do you describe your relationship with the creative process today?
- What do you hope for from The Wheel of Creativity today?
- What are your biggest concerns about your journey through the Wheel?

The reality is that you are in many places in the Wheel at the same time. So it is helpful to choose one area at a time to focus on. Each creative endeavor you're involved in has its own process. So, whether you are building a business, raising a child, composing a film score, writing a book, or becoming a singer, each of those processes is creative; and each has a Wheel of its own. But we'll come back to this later.

How Do I Manage the Wheels in Different Areas of My Life?

Figuring this out is neither the point nor the solution. The mental process of figuring out where you are is a place to begin. It can comfort the mind and relieve the anxiety of not having answers long enough to create space for you to step into. However, the mental understanding alone will not produce the transformation you're seeking. The mind alone does not create, but requires all the other aspects of the human being to join it in creating something new.

Keep in mind that your life is itself one grand creative process, made up of simultaneous processes occurring in all areas of your life. Think of your interests and the roles you play. Perhaps you're a mother or father, daughter or son, husband or wife, business owner or civil servant, dancer or singer or writer on the side. If you think about your roles too much, you could easily start to feel overwhelmed. Yet you navigate the ins and outs of all these roles without thinking too much. This is the way to approach The Wheel of Creativity as well. It is simply who you are as a multifaceted human being.

If you want to sing, you need to:

- Find a teacher.
- Learn proper breathing.
- Practice your scales.
- Learn new music.
- Memorize lyrics.
- Find collaborators.
- Perfect your performance skills.
- Find gigs and venues.
- Promote yourself.

If you want to build a business, you need to:

- Choose your field.
- Define your product.
- Identify your market.
- Research what's out there.
- Find financing.
- Make the product.
- Refine the product
- Promote the product in the market.
- Sell products or services.
- Manage your cash flow.

Having more than one Wheel turning in your life at once is natural. The work is to integrate these Wheels by using whatever is happening to return to the stillness of your own center.

Take time to answer two questions:

1. What do you want to do?

2. What steps do you think/know are needed to make it happen?

Remember that things getting a little chaotic is part of the process. Embrace it. Let go of your illusion that you are in control. When your mind starts to go a little wonky, when you can't figure things out—is it this or that?—go ahead. Jump right in between them. Dive in. Untie the rope that keeps you attached to the shore and set sail. The adventure is about to begin.

How Do I Integrate the Process?

Have you ever played pinball? When I was a child, my father owned a small business called Automatic Amusement Company. He leased jukeboxes, arcade games and such to restaurants and bars. He would do his rounds, sometimes taking me with him; and when I got older, I took my turn at pinball. It is not an exact science—well, perhaps it is for some—but pinball wizards go by feel.

The physical world is a world of opposites.

- Light and dark
- Right and wrong
- Good guys and bad guys
- Top and bottom

How many can you name?

The creative energy of the Universe is founded in two principles: Masculine and Feminine, or active and receptive. If we are ever to free ourselves from the whiplash-inducing pinball game of flipping from one opposite to the other (where we are the ball), we have to learn to integrate these opposites in ourselves, in our minds, bodies, spirits and hearts. And that is what the following practices are designed to help you do.

What are the Key Principles of The Wheel of Creativity?

You are responsible for your life. Rather than a burden, this responsibility is a tremendous gift. This great and glorious adventure of Life is yours right now. Nothing has to change out there for heaven to arrive. The Wheel of Creativity can show you the way, starting with four key principles:

1. Approach everything as a meditation.
2. Identify with the Essence of a thing (or person) rather than the Form.
3. Honor the process of your life, and trust it.
4. Be present in the moment with your body, mind, heart and spirit.

How Do I Practice the Principles of The Wheel of Creativity?

If you recall, each quarter of the Wheel is associated with a domain of the human being:

1. Quarter 1 is Vision, and is the domain of the mind.
2. Quarter 2 is Exploration, the domain of the spirit.
3. Quarter 3 is Incubation, the domain of the heart.
4. Quarter 4 is Cultivation, the domain of the body.

Most of us are more comfortable, more familiar and more practiced in some of these domains than others. The places where we prefer not to spend too much time can leave gaps in our personalities. And each time we get to these places in the Wheel, the process can stall, unless we learn to fill those gaps authentically. These are the areas where we keep producing the same undesirable results—and can't understand why.

The person who fears taking exams may spend a lifetime in an unfulfilling career rather than risk feeling stupid. The person who requires a scientific explanation for everything in life might avoid what nourishes the spirit. The person once burned in love may spend a lifetime longing for but never finding a soul mate. And the person who has never felt physical strength may never develop it.

Because we live our lives through our thoughts, intuitions, emotions and actions in the world, moving through the four quarters again and again as the Wheel turns in your life is integrating. So the practices I've designed offer you a variety of ways to approach and tackle the challenges of each station. With that, let's get started.

How Do I Get the Most out of Each Station?

Start by choosing just one area of your life for this inquiry, and I'll take you through the process:

1. Choose an area of your life where you're struggling.
   - Describe the problem there for you.
   - What exactly is going on? Describe the circumstances.

2. What are you experiencing in this area?
   - List your five top feelings about this area.
   - Why is it bothering you? Describe your reaction using "I."

3. Which principle are you operating in—active or receptive?
   - Are you spending more time doing or being?
   - What is needed now? Do you need to take hold or let go?

4. Which quarter are you spending time in?
   - If you're more active, is it Exploration or Cultivation?
   - If you're more receptive, is it Vision or Incubation?

5. Which of the stations seems to best fit your experience here?
   - Do any of the experiences resonate immediately?
   - Do any of the station voices speak your language?

6. Choose your practices and experiment with them.
   - If you're clear which station you're in, work with those practices.
   - If you're still not sure, work with the practices from several stations and see what you learn.

Daily Creativity Practices

MORNING

- **Get still and listen**. It's so easy to start the day with to-do lists as your first thoughts. Appointments, phone calls, shopping and obligations can sweep you up before your feet even hit the floor. But is that really how you want to greet the world? Even if you have to set the alarm for 4:55 a.m. to get three minutes of solitude in the bathroom, get still and listen to your body, heart, mind and spirit. Where are you in the Wheel today? What needs to be expressed to find beauty in your day?

- **Set an intention.** Every person on earth starts the day on level ground in one area: We all have 1,440 minutes in our day. Through them, your life unfolds before you, and they do not stop for you to get ready. Life is looking to you to focus the precious energy with your name on it. Start your day with a vision for what you want to happen. Set an intention, not just for what you're going to do, but how you'll do it.

THROUGH THE DAY

- **Take an "expresso" break.** The French, along with many other Mediterranean cultures, take regular breaks throughout the day to sit and sip espresso. They stop, sit (sometimes) and watch the world go by. They might chat with a friend or read the newspaper or just watch. But they take breaks. I'm not suggesting you get caffeinated, but rather that you stop at least once a day, notice what's around you, and respond to it. Be present with the world around you. Engage with it. Do something with it.

- **Move mindfully.** If you have control of your physical body, movement is an integral part of your day. Everything from spreading the butter on your toast to washing your hair is an opportunity to be creative, to play, even just to be conscious. So enjoy it. At least once a day, make your moves mindfully. Fall in love with the feeling of your body in space.

- **Check in.** Solitude plays a crucial role in the creative process. But isolation can be a killer. Knowing that you have a "crew" who believes in you and will help you get home can make the difference between a successful and an unsuccessful outcome. Reach out. Pick up the phone. Send someone an email. Offer someone else a hand, but connect with someone.

NIGHT

- **Take stock.** Keep a little notebook by your bed. Before you lay your head down, let go of your day. Are there any things you wish you'd done differently? Things you said that are gnawing at you? Any people you're left feeling uneasy with? Write them down and let them go. In light of your intention for the day, how did it stack up? Don't judge this—it's an inventory: How many bottles are left on the shelf?

- **Be grateful.** Write down five things you're grateful for from today. It could be your new boyfriend, a decision you made or the fact that the truck that almost hit you missed. Some days are easier than others. But list five before lights out. This alone will change your life. Feel your gratitude. Now, sleep well.

Seven Steps to Getting the Task Done

Each station is a road from where you are to infinity, to the eternal, essential elements of who you truly are. The journey of the Wheel is a journey inward. Every station moves you from the outside of the Wheel—finite, spinning, changing Form—to the center—infinite, still, unchanging Essence. You progress from the spin of the circumstances at the outside of the Wheel to finally rest in Source at the center by your willingness to take on the task of each station. Then you return outward again, centered, surfacing at the entrance to the next station.

In order to make this journey fearlessly and with ease, you need to engage all aspects of your human nature. By continually moving inward as you move from one station to the next, your mind, spirit, heart and body are integrated. And different areas of your life are unified.

These seven steps are designed to engage you from different angles. Enjoy them!

1. Inspire yourself. Inspiration can come from anywhere—from a thought while brushing your teeth to a beggar on the street. So take responsibility for letting it in. Throughout these pages, I have shared things I have found to be particularly inspiring. But the best are the things you go out and find for yourself. Expect to be inspired when you are:

- Reading Facebook
- Listening to music
- Attending a play
- Watching a movie or DVD
- Reading a book
- Walking in Nature
- Swimming in the sea
- Sitting in a café

2. Reflect. Reflection is the beginning of self-knowledge and awareness. Some people meditate. Some practice mindfulness. Taking time to quiet your mind and listen returns you to your own inner wisdom. Make space in your week for this. Keep in mind that reflection may occur differently at different points on the Wheel.

- Meditate (sitting or walking).
- Practice yoga.
- Sweep the floor mindfully.
- Keep a journal.
- Sip your coffee slowly.
- Swim, walk or run.
- Stroke your pet.
- Watch the clouds move.

3. Express. Expression is the out breath of the creative process. If you open your eyes, you will see it in the far corners of your life. On page 190, you will find a set of questions for each station designed to lead you into your own true essential nature, where the creative process begins and ends. Use these questions as a guide. Make up your own. Keep notes through the week, and experiment with as many different media as you can beyond words:

- Draw on your shopping list.
- Paint with unusual liquids.
- Document your day in photos.
- Play with dolls.
- Grow an herb garden.
- Make a collage with fabrics.

- Sculpt your body with exercise.
- Make a mask of your image.
- Make your meal beautiful.

4. Embody. The act of grounding your thoughts and feelings in your body is an integral part of being human. And moving your body has a dramatic impact on your quality of life. Linking the two brings magic to your life. But with computers doing so much for us, we now need to make time for things our ancestors did every day. So this step invites you to get up and move consciously, integrating your whole being to achieve each station's task. The only requirement is that you enjoy it!

- Practice yoga.
- Stetch to start your morning.
- Walk, run or bike to work.
- Try competitive sports.
- Dance in your pajamas.
- Explore tai chi.
- Massage someone you love.
- Make love.
- Swim in natural water.
- Climb the stairs and feel the burn.

5. Connect. Connection is the lowest common denominator of existence. From scientific discoveries to spiritual mysteries, all signs now point to the interconnectedness of all things. Remembering this simple fact, in our darkest hours or brightest days in the spotlight, returns us to our place in Life. Use these or make up your own:

- Visit a farm.
- Walk in Nature and listen.
- Ask your friends to dance.
- Listen to your animals.
- Clean your house.
- Spend a day in silence.
- Call an old friend out of the blue.
- Buy your vegetables from the grower.

6. Act. Action is the one sure thing no creative process is complete without. Whether you're in the active or receptive phases of the Wheel, the creative process requires you to bring ideas from Essence into Form. This is the focal point of all the other activities you engage in, where external problems find solutions through you. What makes people prolific in their field ultimately requires that they just do it. Here are some things you can do:

- Find problems to solve.
- Set your intentions.
- Organize your time.
- Contribute to someone.
- Plan the work.
- Work the plan.
- Measure results.
- Practice intentional acts of caring, for yourself and others.
- Let go of outcomes.

7. Celebrate. Celebration is the final step, and one we so often forget. Every success needs and deserves to be honored and acknowledged. So celebrate.

- Rest.
- Play.
- Throw a party.
- Do something extraordinary.
- Smile.
- Laugh.
- Dance.
- Bake cookies.

The Winding Path to Your Innermost Essence

Here are some questions designed to lead you back to yourself. Each set of questions guides you through the experience and the task of each station to its reward, from the external forms of your life to your own true essential nature.

Station 1: Hunger

- In what area of your life do you feel restless or dissatisfied today?
- What do you know clearly that you do not want in your life?
- What would it mean if you told the truth about your hunger?
- What awareness do you need to move forward in this area?

Station 2: Appetite

- What is the opposite of what you said you don't want in Station 1?
- What kind of nourishment do you desire today?
- What is the quality of your desire mentally? spiritually? emotionally? physically?
- Where is your desire leading you?

Station 3: Anorexia

- Where do you feel stuck in your life today?
- Where does the automatic "No" come up in your life? What words does it use?
- What would you love to do if you could overcome this "No"?
- What kind of force is required to move you off the status quo?

Station 4: Launch

- What are you enthusiastic about in your life today?
- Where do you feel a new surge of energy or power?
- What are you leaving behind in order to move ahead?
- What does this letting go free you to do next in your life?

Station 5: Isolation

- In what area of your life do you feel you made a big mistake?
- What kind of discovery are you counting on now?
- How vigilant are you willing to be in order to see it?
- Who is helping you stay on course? Who is your ground crew?

Station 6: Crisis

- Where are you in crisis in your life?
- What forces do you feel are against you as you try to move ahead?
- How will surrender bring you focus here?
- What is the clarity you need to survive?

Station 7: Conception

- Where in your life are you in the embryonic stage?
- What is your spontaneous response to this experience?
- What does being receptive look like in this situation?
- What do you hope to bring forth in the world?

Station 8: Gestation

- Where in your life do you feel like you're waiting?
- What do you feel must happen for things to be okay?
- What would happen if you let go and trust the process?
- What do you want to believe about life but aren't quite sure of?

Station 9: Breakthrough

- What in your life is waiting to be born?
- What needs to shift within you in order to appreciate it for what it is?
- How is this New Thing an expression of you? How is it unique?
- What have you learned about the creative process now?

Station 10: Nurturing

- What are the essential ingredients of unconditional nurturing?
- Where in your life have you experienced tenderness?
- What is the value in protecting the New Thing now?
- How will you know when it is mature?

Station 11: Pruning

- What needs to be cut away for the New Thing to thrive?
- In what area of your life do you feel fatigued?
- What are the essential ingredients of compassionate discipline?
- How will you know when the New Thing is ready?

Station 12: Harvest

- What are you harvesting in your life today?
- In what areas are you on the verge of satisfaction?
- What New Thing are you struggling to release to the world?
- Where do you see your life purpose through what you've created?

CONCLUSION
The Wheel Will Bring You Home

Go confidently in the direction of your dreams.
Live the life you have imagined.
HENRY DAVID THOREAU

As I write these concluding words, I am acutely aware of how much courage it takes to live a human life. Each of us, no matter where we're born, what kind of privileges we are blessed with or whose life we wish we had, has a set of gifts and challenges unique to us. Rich or poor, healthy or sick, intelligent or less so—everyone has something to offer, and everyone has needs to be filled. One person's need is another person's opportunity for abundance. No matter what other people's lives look like from the outside, for better or worse they have their blessings and their curses just as yours does.

It has taken me many years of living to know in my heart that we are all connected. The *Tao te Ching*, a classic Chinese text, raises these interesting questions: "What is a good man but a bad man's teacher?/What is a bad man but a good man's job?" The person I would judge is my greatest teacher. The man who cuts me off in traffic is my angel. The young man who steals my purse gives me some-

thing of greater value to take its place. The one who is hardest for me to love is the one who teaches me the meaning of love.

The longer I have lived, the more I have come to know that Life is a journey. Why do I make this journey? To get there? Sometimes. But I will reach and pass many destinations before my final departure. More often than not, I journey to have the experiences, to participate with others in creation and to leave something of value in the stream of Life.

In this Conclusion, I retrace the steps of my journey, which I began in the Introduction, in the hope that you will see the creative process is always at work, whether you recognize it at the time or not. It is the Hero's Journey, and we are the heroes of our own lives.

Going Home to Leave Home

It was 1981 when I finished graduate school. The United States was in a recession. Jobs in the Midwest **193** were scarce, while Houston was a boomtown. So I returned home to Houston to look for a job.

I got an informational interview with the friend of a friend of a friend of my mother's. Don Macon was an old-timer and a visionary. In his retirement he had built UTTV, a highly sophisticated television system linking the entire Texas Medical Center. I liked him, and I saw an opportunity. He had no job to offer me that day, but I kept the conversation going until finally he said, "Well, maybe I could find you something."

That first job—changing videocassettes in the broadcast control room, alongside a man who could easily have handled it himself—bored me. I straightened shelves and swept floors just to keep busy, until Don's right-hand man noticed. Long before the Internet, I helped develop an embryonic online information service for the medical center. And when the daily newsmagazine producer moved on to another position, I got her job: anchor, writer, producer and supervisor of a small TV-production team. I accidentally discovered that I could love my work.

Severing Ties

After a few years, I returned to Chicago to be with the man I had met while job hunting in Chicago. As soon as I got there, reality hit: Ted traveled 250 days a year. When that relationship eventually ended, I felt like a failure. But I spread my roots into fertile soil and began to grow.

I was working in advertising for the first cellular phone service provider in the United States, and the last organization that would employ me full time. I watched 50-year-old men—20-year employees who were expecting a comfortable and secure retirement—being shuffled off to out-of-the-way cubicles to finish out their terms. I saw their disillusionment with the system to which they had given their lives, thinking they would be rewarded in their later years. The rules had changed.

I learned that it does not pay to delay your life. I realized I did not want to spend my life on other people's dreams, because there was no guarantee

they would include me at the end of the road. I learned that if what you do and how you do it is not your primary reward, then no outside reward will satisfy you.

I had been feeling restless in my position. I found a more rewarding position in the company and went after it. When my boss blocked the move, I knew that trust was broken. I decided to leave the company and go out on my own. It was the biggest leap into the void I had ever taken, but it didn't take long to recognize what a gift she had given me.

I started making contacts for freelance work as a writer/producer. I got my first project via a cold call to a communications manager at Motorola. He had just been assigned an audiovisual project, which he offered me.

That job earned me more than $9,000 in one check and launched my freelance career. I stayed in Chicago for 10 more years, consulting as a writer/producer with corporate clients such as Motorola and Allstate Insurance. I moved from the suburbs to a stylish high-rise in the heart of Chicago's Magnificent Mile, and I saw my business expand into documentary television and film, which challenged and inspired me.

Through a series of happy (and unhappy) "accidents," I fell in love with a new man who introduced me to a creative and spiritual community that supported us both. During our time together, I deepened my understanding of myself and continued becoming more conscious. I studied improv and acting, metalsmithing and screenwriting, voice, guitar and music theory. I expressed the poetry of my life in every way I could. Ben pushed into the rigidities in my heart, but I could not soften them at the time. Finally, after years of working at our relationship, we surrendered to the inevitable and returned to being friends, where we had begun.

Learning to Live in Process

In the year that followed, I trained with Anne Wilson Schaef in Living in Process facilitation. I joined people from all over the world—from California businessmen to Maori elders—who were equally committed to this way of life. They taught me that Life is a process, unfolding naturally through us as part of Nature, to be honored and allowed. During training sessions through the year, I learned levels of honesty, transparency, respect, creativity and love I had never before experienced. I touched the deepest places in myself, grieved all the losses of my life to that point, and liberated my true nature as an expression of Life itself.

Daring to dream, I applied for and received a master's degree fellowship in interdisciplinary arts at Columbia College in Chicago. I would have gone, except for the calling—a clear, specific, intuitive message in my morning spiritual inquiry practice—to go to Los Angeles. And so in autumn 1994, I went without questioning.

The Leap of a Lifetime

I knew one person in LA, and, as I mentioned earlier, by the time I arrived, the house-sitting job she had arranged for us had fallen through. We moved into a studio apartment, and within a week a thief had broken into my car and stolen everything in it. Days later, with the help of a friend from Chicago, I received a call out of the blue offering me a townhouse in a parklike setting in Studio City, California, complete with five loving cats who needed tending.

Somehow throughout this process, I felt completely still within. I felt as if I were being carried along in the palm of God's hand, and I was sure that nothing could touch me there.

I did not go to LA to work in television, but I needed to make money. I faxed out five résumés, and within two weeks I received a call. I got my first TV job in LA.

While millions of people in LA commute for hours, the production offices were two blocks from my townhouse. When my landlord came home from his film production job in Hawaii, another house in our little neighborhood became available. I pruned

my belongings, gave up my apartment in Chicago, and made the commitment to LA. With job, home and friends now in place, I was deeply reminded that I can trust the process, even when I don't understand it.

Doing the Right Thing

About a year later, my mother's cancer metastasized; without my father, she was lost. It was a tough decision, but I left Hollywood to be with her in Houston.

Her final six months were a healing time for us both. As she became more and more dependent on me, she showed me how generously and deeply I could love. It was a gift neither of us would have chosen, but it was the best she ever gave me.

At exactly noon on May 1, 1996, Mom left her body. And again, The Wheel of Creativity took a turn in my life. The events of the years that followed illustrate the 12 stations of the Wheel in the sands of my life. There are always many Wheels turning in your life, just as in mine, and you always have the opportunity to use the stations of the Wheel to help you respond to them.

Moving out, Moving in

I had three weeks to empty Mom's apartment—sort, sell, pack and move her things. I found a larger apartment for myself in LA. I settled in with all her things around me. I found two Siamese kittens to start a family of my own. And I tried to go on with my life, seeing friends and working on a consistent string of projects. But I was not myself.

Hunger. Home disappeared in a flash. I was alone in the world—no parents, no siblings, no partner and no children—and nothing would orient me in the sudden, crazy disorientation I felt. I called a friend and went to visit him on the edge of the wilderness in Colorado, to stare into space for a week or so.

One thing led to another, and Michael and I began a relationship. Part of me knew that I should make no major decisions for a year, but within the year I was living in Colorado full time. From the urban congestion of Los Angeles to a backcountry migration path outside Estes Park, I left Home once again.

Life turned me inward. I began a different kind of spiritual path—a practice of spiritual journeying with an experienced shaman, which I followed for the next two years. I needed to acknowledge and sit with my hunger. But it was difficult. With the competitive noise of LA silenced and the nearest TV job a two-hour drive away, I turned toward my own creative work and began to write.

Appetite. Almost from the beginning, Michael and I struggled. My illusion of making a home with him soon dissolved. My longing grew. I needed to bring my family close again.

When Mom died I inherited everything, including all her papers. There I met her mother, Minnie Lile Thacker, the grandmother I had never known. And suddenly my longing had direction. I needed to find out who this woman was who had been diagnosed in 1930 as schizophrenic and was institutionalized, shocked and lobotomized, and spent her last days in a mental hospital in north Texas.

I needed to know her story to know my own. I spent a month driving 4,000 miles of back roads in Texas, chasing every scrap of information—towns that no longer exist, people who had sat on her lap as children, places she had visited as a child herself. And then I spent the next few months, while Michael was coming and going, writing, expressing, transforming the story of her life into a screenplay.

Anorexia. I kept trying to get back Home, but it was no longer there to go back to. Michael and I went our separate ways. Between the choice not to make the two-hour commute for work and the tech-stock crash, most of my moderate inheritance was gone. Within two years, I was on my own, hurt and angry, again.

Gradually, I rebuilt my life. I leased a three-story townhouse on the edge of Boulder, overlooking a cattle farm that had somehow survived urbanization. It was a luxurious time of homemaking, cooking, gardening and nightly log fires. Life was rich and

grounded and good. I needed the nourishment. But everything has its costs.

I took a freelance project that stretched me beyond my comfort zone and experience, as producer of a documentary series. Everyone told me the previous producer worked 80-hour weeks. But I needed the job. After several months—mentally, physically and emotionally exhausted from the strain—I was asked to resign. I was devastated, ashamed and—at the end of the day—relieved.

Go. That was the first of three events that closed the door on Boulder as my home. The second was notice from my landlords that they wanted their house back. The third was a financial gift from Michael. I took these three things as my sign. And I learned that while sometimes I choose to leave Home, sometimes Life chooses for me.

That was the moment. At the time, I saw it through eyes of desperation; now, I know it was a gift. It was spring 2001. I had known for a long time that I needed to leave Boulder. I just didn't know where to go. Nothing fit. No place called me. Letting go of the shore was a process for me.

A White Girl's Walkabout

As home, love and income were all lifted from me at once, I finally surrendered. I loaded a few suitcases into the back of my Jeep, put the rest of my personal possessions in storage, and set out on what Australian Aborigines so beautifully call walkabout. In this powerful rite of passage, adolescent aboriginal males spend up to six months in the wilderness, retracing the steps of their elders. Mine would be six weeks to points in Europe undetermined.

I drove with wings to Texas to visit family, then on to Mississippi for a month with dear friends, and finally to Chicago, which I had left on another hunch six years earlier. I postponed my flight to Europe 10 times. I needed to say what I would later realize was goodbye.

Launch. When I finally got on the plane at Chicago's O'Hare International Airport, it was August 24, 2001. I was excited and scared at once. I could see only my back as I moved ahead, disappearing over a distant horizon. But I could not see myself returning. And that terrified me.

After two days on my own in London, I met a dear friend in Greece. The moment we reached the far side of the tiny Greek isle of Skyros, my unraveling began. Creativity mixed with compassion, sun and sea at a holistic retreat at the end of a dirt road through the forest. Fresh, clean vegetarian fare and daily doses of ouzo showed me new recipes for nourishment. Between courses in watercolor, clowning, chanting and yoga, I ate sensual figs, picked fresh from their trees by the wild and sexy bronze Greek gardener. I toasted the golden setting sun with ouzo. I disappeared into the breeze of the hammock beside the hand-laid labyrinth. I showered outdoors with the hot sun on my skin. I sunbathed topless on a lonely beach. I didn't know why, but I couldn't stop crying.

It could not have been a more perfect preparation for what was to come next. Creating this much distance from all that I knew began my liberation from who I had always been. I could not have foreseen where my life would take me from there.

Isolation. My friend and I spent our last night together in a five-star hotel in Athens. On the morning of September 10, I woke so terrified I was hallucinating. I called a friend in the States for help. "Keep it simple," was her wise reply. We took separate taxis that morning: I was bound for Florence, my friend for home. I could not understand what was happening to me. I could only keep moving forward, pushed by the dissolving road behind me as programs ended, hotel reservations concluded, and the only person I knew in Europe headed for home.

My trip to Florence was frantic as I tried desperately to find a room. It was September, and Florence was heaving with tourists. I raced through Rome airport with calls to hotels in a language I did not speak on a pay phone I did not know how to use. I was on the edge of despair when, finally, after numerous failed attempts, a merciful Florentine hotelier found one room for one night of the week I was to spend there; that was all she had.

I arrived in Florence two hours later. An Italian taxi driver who liked Americans delivered me to the long shadow of the Duomo and my room at the inn. That tiny little sliver of land in the midst of my vast, uncharted ocean was enough for me.

Crisis. The next day I returned to my hotel at three in the afternoon, hoping for a room. When I turned into the lobby at the top of the stairs, I saw the archway to the bar, and a man standing there whose ashen face told me someone had died. It was September 11. The emotional explosion was so huge that resisting was not an option. I was frozen in my tracks. Everything else fell away, and Focus happened of its own accord.

I took an empty chair in the bar. For the next four hours, I sat frozen there as those images we shall never forget, repeated again and again on the TV screen, burned the backs of my eyes. For four hours I sat, clinging to a river of strangers coming through in 15-minute intervals who were as lost as I, trying to make space in our minds for the unimaginable.

Chaos. I was weightless, untethered. Now I knew why I had been so scared. Life as I had known it was changed forever.

The hotel did manage to find me a room, and for three more days I stayed in Florence and found comfort in the golden steps of the Medicis and the shadows of Michelangelo's divinity-in-stone. I got lost in the mayhem of the market. I ate pasta and drank Chianti in the cool night air. But I was raw; and by then, it was clear that I had to get out of Florence. I ended up on a train to another unknown, a childhood memory of the young receptionist at my Florentine hotel.

The Calm After the Storm

Conception. I arrived in Tuscany at sunset. The taxi floated through the silent landscape like a lace curtain in a warm breeze. Cypress trees stood at attention and cast long, purple shadows across softly flowing roads once traveled by Roman regiments. I took a very deep breath and let in the wonder.

Chianciano Terme is a remote town near Siena where Italians go to take the healing mineralized waters that flow freely from five subterranean springs. My hotel was moderate, though elegant for an earlier era, and maintained with tender loving care. As night fell, I waded into the stream of Italian families on their evening promenade. They were not my family, but they comforted me.

On Friday I found myself in a park, lured by a jazz band in the gazebo. People were scattered on plastic chairs across the mosaic terrace, attentive and tapping their feet. Suddenly, the lead singer spoke a few Italian words, and everything stopped. At the stroke of noon, every person paused in silence to express the world's mourning with Manhattan as only Italians can. I must have been the only American in the crowd, but I couldn't have felt safer. I stopped and I rested. The healing waters moistened the soil of my heart, and Life planted the seed of a new life there.

After four days, I boarded a train for Rome to catch the *couchette* (overnight sleeper train) to Ville-franche-sur-Mer, a picturesque fishing village on the French Riviera. The mother of a friend in LA had invited me to spend three nights with her.

Gestation 1. After those few days with Karin and 10 days in a hotel, I still was not ready to move. I longed to lie on my back in the sun with my eyes closed. I recognized this as what I had left the United States for.

Karin made one phone call, and I had a gorgeous flat with a view of the bay and below my terrace an artist's studio in a walled garden. I unpacked my suitcase, closed the door behind me and made myself at home. I had no idea how long I'd be there. Gradually, the urgency to know my purpose and my place on earth diminished in the beauty of day-to-day life, *la vie quotidienne*.

A handsome and gentle French policeman with piercing green eyes invited me to coffee. Over the next few months, Olivier held my hand as I walked on new ground and discovered a new way of life. The unfamiliar sights and sounds of the Côte d'Azur spoke to me in a voice I had long forgotten. But it was the Mediterranean Sea that kept me there.

For six months, I was nourished by everything in this world. I experimented with French recipes whose words I did not know, got lost in local markets and rekindled my love of entertaining. I sketched, taking courage from Friedrich Franck in his book *The Zen of Seeing*. Franck speaks of drawing as meditation, a practice of connecting through eye, hand and page with the world before me, allowing it all in.

When high season arrived, my rent quadrupled. A room in a sculptor's villa atop the steep hills rising up from Villefranche Bay gave me a little cell away from city life, surrounded by Nature, animals and artists. As four more months passed, the thick red journal I had purchased for the trip filled up with thousands of words, tiny drawings and marks to say what words could not. There were favorite magazine clippings, scraps of fabric, museum tickets and the like, from cover to cover.

Finally, after years of rigid direction of my life, I was allowing myself to be guided by my heart and its connection with forces greater than myself. It was as if a river of silver ran through my heart, moving me to each new action on a current that came from beyond me.

No Place Like Home—Wherever That Is

Gestation 2. In July 2002, I went back to the States for a visit. On my first day in Los Angeles, bleary-eyed with jet lag, I met with a long-time client. Out of the blue, a quick hello to her boss produced the offer of my dream job; but it was in Boulder. I wrestled with the decision and decided to go for it. Ten weeks later, the dream job disappeared as abruptly as it had appeared when we were unable to agree on money.

Everywhere I looked, there were walls. I had reduced my entire life to a tiny room in the beautiful home of a dear friend in exchange for some chores and a few dollars for utilities. Along with occasional trips to Starbucks with my laptop, my friend and her dogs were just about all that kept me sane. But I later realized that walls have a purpose too: to contain the new life growing within them.

I waited much longer than I had imagined I would for what would come next. But through that year I learned that there is a gift in losing it all. When all my dreams, achievements and successes disappeared, all that was left was who I was. And I learned that I myself have value; there is value in my just being there with my friends. It was then, in those dark days, that I began to formulate the ideas that would become this book.

Breakthrough. At the end of that year in LA, I woke up one morning to find an email from a communications director whom I had met in Nice two years earlier. She said she had a project available for which she thought I might just be perfect. Coincidentally, I had a flight booked to Nice the next week. As if I had planned it in advance, I made an appointment and went for the interview.

Return. The part-time freelance position was an opportunity for a new life, and it required a commitment. If I had not desperately needed the money, I would never have said yes. I was worried about the French, which I did not speak. But I did need the job, and I did say yes. And so I was required to break through to a new level of living.

Nurturing. When I moved back to Nice, I lived with Olivier while I started over. Because I did not understand French, the job initially took me four days a week to do what I eventually accomplished in one. I spent months of sleepless nights attending to this baby. But with a grateful heart, I did what was required to nurture it. Eventually it began to mature, and my skill with it. And things got easier.

My life with Olivier—sensuously simple in the Mediterranean way—nourished me and supported me to find my feet again. For me, the little things have always made me feel at home. Little by little I collected bits and pieces for a new life, saving money and stabilizing myself from a very precarious position. I prepared to build the foundation on a new shore, carving the stones one at a time.

Pruning. Nurturing and Pruning, fathering and mothering energies, often go hand in hand. I moved between tenderness and fatigue here, between protection and discipline. I worked very hard, and my client base grew. I humbly accepted what was offered and allowed it to nourish me in ways I would never have chosen or planned.

At the same time, my identity—who I had thought I was—was being transformed. There was work to be done to let it go, to cut away what no longer fit, to reveal a new and deeper expression of myself. It is a delicate operation, this Pruning. One of the things I had to let go was Olivier.

Harvest. On the ides of March 2005, I moved into my own flat near the port in Nice. It was a celebration of a new me! Friends gave me furniture, dishes, bedding. I bought what I could from Trocs and Depot Vents or rescued the occasional street treasure. I shipped one container of my most precious possessions from the United States: two purple velvet chairs my mother had recovered at least three times, two handmade chairs handed down through my father's family for 200 years, my Total Gym and 10 boxes of books. Row by row, I tended the field in an entirely new land and harvested a new life there. That brought me Home again, ready for a new cycle to start.

Home Again: The Start of a New Cycle

I could never ever have imagined that the journey I began four years earlier, when I closed the door on my storage unit in Colorado, when I woke hallucinating in the Athens hotel room, when I arrived on my friend's mother's doorstep in France, would lead me here.

But this journey—described to show you the path—is one we all take. Sometimes it's physical, sometimes emotional, sometimes geographical and sometimes metaphysical. But wherever you are on your journey today, The Wheel of Creativity keeps turning, and one destination gives way to another, taking you ever deeper within yourself.

The Woman Who Jumps

Later that year, my dear friend Anne asked me to join her on a cruise vacation she had won in a raffle. For 10 days we shared a lovely cabin on an elegant four-masted sailing ship, wonderful meals and beautiful Mediterranean ports from Bonifacio to Capri.

There was a man on the ship—a tall, dark and handsome Croatian man with a sparkling smile and glistening black eyes—who served us dinner. Franjo was a good man, I would come to learn, his character forged in his early 20s through seven years of war. A friendly flirtation gave birth to something deeper, and in that most predictable of all vacation stereotypes, I fell in love.

I felt feelings I had not felt in decades. I saw myself standing on the edge of a precipice. I knew this love affair would probably not be permanent. I knew there would probably be pain. And I knew I had a choice: I could be the woman who stands on the edge, saying, "No. I will take care of myself." Or I could be the woman who jumps. And that's the woman I chose to be. "Don't say no to love" became my mantra.

I entered the Wheel again, and this time the revolution came to my heart. Every Saturday for the next two months when his ship was in port, we met at a café in Cannes. We sat a while and sipped cappuccinos as if we had all the time in the world. People noticed us. I gave my heart, my mind, and my 49-year-old body to this 31-year-old Croatian hero who told me his story and gave me his love. I was in love for the first time in 25 years. And it inspired me.

That autumn, Franjo's ship crossed the Atlantic for the Caribbean. Then he went home on leave. As the only son of his Croatian family, he was expected to take care of them, so our relationship was not an option for him. We both moved gently on. I saw him once more about a year later, and we shared a quiet moment of appreciation for the past. The

Wheel came full circle again, opening me deeper to Life in a place I had kept firmly sealed for 25 years. Its blessings were rich.

The Beauty of Being

My heart was wide open. That inner glow that connected me with my own vitality was showing up in other ways as well. I took care of my body. I ate the best food. I moved my body for the pleasure of it. I indulged in yoga. I swam in the sea. I danced alone in the night for all the light in my life. I took up singing again with a sparkling Austrian opera singer and found the depth and breadth and height of my voice.

All these things flowed from my open heart, and what they were teaching me renewed my focus on this book. By August 2006, I had put together the first Wheel of Creativity Weekend, a two-day workshop for women, in the south of France. The pieces of my life were both the groundwork for the book and the seeds of ideas planted and gestating, without my even knowing about them.

Love and Work

In September the following year, Anne's handsome, seafaring brother and his children came to visit. While Ian's two 20-something children stayed in a bed and breakfast near Anne, Ian chose my friend's empty flat around the corner from me.

Over the next 10 days, I spent a sweet, warm, lighthearted time with their family. A bet about a song resulted in a romantic dinner at my favorite cliffside restaurant overlooking the sea. Having not heard from Franjo in nine months, I was free. I was more open than I'd been in 25 years. And Ian was entranced.

On the last morning before Ian left for home, we met for coffee. He announced that he wanted to start a relationship with me. I was honored and surprised. He was a man of character, and that attracted me most of all. But I also wanted someone who was there.

Two weeks earlier, I had sat over tea with a dear friend and made a list in my journal of 50 qualities I wanted in a man. She gave me a rose petal blessed by her spiritual guru to put with that page. Six days later, Ian arrived in Nice. The creative process was engaged.

After he went away, I heard my own words, "Don't say no to love." I sent him a text message to say I would keep the door open.

Ian was a captain, a man of action. Within two weeks he was back in Nice for a weekend visit. Within a month, I was in London with him at the theater, in his home, on his ship.

We spent New Year's Eve at a spa in the English countryside, and it was there at four minutes before midnight that he got down on his knees in the library of the old stone manor and asked me to marry him. The adventure of life took a new direction for me, in matters of the heart as well as matters of work.

Settling Into the Heart Where Home Is

After three long years, I finally let go of the French project. It had served me well, but it no longer fit. Life responded with three new clients who kept me working, creating and earning at a level I had never achieved. They were interesting projects on meaningful and useful subjects. And they restored balance in my life. I came to love my work again, and my life blossomed.

In 2007, two women committed to go through the entire Wheel with me, one stage each month for a year. They were my focus group, and they helped me express, explore, test and refine the building blocks of this book.

The sessions were magical. We each brought our present moments, our vulnerability, our imperfections and our humanity, I as much as they. My vision of The Wheel of Creativity and its 12 stations took form as we explored ideas together. I incubated them deep within me. I spent the months in between doing research, recording my thoughts and experiences, and developing exercises. Finally I harvested a workable model for the outside world.

In March 2008, Ian and I were married beneath an ancient bois d'arc tree on a friend's farm in Texas. At

age 52, I was certain. Ian continues to be my greatest supporter, my faithful friend and most precious companion.

For an independent girl who could not tolerate vulnerability, my world has expanded with the lessons only intimacy can offer. It's what my mother tried to suggest to me as "interdependency," but I could not hear. For the first time in my life, I was moving from an I to a We, not by putting myself out on a limb but by stepping out on the bridge he was offering me. And that was another first.

It has been four years now. I split my time between France when he's at sea, England when he's at home, and the United States, working, creating, loving wherever I am. At times I marvel at the perfection of Life's design, at how much I'm able to achieve when he is away. My life today gives me time to focus and achieve, and time to slow down and receive. I could not have imagined it better.

The Wheel Will Bring You Home

When I look back to where it all began, when I left Boulder, Colorado, with no place to go and no place to go home to, I toast my life for its magnificent artistry. I weep with appreciation for its good will. And I relax in the knowledge that a life surrendered to this process is a life elevated to the heroic. The Hero's Journey, so beautifully presented in universal mythologies across cultures and millennia, is a journey we all take.

These are the streets where I have learned what it means to be creative, with my voice, with my heart, with my life. Through each stage of the journey, I learn who I am collaborating with and what is needed for that collaboration. The journey continues, and the longer I live, even as my body ages, the more alive I become.

Mine is the story of a girl who left home, knowing only that she needed to leave, not knowing where to go or for how long. What she did not know became her guardian and guide, her journey became her life, and the new land to which she went brought her Home to herself.

My Mother's Legacy

My mother fought for her last breath. Two days earlier, she had looked at me with desperate eyes and said, "I never got my turn." She was a gifted, caring, intelligent woman driven by something outside her. For all she did for others, she died feeling she had not found her place.

My grief for her will never end, but with her dying words she gave me the legacy I treasure most of all, the keys to the secret garden. She gave me an imperative to find my place in the unfolding of Life, the courage to take pleasure in that place. Because of her life, I learned that my gift to the world comes like an arrow from my heart, pierced by longing and fueled by love.

Your Life, Your Gift to the World

Life is a creative process. You are not here at the whim of some all-powerful figure or absentee landlord. You had a choice in the life you're living, and you have a choice in how it affects you and what you do with it. You have a choice about the impact you make on everyone whose path crosses yours and the legacy you leave behind.

Each place and each time period of life contributes to your understanding of what you're here to do. Everything you have lived has meaning. There are no mistakes, no accidents, nothing wasted, and nothing that should have been different. You're not in charge, but you can collaborate with the unfolding of Life itself.

Each generation has a different set of challenges based on the actions and nonactions of the previous generation. The earth on which we live is a collaborator, too, just as we are. We are interdependent. Life flows through us all equally—freed or blocked by us—and we are responsible for our place in its unfolding. This privilege is the definition of purpose, the meaning of life and the greatest adventure of all.

You are here. Take your place. Live the adventure.

CPSIA information can be obtained
at www.ICGtesting.com
Printed in the USA
FSOW04n2340121117
41006FS